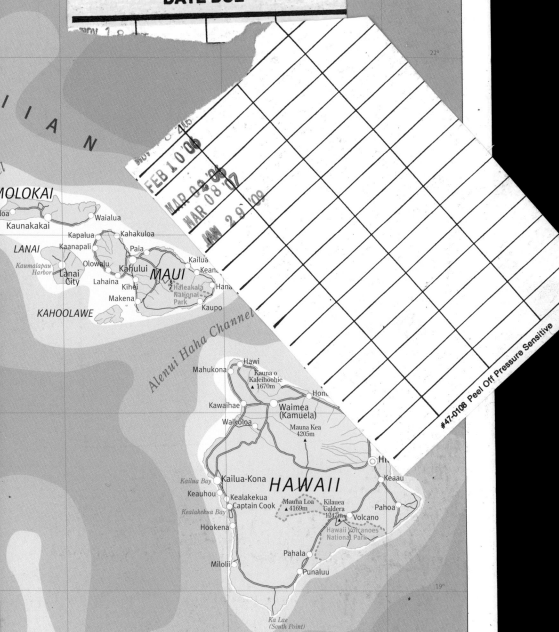

MOLOKAI

Kaunakakai
Waialua

LANAI
Kapalua
Kaanapali
Kahakuloa
Paia
Olowalu
Kaumalapau
Harbor
Lanai
City
Lahaina
Kahului
MAUI
Kihei
Kailua
Keana
Makena
Haleakala
National
Park
Hana

KAHOOLAWE
Kaupo

Alenui Haha Channel

Hawi
Mahukona
Kauna o
Kaleihoohie
▲ 1670m
Kawaihae
Waimea
(Kamuela)
Hon
Waikoloa
Mauna Kea
4205m

Kailua Bay
Kailua-Kona
HAWAII
Keaau
Keauhou
Kealakekua
Captain Cook
Mauna Loa
▲ 4169m
Kilauea
Caldera
1247m
Pahoa
Kealakekua Bay
Volcano
Hookena
Hawaii Volcanoes
National Park
Milolii
Pahala
Punaluu

Ka Lae
(South Point)

157°
156°
155°

22°

19°

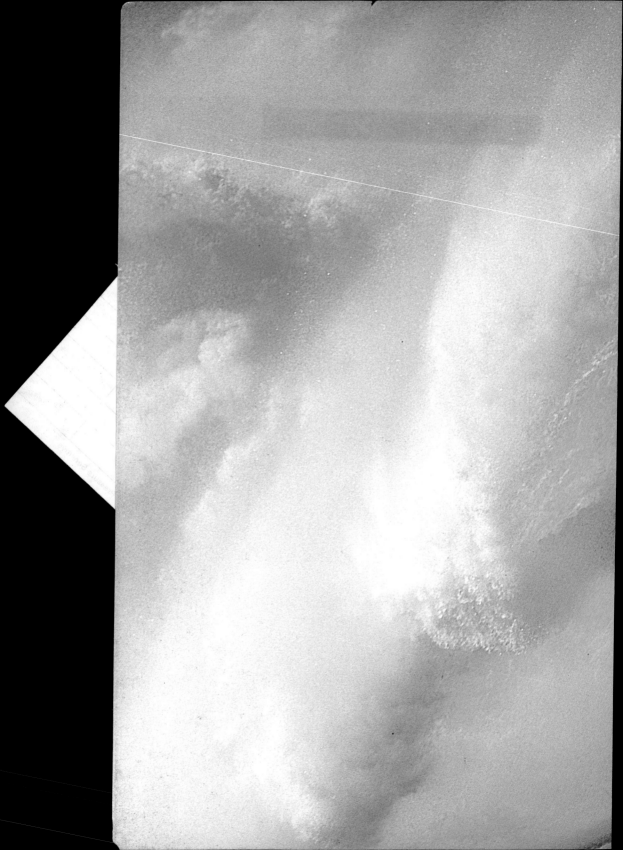

Surfing
Hawaii

The Ultimate Guide to the World's
Most Challenging Waves

written and edited by
Leonard and Lorca Lueras

with editorial and
photographic contributions by

Erik Aeder, Carlos Andrade, Walter Andreae,

Bernie Baker, Nick Beck, Steve Bingham,

Art Brewer, Joe Carini, Jason Childs,

Chris Cook, Jeff Divine, Dana Edmunds,

George Frayne, Peter French, Mana, Barry Morrison,

Carey Smoot, Sean Thomas, Grady Timmons,

Brett Uprichard, Tim de La Vega and Steve Wilkings

PERIPLUS

Published by Periplus Editions (HK) Ltd.

ISBN 962-593-540-1
Printed in Singapore

Distributors:

Asia Pacific
Berkeley Books Pte. Ltd.
5 Little Road, #08-01
Singapore 536983
Tel: 65-280-3320
Fax: 65-280-6290

Indonesia
PT Java Books Indonesia
Jl. Kelapa Gading Kirana
Blok A14 No. 17
Jakarta 14240
Tel: 62-21-451-5351
Fax: 62-21-453-4987

Japan
Tuttle Publishing
RK Building, 2nd Floor 2-3-10
Shimo-Meguro
Meguro-Ku, Tokyo 153
Tel: 81-35-437-0171
Fax: 81-35-437-0755

North America
Tuttle Publishing
Distribution Center
Airport Industrial Park
364 Innovation Drive
North Clarendon, Vermont
Tel: 802-773-8930
Fax: 802-773-6993

Cover: The soul of Waimea. *Photo: Jason Childs*
Pages 2–3: The power of sheer power. A Waimea Bay shorebreak wave such as this one can easily buckle or snap a surfboard or person into equal parts of its original whole. *Photo: Jason Childs*
Pages 4–5: On a tamer note, Windmills on Maui can turn ocean power into a thing of beauty. Nice positioning beneath a mirror-glass curtain. *Photo: Erik Aeder*
Pages 6–7: It's a "Standing Room Only" kind of day at the legendary Waimea Bay. *Photo: Jeff Divine*
Pages 8–9: Waimea's outside power retires inside in a frenzy of whitewater. *Photo: Jason Childs*
Pages 10–11: At its glistening apex, just before it breaks, an ocean wave is a form of poetry in non-motion, a natural force exquisitely frozen in time. This one rose at Sunset Beach. *Photo: Bernie Baker*
Pages 12–13: Tow-master Rush Randle jet-skis away from center stage as surfers Dave Kalama (left) and Laird Hamilton (right) drop into Peahi, the Maui surf spot known as Jaws. *Photo: Erik Aeder*
Pages 14–15 (Title page): Ross Williams blurs all distinctions while performing in a now-you-see-me, now-you-don't, magical, el mysto in-and-out surf act at Back Door on the North Shore. *Photo: Bernie Baker*
Opposite: Gerry Lopez and surf pooch ponder the beginning of yet another endless winter on the Polynesian surfing isles known as Hawaii. *Photo: Dana Edmunds*
Pages 18–19 (Dedication): Waimea again, this time as seen from the beach. *Photo: Jason Childs*

Dedicated to Lono,
God of the Heavens and Weather Phenomena

Above: Maui barreler Lloyd Ishimine breaking through a giving Honolua Bay tube. *Photo: Erik Aeder*

SURFING HAWAII

CONTENTS

Right: Perfect day, perfect Pipeline. *Photo: Jason Childs*

The Hawaiian Islands

Surfing's Birthplace

Surf Season

Access

Sea Bottom

Special Gear

Hazards

Medical

Highlights

During modern times, the sheer spectacle of surfing in Hawaii—and the associated glamour of being an accomplished surfer in Hawaii—has captured the collective fancy of sports enthusiasts, fashion trendsetters, marketing moguls and even intellectuals throughout the world in many special ways. All have been fascinated by what to them are otherworldly visions of brave young men (and sometimes even women) who regularly go to Hawaii to paddle out into the warm but fickle seas and attempt, almost irrationally and obsessively, to catch and ride what are perhaps the most challenging and dangerous ocean waves ever created by the forces of Nature.

Indeed, what adventurous person on Earth worth his or her guts wouldn't like to experience what all good surfers do when they dramatically take off and drop into a perfect Hawaiian wave vector? Who wouldn't want to be swept along so quickly by such a pure form of natural energy?

One can experience this phenomenon vicariously—by watching it on film, or even by traveling to Hawaii and studying it at beachside through the lenses of a high-powered camera or a pair of binoculars—but, well, that's kind of cheating. It's like enjoying sex by only watching it. It's not quite the same, dude, unless you get to actually—and indeed very personally—do it all yourself.

Former Hawaiian surf champion Paul Strauch once confided to an interviewer that, to him, surfing in Hawaii—or surfing anywhere, for that matter—was as pleasurable—and sometimes even better—than sex. "Surfing," he mused during an interview about his surfing career in Hawaii, "is very much like making love. It always feels good, no matter how many times you've done it."

Strauch's words may seem farfetched to a non-surfer, but if you ask serious surfers whether they would rather have a day of perfect Hawaiian waves or a day of sex with someone gorgeous, they will invariably choose the former. After all, beautiful men and women will always be around, but perfect waves, well, they don't make their magical appearance very often.

Irrational Dedication

Strauch's ancient Hawaiian ancestors also had very similar feelings about their favorite oceanic sport, and they even used to chant poems about surfing's sublime pleasures. Though most modern-day surfers are probably unaware of its history, the aquatic pastime of stand-up boardsurfing has been enjoyed in Hawaii since perhaps as early as the Middle Ages, though it wasn't until the late 1770s that any *haole* (or outsider) had the opportunity to witness this uniquely Hawaiian watersport live. By this time, native Hawaiians had already organized themselves into serious surfing *huis* (or clubs) that were sponsored by royalty, and were meeting regularly to compete in what may well have been among the world's first athletic events.

Opposite: It's winter contest time on the North Shore and *the* place of truth is, as usual, the powerful and inimitable wave known to all as the Pipeline. In a fine three-shot sequence recently captured at the Pipe, a rapt gallery of wave-watchers looks on spellbound as talented local boy Johnny Boy Gomes smokes his way through a proper Pipeline tuberino. *Photos: Art Brewer*

Indeed, long, long, long before anyone had even dreamed of the high-tech foam and fiberglass waveriding craft of today, the people of Polynesia—and particularly the Hawaiians—had been gathering at their favorite surfing beaches to have fun in the sun and to demonstrate their waveriding prowess. Meanwhile, the enthusiastic spectators onshore would cheer, have a feast and place bets on their favorite surfing heroes.

Even the typical 21st-century surfer's seemingly irrational and obsessive dedication to the sport is nothing new. Hawaiian chants recall fine surfing days when Hawaiian waveriders would drop whatever they were doing—work, family, everything—in order to ride good waves. When the surf was up and pumping, wrote the prominent Hawaiian scholar Kepelino Keauokalani (1830–1878), all responsibilities were put on hold: "All thought of work was at an end, only that of sport was left . . . all day there was nothing but surfing, Many [surfers] went out surfing as early as four in the morning."

A Magical Surfboard

If distant storms didn't generate suitable waves, anxious Hawaiian surfers would often enlist the aid of a *kahuna*, a sorcerer or shaman, to literally pray for good surf conditions. The *kahuna* would chant loudly to the sea gods and lash beach vines, "unitedly upon the water until the desired undulating waves were obtained." According to one chant, in some parts of Hawii, people would even build grand stone *heiaus* (or temples) at which they prayed and left offerings.

In the archives of Hawaii's Bernice Pauahi Bishop Museum, the world's leading repository of Polynesian history, there is a 1919 archeological study written by John Francis Gray Stokes (1876–

1960) that describes an ancient seaside *heiau* at Kahaluu Bay on the Kona coast of the Big Island of Hawaii. This temple was identified by Kona Hawaiians as a "*heiau* for surfriders, where they could pray for good sport." Stokes doesn't write a great deal about this temple, which was known as Kuemanu, except to say that within its confines was a bleachers-like terrace, where spectators could sit and watch surfing, as well as a brackish stone pool where surfers could relax and bathe after a day of riding the waves.

In one chant that has been dated to the 12th century, Hawaiians celebrated the surfing prowess of a great chieftain, and in another mythic poem, poignant stanzas relate the story of a serpent-sorceress who fell in love with a handsome young surfer. To keep him as her lover, she gifted him with her long and passionate tongue, which she transformed into a magical surfboard.

Because early Hawaiian traditions were passed down orally in the form of a series of memorized chants, there are no early written accounts about surfing. However, archeologists and art historians have discovered ancient Hawaiian petroglyphs (or pictures incised into volcanic stone) that depict cartoon-like surfers on surfboards. These petroglyphic surfers may or may not predate the arrival of the white man (or *haole*) in Hawaii during the late 18th century. Ancient surfing scenes (as recounted in recorded chant sequences) were apparently fun, bitchy, fanciful, and sometimes even violent. Woe betide the weaker of two surfers in one chant who became entangled in a love triangle involving a powerful woman chief. Even worse was the plight of an enthusiastic surfer of lower caste who dared to ride waves that were *kapu*-ed (declared off-limits or taboo) by an avid surfing *alii* (high-caste chief).

Opposite: This earnest-looking Hawaiian man poses with his family alongside a grass shack in what may well be the first known photo portrait of a surfer and his surfboard. This superb study was taken by a photographer named Theodore P. Severin around 1890. It is now in the archives of Honolulu's Bernice Pauahi Bishop Museum.

A collection of these Hawaiian surfing stories—along with similar Polynesian lore from Samoa, Tahiti and New Zealand—would fill a medium-sized book. Such an anthology would firmly establish that surfing was indeed a very important part of day-to-day life in the middle and south Pacific islands inhabited by the seafaring Polynesians. Such accounts would also fuel speculation about the origin of surfing, since, despite the recorded oral history, nobody can quite pin down just where this maritime dance form was born. Who on this planet first meditated on the recreational use of gravity and moving-wave vectors? And who shaped the first surfboard, paddled into that first rideable wave, then actually stood up on that surfboard and rode it towards shore?

The First Surf Reporters

The great British explorer and navigator, Captain James Cook, wrote in his journal in 1777 about a curious Tahitian water sport called "choroee", in which Tahitians in small outrigger canoes paddled into and rode ocean waves. However, it wasn't until Cook visited Hawaii a year later that he saw actual stand-up boardsurfing.

Unfortunately, Cook did not get to write about this sighting because he was killed in 1779 by a group of angry Hawaiian natives who attacked him and four of his marines in the shallows of Kealakekua Bay on Hawaii's Kona coast. However, Cook's second-in-command, Lieutenant James King, took quill in hand and charmingly described the spectacle that was surfing in "Stone Age" Hawaii. In Volume III of the British Admiralty's report on *A Voyage to the Pacific Ocean*, King noted that in Hawaii, "Swimming is not only a necessary art, in which men and women are more expert than any

Left: It was the legendary beachboys of Waikiki who re-popularized and saved Hawaii's cultural heritage of surfing early this century, after it had endured years of discouragement and neglect. This early Hawaiian surfer was photographed by the Honolulu photographer Frank Davey at popular Waikiki Beach below the brow of Diamond Head around the 1900s. He is wearing a stylish loincloth and holding a short *alaia* surfboard that was the waveriding vogue in Old Hawaii.

Right: Waves, waves and more waves is what surfing in Hawaii is all about, and the spectacularly beautiful islands are home to some of the finest and most challenging waves in the world. In this particular surfing triptych, we pause to contemplate the beauty of three entirely different Hawaiian wave moods as captured by three photographers on three different islands.

Top:
Photo: Joe Carini

Center:
Photo: Art Brewer

Bottom:
Photo: Erik Aeder

people we had hitherto seen, but a favourite diversion among them."

About surfing, an "exercise" which "appeared to us most perilous and extraordinary," King wrote: "The boldness and address with which we saw them perform these difficult and dangerous manoeuvres was altogether astonishing and scarcely to be credited." An accompanying engraving by a ship's artist includes a detail of a Hawaiian native paddling on a surfboard towards the ships that Cook had brought on his historic expedition. Even though this paddler is not actually surfing, he is part of the first artistic study ever done of a surfer and his surfboard.

Cook and King were the first (but not the last) author-explorers to become entranced by this "astonishing" activity. During the next hundred years and more, dozens of missionaries, adventurers and authors would visit Hawaii and record their impressions of this uniquely Hawaiian sport.

Unfortunately, many of the first and most influential reactions to surfing were penned by overly-zealous Christian missionaries who found many social phenomena associated with the sport to be un-Christian. They frowned upon surfing's semi-nudity and sexual connotations, and they did all they could to make the sport *kapu* (or taboo). The drinking, gambling and merry-making that usually took place at ancient-style surf contests, as well as the "lascivious" displays of *hula*-dancing, were all strongly discouraged.

Surfing also suffered along with the general decimation of the Hawaiian population during the years following the coming of the foreigners. When Cook "discovered" Hawaii in 1778, it was estimated that there were around 300,000 native Hawaiians living and thriving on the archipelago's six major islands. Within the first century of exposure to the West,

Right: In a different kind of vintage photograph, this one from the recent 1970s, local Pipeline surf artist Gerry Lopez strikes an authentic Country-style pose, complete with surf dog, chickens, ducks and what was then a newly-shaped, primo and then state-of-the-art Lopez Pipe Model surfing board. *Photo: Dana Edmunds*

INTRODUCTION

however, thousands of Hawaiians died of both serious and minor diseases. By the 1880s, the Hawaiian population had shrunk to about 40,000 people. This fact alone explains why surfing diminished in Hawaii during the late 19th century.

"Destitution, Degradation, and Even Barbarism"

In 1847, Hiram Bingham, the leader of the first party of 14 Calvinist missionaries to arrive in Hawaii from faraway New England, wrote, "The decline and discontinuance of the use of the surfboard as civilization advances may be accounted for by the increase in modesty, industry or religion, without supposing, as some people have affected to believe, that missionaries caused oppressive enactments against it."

This was the same Bingham, however, who, upon arriving in Hawaii, had written from shipside: "The appearance of destitution, degradation, and barbarism, among the chattering, and almost naked savages, whose heads and feet, and much of their sunburnt skins were bare, was appalling." He continues: "Some of our number, with gushing tears, turned away from the spectacle. Others, with firmer nerve, continued their gaze, but were ready to exclaim, 'Can these be human beings?! . . . Can such things be civilized?'"

Hawaiians had to endure difficult and painful times indeed, but despite the terrible decimation of their people and the suppression of their traditions, other, more sophisticated visitors came to Hawaii and were charmed by what they saw on land—and at sea.

In 1825, for example, the British captain George Anson Byron, master of HMS *Blonde* (and a cousin of the great poet George Gordon, Lord Byron) reported that in Hawaii during the 1820s, a surfboard was a very fashionable part of a young male Hawaiian's estate: "To have a neat floatboard, well-kept, and dried, is to a sandwich islander what a tilbury or cabriolet, or whatever light carriage may be in fashion, is to a young Englishman."

At about the same time, an open-minded missionary named William Ellis witnessed the act of surfing and noted (in marked contrast to many of his clerical colleagues) that for one "to see fifty or a hundred persons riding on an immense billow, half immersed in spray and foam, for a distance of several hundreds yards together, is one of the most novel and interesting sports a foreigner can witness in the islands."

By the 1860s, even the famed American author Mark Twain had visited Hawaii and succumbed to the siren call of the surf. In *Roughing It*, a humorous collection of newspaper articles published in 1866, Twain described his first and last surfing experience. "I tried surf-bathing once, subsequently, but made a failure of it. I had the board placed right, and at the right moment, too; but missed the connection myself. The board struck the shore in three-quarters of a second, without any cargo, and I struck the bottom about the same time, with a couple of barrels of water in me."

Like most novice surfers, Twain was frustrated in his attempts to ride the waves, so he just watched in awe as a Hawaiian (or "heathen," as Twain called him) came "whizzing by like a bombshell! It did not seem that a lightning express train could shoot along at a more hair-lifting speed," Twain exclaimed.

Heenalu, The "Royal Sport"

During the 1800s, there also emerged a number of prominent

Hawaiian scholars who began recording the many fast-fading Hawaiian chants. Among them were Kepelino Keauokalani, Samuel Manaikalani Kamakau (1815–1876), John Papa Ii (1800–1870) and David Malo (1793–1853). From their voluminous accounts and records of Hawaiian events, the subject of surfing—in both a practical and historical context—emerges time and time again. Ii even describes in great detail how and from which indigenous woods various ancient surfboards were made as well as how board designs differed, depending on what kind of wave a person wanted to ride.

In these accounts, the Hawaiian word that was most often used to describe surfing was *heenalu* (or wavesliding), and a surfboard was known as a *papa heenalu* (or wavesliding board).

As historians, these four men contributed a great trove of information for surfing historians to draw from, but despite their efforts, it wasn't until the so-called "popular press" and internationally famous authors began to write about this unusual Hawaiian sport that surfing really began to attract the attention of the outside world. Indeed, surfing's greatest publicity coup probably took place in 1907, when the popular American author Jack London wrote a widely circulated story entitled *A Royal Sport: Surfing at Waikiki.*

London, who had attempted surfing during a holiday in Hawaii that summer, stood up on a moving surfboard, experienced what he described as "ecstatic bliss," and, in response to this waterborne euphoria, began to describe a Waikiki surfer as a "Brown Mercury" who emerged from an "invincible roar . . . not struggling frantically in that wild movement, not buried and crushed and buffeted by those mighty monsters, but standing above them all, calm and superb, poised on the giddy summit, his feet buried in the churning foam, the salt smoke rising to his knees . . ."

Above: A poignant beachside memorial to the much-admired Hawaiian surfer, Eddie Aikau, who tragically died at sea in 1978 while attempting to secure help for his fellow crewmen who'd been stranded aboard a traditional Hawaiian sailing canoe named the *Hokulea.*
Photo: Jeff Divine

London's colorful descriptions are often credited with stimulating an overseas interest in Hawaiian surfing. This new enthusiasm was heartily supported by a new Hawaiian industry—tourism—which began extolling the virtues of exotic Hawaii in propaganda distributed throughout the world. To attract more visitors to the islands, local businessmen and government leaders were promoting the islands' *hula*-dancing, music and surfing as part of a glamorous, Hawaiian-style vogue.

Walking On Water

As a result of London's popular surfing story *Brown Mercury*, many individual surfers began to make a name for themselves. An Irish-Hawaiian Waikiki beachboy named George Freeth (1883-1919) was invited to conduct the first ever surfing demonstrations on the US mainland at Southern California's Redondo Beach. Freeth's West Coast promoters introduced him as an "aquatic attraction" and as "the man who can walk on water." In the wake of this publicity, Freeth remained in California for some 12 years. While he was there, he taught numerous people how to ride the waves.

Sadly, Freeth died young "as the result of exhaustion from strenuous rescue work" he performed on California's busy beaches. On the plaque beneath the bronze bust erected in his honor at Redondo Beach, Freeth is identified as the "First Surfer in the United States" and as a person—of Royal Hawaiian and Irish ancestry —who "as a youngster revived the lost Polynesian art of surfing while standing on a board."

Freeth's pioneering accomplishments on behalf of his people and their favorite sport were, as Lieutenant King had said more than one hundred years earlier, "astonishing." But only five years after Freeth had turned California onto surfing, another young and talented swimmer-surfer suddenly appeared big-time on the international watersports scene. This man was Duke Paoa Kahanamoku, and he carried Hawaiian surfing to even greater heights by popularizing it throughout the world. He surfed before rapt audiences in many parts of America, and, in 1915, achieved a special renown by becoming the first person to demonstrate surfing in now surfcrazy Australia. Much more is written about the legendary Duke later in this book.

—*Leonard Lueras*

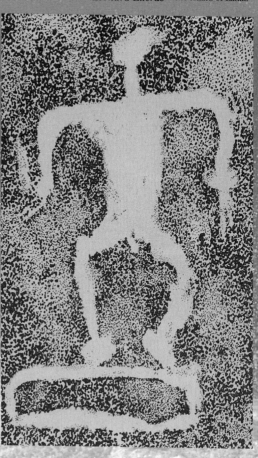

Left: Early authors who wrote about surfing used to describe surfers as men who could "walk on water." Nowadays, a cooler thing to do is to "walk on air", as five-time world surfing champion Kelly Slater does here in a recent airsurfing demo on Oahu's famous North Shore. *Photo: Jason Childs*

Below: Slater's antics at left are reminiscent, in a balletic way, of the figure in this ancient Hawaiian petroglyph from the island of Lanai.

Left: Yet another surfing triptych, this one about three decidedly different Hawaiian surfing situations. A rude North Shore pause (**Top**) is followed by what may evolve into an even ruder late Pipeline scratch-over (**Center**). Both of these precarious waves make way for good fun on a playful little sandbar (**Bottom**). *Top and center photos: Jason Childs; bottom photo: Jeff Divine*

Following pages: Sunset highlights the mood in these two pictures. *Top photo: Brett Uprichard; bottom photo: Dana Edmunds*

INTRODUCTION

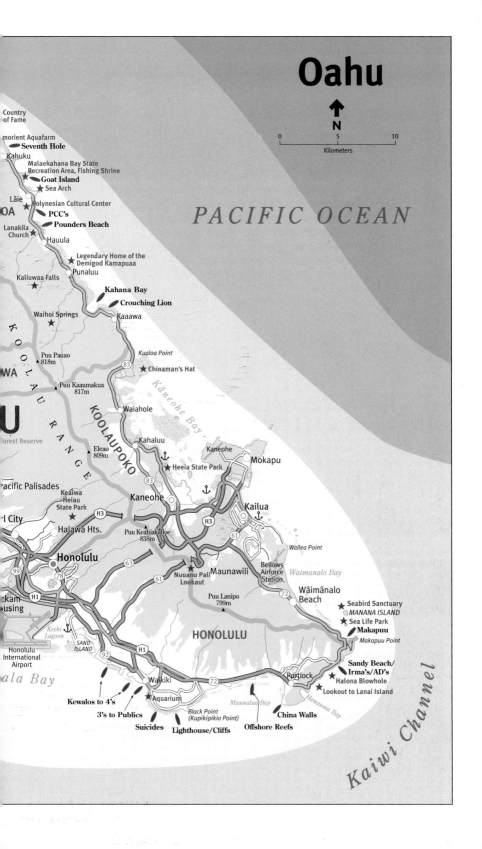

Introducing Oahu
Surfing's "Gathering Place"

The island of Oahu is known as "The Gathering Place" because of its longtime role as Hawaii's financial, social and political center. Its main port city and Hawaii's capital, Honolulu, the "Sheltered Haven," has always been of strategic importance both as a commercial and military destination because of the commodious size of its two beautiful harbors, Pearl Harbor and Honolulu Harbor.

Indeed, while Oahu is not the largest Hawaiian island, none of the Outer Islands is as developed as it is, and no other Hawaiian city approaches Honolulu in importance. This is probably why some 85 percent of Hawaii's population live on Oahu, and why most business and decision-making takes place in this so-called "Crossroads of The Pacific."

Not surprisingly, Oahu is equally important when it comes to surfing in Hawaii. While reasonably good surf can be found on all the Hawaiian islands, for some odd reason—perhaps as the result of a its special geological features—Oahu has also always been the prime gathering place for surfers in Hawaii.

The island of Oahu is without doubt the most surf-rich place in the Hawaiian chain (and perhaps in the world). It has the largest number and finest selection of summertime breaks in Hawaii (the Ala Moana Bowl and Number Threes are prime examples), and its North Shore beaches constitute what is arguably the finest single stretch of good surfing beaches in the world, with such spectacular surfing spots as Sunset Point, The Banzai Pipeline and Waimea Bay, to mention but a few.

And while Oahu is not a big island in terms of size, it is very Big Time when it comes to surf. It is the greatest surfing destination on the planet, whether you are a novice surfer or an accomplished waveriding veteran of North Shore winters past.

Oahu's "Town and Country" wave menu features the entire surfing enchilada—from smooth and shallow reef rollers that majestically fan into famous Waikiki Beach (perfect for beginners and experienced surfers) to pounding, body-whomping beach breaks (that fiercely snap, crackle and pop) to the most prestigious big-wave and tuberiding spots known to surfing man and woman.

Yes, it's all here, surf-sniffers, but for now—and for the sake of proper introductions—it is time for us to *hele* on (move forward) into the heart of this book, a magical mystery tour of Oahu that will attempt to familiarize you with the waves of the sleepy but roaring North Shore ("The Country"), the more urbane South Shore ("The Town"), the dry, wild and savage West Side (from Ewa to Makaha and on to Yokohama), and, finally, Oahu's verdant, windy and wet Windward Side. Aloha, brah! Time to move on, enjoy, and hopefully surf your butt off!

—*Leonard and Lorca Lueras*

Preceding pages: In the islands it's inevitable that sooner or later you're going to get burned. One person's stoke, you see, is sometimes another person's bummer. *Photo: Jeff Divine*

Opposite: Oahu is truly the gathering place, as you can see from this shot of a beachboy gathering in the heart of Waikiki. *Photo: Brett Uprichard*

Following pages: A hilltop view of the Sunset Beach Arena on a good and not-too-crowded day. *Photo: Art Brewer*

The North Shore
Surfing's Proving Grounds

Winter, between October and April

Easy, the main Kamehameha Highway runs parallel to most of the coastline

Mostly reef, but also some sand-bottomed breaks

Big-wave boards, a springsuit and a very serious go-for-it attitude

Crowds, locals, punishing surf and dangerous surf breaks

Drowning, kissing the reef and harsh poundings in the water

Pipeline, Sunset and Waimea; *the* surf experience

On Hawaii's North Shore, waves are not measured in terms of linear feet, but in increments of fear.
—A popular early '60s comment by a surf filmmaker

Surfers come to the North Shore scared. If you "no scared", it usually means you're not pushing your surfing anymore, at least not in large surf—and that's fine . . . If you are still charging, chances are that you came to Hawaii with some healthy fear, because you know you're going to be putting yourself into some challenging situations.
—Pete Johnson in *Transworld Surf* magazine, December 1999

Every now and then, we would hear reports through the grapevine of big-wave riders on the North Shore drowning, and for the first time I began to understand why so many of the great California surfers never gave the North Shore a try, or if they did, they came back home and never tried it again.
—Former California surfing champion and artist Mike Doyle in his memoir *Morning Glass*

Yes, a lot has been said about the North Shore, a stretch of coast often referred to as "the seven-mile miracle." Surf publications rave about this coastline rich in baby sand shells, and there isn't much that hasn't already been said or written about it. I mean, people even write long and effusive poems about the place.

Whatever its poetic or popular mystique, one thing is for certain: the North Shore of the Hawaiian island of Oahu is, without reservation, the most famous and revered place in the rarefied world of surfing. It is a Mecca to surfers worldwide. This has to do with the fact that the North Shore is home to some of the best, heaviest, most monstrous and challenging surf in the world, and also with the caliber of surfing exhibited there by both Hawaiian and visiting surfers. What these mad watermen do there is of a performance level rarely seen in other parts of the world. For all True Believers, no other place on Earth captures the essence of being a surfer as well as the North Shore. If there was ever a place that surfing is immediately identified with, then the North Shore of Oahu is truly it.

Between the winter months of October and April, Oahu's North Shore experiences an annual bombardment of waves and an invasion of pros, schmos, and bros all intent on tapping into prime North Shore surf. Many are there to simply savor the experience of watching a flawless 10- to 12-foot seething Pipeline being gutted by the world's best. Others watch in awe as towering walls of water at 20-feet plus smash into Waimea Bay.

While some people are content to just be spectators and to study the small-wave maestros offering sneak previews of the next era of performance surfing, others are not. Out in the water are packs of seemingly deranged nutcases rushing the waves with reckless abandon. For those surfers who are being paid big bucks to give their sponsors as much name and

51

Preceding pages: Watch in awe as Ross Clark-Jones and Arnold Dowling take the plunge on a big Waimea beast. *Photo: Jason Childs*

Opposite: Once you're in the Pipe, there's no turning back, even if it means annihilation. Chris Strother confronts a moment of truth. *Photos: Jason Childs*

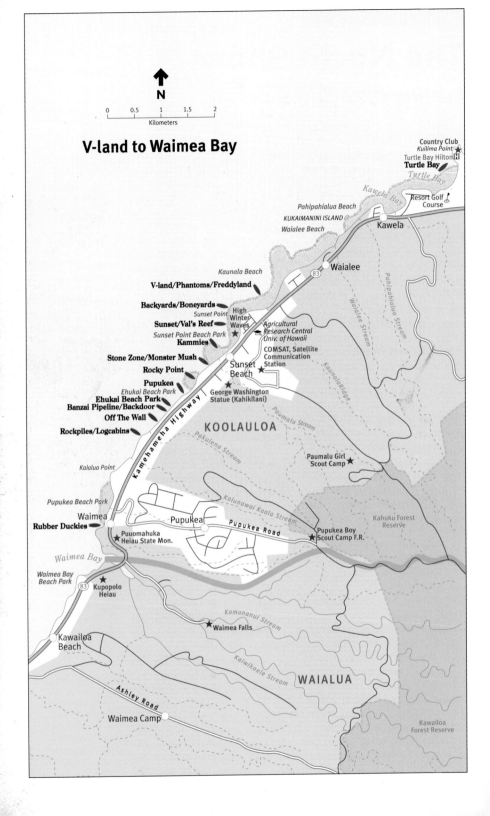

V-land to Waimea Bay

N

0   0.5   1   1.5   2
Kilometers

Country Club
Kuilima Point
Turtle Bay Hilton
Turtle Bay
Resort Golf Course
Kawela Bay
Turtle Bay

Pahipahialua Beach
KUKAIMANINI ISLAND
Waialee Beach
Kawela

Kaunala Beach
83 Waialee

V-land/Phantoms/Freddyland

Pahipahialua Stream

Backyards/Boneyards
Sunset Point
Sunset/Val's Reef
Sunset Point Beach Park
Kammies
High Winter Waves
Agricultural Research Central Univ. of Hawaii
Waialee Stream

Stone Zone/Monster Mush
Rocky Point
Pupukea
Ehukai Beach Park
Ehukai Beach Park
Banzai Pipeline/Backdoor
Off The Wall
Rockpiles/Logcabins
COMSAT, Satellite Communication Station
Sunset Beach
Kaunala Ridge

George Washington Statue (Kahikilani)

KOOLAULOA

Paumalu Stream

Kamehameha Highway
Pakulena Stream

Kalalua Point

Paumalu Girl Scout Camp

Kalunawai Kaala Stream

Pupukea Beach Park
Waimea
Rubber Duckies
Pupukea
Pupukea Road
Kahuku Forest Reserve

Puuomahuka Heiau State Mon.
Pupukea Boy Scout Camp F.R.

Waimea Bay

Waimea Bay Beach Park
83 Kupopolo Heiau

Kamananui Stream

Kawailoa Beach
Waimea Falls

Kaiwikoele Stream

WAIALUA

Ashley Road

Waimea Camp
Kawailoa Forest Reserve

logo-sticker exposure as possible, surfing on the North Shore also means big business. They perform for the cameras, go for the gold in contests, and try to etch their name into the annals of North Shore surfing. Then there are the local boys, a homegrown contingent of waveriders who have seen surfing fads come and go like the crowds that congest their surf spots every year. They reluctantly put up with this visiting circus, perhaps because they simply love state-of-the-art waveriding.

One thing you'll definitely notice on the North Shore, particularly at the prime surf spots, is that anyone picking up set waves is usually surfing way above your average Joe. Imagine yourself on the beach at Ehukai on a sunny surf day, say around early December. The lineup immediately in front of you will probably be chock-full of all your heroes trying to outdo each other on every breaking wave and be *the man*. Think

Tom Curren, Johnny Boy, the Irons brothers, Tommy Carroll, the Beschen brothers, and, if your timing is right, even Mr. Kelly Slater himself—live, in technicolor, and redefining what ripping is all about. Yes, they will all be here, along with droves of undergrounders, low profilers, upcoming amateurs, hotshot unknowns, visiting movie stars and even your common everyday surfer.

Contest time can be especially thrilling, as Hawaii is the last stop on the Association of Surfing Professionals (ASP) pro tour, and the final shot at world-ranking for world-title contenders. Hawaii is also an important "last chance" competition venue for surfers trying to qualify for the upcoming world tour. Performance levels are balls out because everyone is trying to get as mental and upside-down as possible to prove that they've got what it takes to rip the North Shore. Not to mention the pack of photogs, media hounds

Above: Signs like this on the North Shore are to be taken seriously once winter swells begin their annual migration to these mid-Pacific beaches. *Photo: Brett Uprichard*

Above: ". . . and whatever you do, don't blow it in front of the photog (or photogs)!" Nobody misses a trick when every move is being watched by a beachside photo-studio crew such as this one. *Photo: Erik Aeder*

and videographers on the beach, all trying to get "the shot" as well as footage of today's, yesterday's and tomorrow's surfing stars. Contest time is often likened to an aquatic circus, given the documentarians, groupies, personalities and assorted freaks of the surfing world who descend upon on this small stretch of coast just between Kahuku and Kaena.

Without a doubt, not only is Oahu's North Shore the Circus Maximus of surfing, it is also the raw essence of the surfing experience. The surfers, the surf and the vibes here are unique, unlike those anywhere else in the world. Just being at the North Shore and taking part in the scene instills in one a sense of belonging to a special tribe of people.

It's hard to describe the feeling of anticipation you're filled with as you're driving out of town on Oahu's H-2 Freeway for the very first time and heading towards the North Shore. Excitement builds with each passing road sign, along with your thoughts and expectations about the pounding surf that's just ahead.

A Place Called "Country"

The further north you drive, the more you'll notice that you're moving into "Country" domain. The highrise buildings gradually recede as you go past the Aloha Stadium and up through Mililani Town, Wahiawa and the olive drab military boys at Schofield Barracks. Eventually, near Leilehua, you will reach the blood-red dust of a Dole pineapple plantation that frames both sides of the Kamehameha Highway.

As you proceed along this razor-edged roadway, you eventually come to a hill with a wide-angle overview of the North Shore. This particular panorama has been ogled by visiting surfers for many decades, and on a day blessed with waves, you can see rolling lines of whitewater pushing over outside reefs, painting a picturesque surfer dream scene. One's heart beats against this vast open ocean backdrop set in front of lush green hills and great blue skies. This is your initial *aloha* to a part of Oahu known as the North Shore, or, more simply, The Country.

nent surfboard shaper Dale Velzy. The surf break Velzyland is found just in front of these unsightly cave-like dwellings. The buildings offer no indication as to what can be found in the water, though, because Velzyland, or V-land as it's commonly called, just happens to be one of the most unreal small-wave rights in the world. Waves here are generally smaller in ratio compared to the rest of the North Shore, but V-land's shallow finger of reef makes sure that anything that rolls over it is guaranteed to pack a punch. What you'll find here is a twisting right-hander that bowls over a weird reef, creating funky double-ups and reform sections that can throw grinding barrels. Rippable cutback sections are also on the menu, and these features all work together to make Velzyland the high-perfomance wave that it is.

Crowds are an endemic problem here, and can lead to much frustration. You can remedy this by jumping on the sectiony lefts which peel off the main peak. They are definitely worth the ride, and can even barrel like the right just opposite, but the reef is not as well-shaped, and waves tend to close out. Paddling back out can be tricky, and you may find yourself ducking whitewater for what seems like an eternity. You can also sit on the inside of the right, in the hope that more aggressive surfers snatching waves up on the outside will blow their ride, leaving the remainder for the droves to pounce on. The inside, though short, can still produce gaping barrels before going into the channel.

An awkward phenomenon at V-land is that no matter how big the surrounding swell may be, the waves breaking will be no bigger than 6 feet. This is due in part to an outer reef that breaks the swell down outside of the takeoff spot, redefining it into an intense double-up over the aforementioned

For logical and geographic reasons, our run through the key Country surf spots will commence at the extreme Windward side of Oahu's northern surfing grounds (in the Turtle Bay area) and then continue on downwards through the heart of the famed North Shore. Because of the reef configurations here, many proper surfing breaks on the coast often appear side by side, so identifying them can sometimes be frustrating. But with a bit of guidance, your disorientation will be easily resolved.

Dale Velzyland

The surf spot furthest north worthy of mention is a break fronting the **Turtle Bay** Hilton, which features a sometimes fun right-hander in the bay when winds are light or from the south.

As you hit the border of the surf-central town of Sunset Beach, you will notice a slew of identical brown townhouses lined up just off the *makai* (or ocean) side of the highway. This area is known as **Velzyland**, named after the emi-

Above: Local boy Nainoa Surratt looking for a sweet wave setup on a Velzyland vector. *Photo: Bernie Baker*

Top right: Todd Holland going for a long hard North Shore drive. *Photo: Jeff Divine*

Bottom right: Camera shy? "Not," says Sunny Garcia. Except for the odd stickers, Sunny's approach is still quite the same these days. Blow-up on the North Shore. *Photo: Art Brewer*

dangerously shallow inside reef. When it starts to get really big, Velzyland becomes washed out and unrecognizable under surges of whitewater.

Phantoms may sound like a spooky name for a surf spot, but according to the nutcases who are stoked to be surfing there, it lives up to its name. Located directly outside of Velzyland, Phantoms doesn't start showing true form until waves start cranking around the 15-foot and up range. What you'll find here is a short right peak with a left that can form lengthy rides. Phantoms is not as regularly surfed as other big-wave breaks, but can still reach unreal proportions. Tow-ins are conducted as well. A surfer named Jim Broach died while surfing out here on a big day in the early 1990s. Apparently, a rogue 25-foot set caught him and his fellow surfers inside and absolutely pounded them. When the sea had calmed after the set, all that was found of Broach was his surfboard. Searches were conducted in vain, and he became one of the rare casualties of big-wave surfing.

On a less threatening note, there are waves in the immediate vicinity for those unwilling to take on lunging 20-foot walls of water. Those not amped on the big stuff

can seek refuge at **Freddyland**, just across the channel from Velzyland. On bigger and smaller days, Freddy's will usually still have a manageable wave peeling off that is perfectly suited for beginners and those shy of big waves. The wave here is a rolling peak breaking over reef, with lefts going longer than the rights.

Backyards & Boneyards

The little headland between Sunset Beach and V-land is a quiet little neighborhood of houses lining backroads with children playing in the street. The backyards of some of these beachfront homes occasionally feature really good waves breaking off the fronting reef. And what better name for a backyard surf spot than, yes, **Backyards**. Surfed at times as a place of refuge from the mindboggling "Country" crowds, Backyards on its day can pump. You can choose between the rights breaking toward Sunset, or the lefts looping toward Velzyland. Either can produce long roping rides, or even barrels, that can hold quite some size (up to 15-feet plus). Waves tend to be sectiony, and it's never fun when a 10-foot wave you've struggled into closes out in your face. But on good days, you'll see less of these and more makeable rides.

Beware of the shallow inside section of the right, aptly named **Boneyards**. When the surf is overwhelmingly crowded at Sunset, the waves coming in on the reef here may just entice you to make the paddle over. Backyards is also a favorite haunt for windsurfers who attack the waves on the windiest of days. It's quite awe-inspiring watching them go when the swell hits solid size.

The real name of this stretch of beach, better known to the world as Sunset, is *Paumalu*, a Hawaiian name that means "taken secretly"

Right: Eating it sucks, but, well, nobody's perfect. Bruce Irons (**Top**) and Mark Healy (**Bottom**) show you what happens when you swallow without chewing. *Photos: Jason Childs*

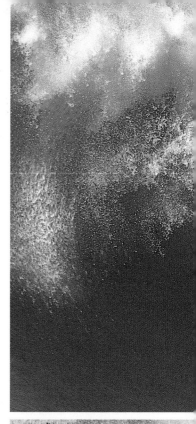

and honors the memory of an unfortunate Hawaiian woman whose legs were bitten off by a shark along here. **Sunset Beach**, originally known as the Sunset Tract (and before that as the Pupukea-Paumalu Beach Tract), is a romantic name given to the area during the 1920s by a real estate developer who had noticed that it was one of the nicest places on Oahu to watch the sun's final rays slowly leave the sky.

Whatever the name's origin, Sunset is one of the most challenging surfing venues in the world. Under 6 feet, the waves here break over an inside reef close to its palm tree-dotted point and form an enjoyable performance right called **Sunset Point**. At this playful size, you'll find all sorts of people having fun: longboarders, boogeyboarders, *keikis* (children), etc.

But as the swell here rises, the action shifts dramatically to a deep-water outside reef where ocean swells channel into thick, ever-shifting and fast-moving surges of water that force their way towards shore with waterfall-like lips. Add the prospect of 15- to 25-knot trade winds that blow huge plumes of salt spray high above the face of these monstrosities (holding you up in vertical drop mode and blinding your eyes until the very last second) and what you have here, would-be surfer, is one of the great surf spots in the world. If you want to be shit-scared by Nature in all her primeval glory, this is a great first-time-in-big-waves testing and prove-yourself ground.

Technically, there are two main peaks that are surfed at Sunset on a good day, both partial to swell direction. On west swells, a fast mountainlike peak rises towards the channel and peels off menacingly, crushing anything that's caught in its path. Sometimes, a left will shoulder off from the peak, and though you can ride it, you can also end up in a very bad spot over

Left: Each year, the North Shore deals out the slaps. Injuries and even fatalities can occur, regardless of one's ability in the water. Always check with the lifeguards if you are ever in doubt, and even if you aren't. *Photo: Jason Childs*

Above: A "Surfer's Crossing" indeed!
Photo: Joe Carini

looks from the beach, so you may want to consult the lifeguards before paddling into something way over your head. Or you may want to stick to **Val's Reef** over the inside with the local groms before heading out into the open sea.

Crowds are an everpresent dilemma at Sunset, and on some days, you will see more than a hundred tiny heads bobbing in the water. Whatever your intentions, Sunset requires top physical conditioning, a primo set of lungs, a big board and even bigger balls. Getting caught inside and pounded is a fact of life when surfing here, as are broken boards. To actually wire Sunset's shifty peaks takes years of dedication.

Paddle straight out from the beach, but time your entries and exits carefully so as to not make a fool of yourself in the heavy inside shorebreak.

the reef and be imminently prone to getting caught inside and being brutally spanked by a very sneaky clean-up set.

Up the reef, however, is Sunset's classic north peak, a sea mount fueled by good north swells which break way outside, and which can present the most diffident of waverunners with a big and contentious wall that can run on through to the inside. This inside section is yet another story because this realm of the reef can push waves into some of the most intense and fat barrels around. Making it through one of these mothers is yet another crapshoot, usually rated at about a 50/50 chance of survival. Woe to those who find themselves inside a thick barrel that claps shut on their head and pile-drives them into the shallow reef below. Those who emerge from such a sick insider are deemed legends, and will surely be buzzing from the resultant euphoria and adrenaline rush for the rest of the day.

Northwest swells do this place the most justice, and anything from 6 to 15 feet is fair game. It's always bigger out there than it

More Than Just A Market

Back on shore, let's repair to Kammies Market, a local foodery that has become a bit of an institution in the Sunset Beach area (and which caters to all a surfer might need). Kammies even serves up waves. Well, not exactly, but the fun left/right peak parallel to the store is called **Kammies** and can fulfill your desire for waves on smaller North Shore days. The waves out here can be bowly and fun, so just check it out from the beach, brah. Usually not too crowded either.

The next two spots going towards Haleiwa from Kammies are **Stone Zone** and **Monster Mush**. Both are better on small swell days when almost every other spot on the North Shore is manageable. They can also sometimes be a great escape from the madding crowds. Stone Zone can have juicy fun peaks and Monster Mush features a usually mushy

right-hander and left. The Mush is right across from Rocky Point, which we will discuss next. Again, think small.

If there was ever a spot made for shooting pictures and for catering to the needs of a photo slut, it would have to be **Rocky Point**. That's not to say that the waves at Rocky's suck; it's just that they get really, really, REALLY crowded. On any given sunny day with decent waves, you're sure to find enough cameramen on the beach to convince the clueless that a major motion picture about surfing was being shot. Rocky's features an unreal left that is super shredable, uniformly hollow, and which can link up and peel a fair way on down the beach. A short right completes this peak, but if you're looking for rights, paddle a tad on down to **Rocky Rights**, where dreamy rights peel off like something out of the World's Most Rippable Waves textbook. Beware of the rocky beach and inside waters when floating closeout end

sections, or when paddling in or walking out. Inside of the rights is a big rock sticking prominently out of the water which you should avoid at all costs. The most auspicious and safest paddle out to Rocky's is from the little sand beach just north of **Rocky Lefts**. When big winter swells bomb this coast, all the sand that settled here during the summer gets washed away (thus revealing the rockiness). Best ridden at under 8 feet.

Those looking for cheap thrills in life should head just across the way from Rocky Rights to the peak at **Gas Chambers**. Fast-breaking lefts and rights are the go, and roomy barrels can be snagged if you're patient. Making it out of them is hard, and trying not to hit the reef when eating it on the inside is just as difficult. Chambers is one of those places where wearing a condom-like helmet isn't such a bad idea. The lefts sometimes close out with Rocky Rights, so choose your waves wisely—you may just score a spitting dream.

Above: And on a mild day at Waimea Bay, it's crosstown traffic, or perhaps— "Ho! Hey! Going! Got it!"—more like a misplaced Malibu on Oahu's constantly busy North Shore. *Photo: Jeff Divine*

OAHU

THE NORTH SHORE

Pupukea is another one of those rock bottom spots that fills in with shifting sand from summer. Whether it's sand or rock that you're surfing over, Pupe's still comes up with the goods, delivering thick rights and lefts that spiral up and down the beach. As perfect for high-performance waveriding as any other spot. Pupukea handles up to about 8 feet solid, and even at that size will still be manageable, though quite heavy. The beach is also a favorite place to sift and burrow for cute little puka shells, or to just hang out and get a tan. Pupukea is situated just to the right (towards Sunset) from Ehukai Beach Park.

The breaks fronting **Ehukai Beach Park** usually materialize over a sand bottom until a proper monster swell buffs the bottom clean and leaves only a bare butt reef below. Smaller days yield fun peaks up and down the beach at Ehukai (in front of the beach park) and at **Gums** (a spot just before Pipeline). The grand Pipeline itself is in full view and just to the left of this little beach park.

Pipelines

The Banzai Pipeline is without a doubt the most famous wave in the world, and it conveniently does its extraordinary thing just to the left side of Oahu's Ehukai Beach Park. You'll know it when you see it: super thick, swift-moving mountains of water that unload their strength with pounding vigor over an obscenely shallow lava reef below. All the rumors, stories, video clips and photos that you've ever seen of the place will come into focus before your eyes on any day that da pipe is in action. Some of the most colossal, fear-inducing, liquid-tripping, awe-inspiring, simply straight-up insane left-hand tubes on earth—ones that can make you poop your pants in a heartbeat—spin through this place with great regularity. (Whew, that was a mouthful). Eh, but how you figgah, brah: no other wave in the world has been as ardently documented as this one, and we ask you to watch and you will very soon learn why. This place f★#king smokes, brah!

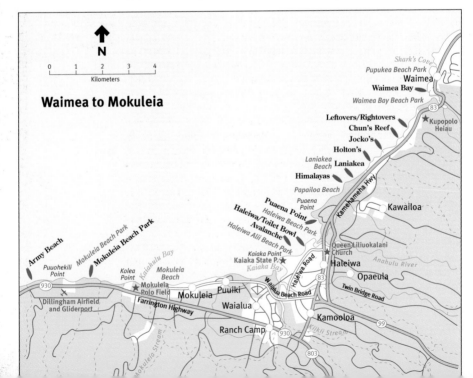

As the wave action rises here, you surf over different parts of the volcanic reef. Under, say, 8 feet, most of the surfing is done on the inside reef. As the swell rises, **Second Reef Pipe** awakens, presenting big rolling faces that lead to mental double-ups over the inside. Waves that cap over the second reef but don't quite break unload straight over the inside with an extra force that seems to have come from the depths of a watery hell. When Second Reef Pipe is happening and online, just the sight of it causes mouths to drop and remain wondrously agape. When the action gets serious, **Third Reef Pipe** comes into "play," peaking way outside and steamrolling in down the line. Heavy stuff.

To actually surf Pipe, you've got to have a considerable number of years of surfing heavy waves under your belt, along with an advanced level of tuberiding skills and a gung-ho, go-for-broke attitude. You also need boards that can negotiate the supersteep and sucking drop, and also be able to

explore the immense magnitude of a Pipe-bomb cave. Above all, you have to really want one of these beasts. There are basically two groups of people out on the Pipe. The first group are those who are addicted to and desire Pipe-drainers like junkies looking for a fix. The others are just, well, out there, but not quite sure if they've made the right choice by stroking out to the lineup, or if they actually do want to confront these demonic waves. You can almost see it in their eyes as they paddle out—whether they've got the fire or not.

Backdoor Pipeline (or **Backdoor**) is a consequential right that reels off the peak, and it is just as intense, if not more intense, than the celebrated lefts. The reef is even shallower here, sometimes drying out at the end of some rides. Some say the drop is even more nuts than the Pipe proper. Gaping right-hand barrels that lunge right off the drop call for little more than a straight drop into the mouth of the beast, and then a fast drive for the exit as you pray hard for the door to stay open.

Above: Big Isle slasher Shane Dorian may be one of the most famous and highly-paid surfers in the world, but he didn't get there by sitting on his couch. Yes, presenting Shane, moving fast on the North Shore. *Photo: Art Brewer*

Above: To Pipe or not to Pipe?
Gerry Lopez and Howard Farrant contemplate
one of the Pipeline's many moods.

Successfully making your wave frontside is a true accomplishment, while managing to emerge unscathed backside is the stuff of legends. You should also keep in mind that what makes Pipe and Backdoor barrels throw the way they do is the hellishly shallow lava ledge that sits no more than 6 feet under the takeoff spot, even during those 10-foot plus dredgers. The bottom contour is actually quite flat in most places, with the exception of lava caves that have formed the basis of countless horror stories about surfers who were caught inside one after a particularly heavy wipeout. Try diving here on a flat day and see for yourself. In fact, the bottom is so obviously dangerous that Gerry Lopez, one of the greatest Pipeline riders in history, once said: "It's not a matter of *whether* you're going to get hurt surfing out there, but more a matter of *when*."

Before attempting to take on the Pipeline, be honest with yourself about your abilities. Are you really ready for it, and are you willing to take on the consequences? Remember that the poor souls out there getting shacked out of their minds and blown into the channel by the fire hydrant-like spray are some of the most accomplished tuberiders in the world. Many are even well-paid to specifically surf Pipe/Backdoor, and it's their job—with skills in check—to make impossible, near-death situations look like a stroll through the park.

Crowds here may be among the worst in the world. Imagine sitting shoulder-to-shoulder with Strider, Liam McNamara, Johnny-Boy, Mike Stewart, Braden Dias, Pancho, Derek and Mike Ho, and Shawn Briley, as well as an entanglement of other surfers, body-boarders and longboarders, some of whom are the best in the world. In a pack like this, the odds of snagging a decent wave fade fast. Scraps are what you'll normally end up with, but you never know. You may just catch for yourself one of those serendipitous moments when Mother Nature decides to cut you a break and flings a big green gem at you.

The paddle out is easy enough, but just be sure to time the sets (as in every surfing situation, but especially here) to make sure you don't get caught inside before scratching on out to the lineup. If you hit the water facing the break, the rip current will immediately sweep you towards the Pipeline channel. From that point onwards, it's all up to you.

The next spot over from Backdoor is one more high status venue in the world of surfing. **Off The Wall** is another of those places specializing in gutsy barrels. The main part of the wave is an accelerated right that bowls from takeoff to wave's end. Waves are super quick, and it takes years of adapting to figure out which ones to pick (kind of like mushrooms in a field). A right pick and you're flying through tunnel vision with an exit. But a wrong choice equals the above sans the exit. Beware of the shallow inside, and crowds that are always a nuisance. Lefts that drive toward Backdoor can be an option, but they tend to clamp shut over a shallow inside section. Getting caught inside here is also not in your best interest. Off The Wall (or OTW) got it's name from the concrete wall facing the break at the end of the public right-of-way going towards the beach. The steep drops characteristic of Off The Wall may also have contributed to its name.

Insanities is yet another properly-christened peak that looks straight into the right at OTW. Its waves can jack and sometimes get good, so keep an eye on it.

The left straight out from the outcrop of rocks on the beach (right by the lifeguard tower) squeezes out some serious juice. **Rockpiles**, as it's called, features a thick left that doubles-up and warps over a boil in the takeoff spot, and then rolls down the line. Big barrels are a possibility, but risky. Getting caught on the inside may push you over the rocks, so beware. From the beach, the size of the waves can be deceiving, and they are guaranteed to be bigger once you get out the back. Rockpiles handles some serious size, and usually has a minimal crowd of surfers. Totally in view from the coastal highway.

The right winding off of Rockpiles, **Logcabins** by name, is a thumping wave that can turn on in small to medium north swells. Shallow rock patches line the bottom here, so extreme caution should be exercised. When going off, Logs can be as intense and tubey as anywhere else on the North Shore. Logcabins may have been named (uh, duh?) after the log rental house on the beach facing this break.

Below: When the Waima river reaches its maximum capacity, the boys head down with their shovels and dig a stream to the ocean. As the flow strengthens, a stationary wave forms over the sand. Great filler-fun, but take heed of the less-than-sanitary water. *Photo: Mana*

Above: Waimea Bay (say "wy-may-uh"). A sacred panorama in the world of surfing. *Photo: Steve Wilkings*

Rubber Duckies, once voted the "Stupidest Surf Spot on the North Shore" in a *Surfer* magazine survey, is nothing to get excited about. A sometimes mushburger right that is rarely ever good comes in on a reef at the beach called Three Tables. Possibly fun on a longboard, but you are probably better off just relaxing on the beach with your rubber ducky.

Winding up at Waimea

Waimea Bay is a beautiful crescent-shaped bay that on big swells holds what may be the premier big-wave right in the world. Under 15 feet, the wave here hugs the point and is known as **Pinballs**. When waves start hitting the 18-foot and up range, however, the activity shifts to the outside and true Waimea jumps into gear. The whole deal here is about making the drop and then escaping to the safety of the deep channel, a ploy that is way easier said than done. Waves hitting the outside boil can jack and lunge with great ferocity, creating a complex drop, one that can get even harder when it is being blasted by stiff trade winds. These mountainous entities have been known to form barrels big enough to drive a truck through. If all this wasn't enough, there is even a freak left that sometimes shoulders off the right (but which is not recommended), and which has so far only been attempted and made by two all-around wave maniacs, Shawn Briley and Marvin Foster. Waimea comfortably holds swells up to the 25-foot range and sometimes bigger. At this height, the Bay reaches its capacity and may start closing out. The crowds that clog the lineup definitely make surfing here even more dangerous than it should be, and, as some Waimea vets say, have killed the mythical magic of the place.

The inside and close to the beach Waimea shorebreak is world-famous for its necksnapping power. Surfers paddling in and out of the Bay have to deal with this phenomenon first, which can be rudely annoying because this fierce sandpounder reaches up to 15 feet on the face on seriously big days. Boogeyboarders and bodysurfers take much pride in riding these liquid time bombs, locking into enormous, frothing sand-dredging pits before they implode on the shoreline. Some stand-up surfers even take their chances here, usually on smaller days. Breaking your board and/or back may result from a session out here, so the buyer of such goods should beware. On days when the Bay shows its stuff, it seems as if the whole island stops to watch. Traffic along the Kamehameha Highway creeps slowly by the lookout cliff as drivers rubberneck and try to see the breaking waves, and park-ing spots around the cliff and beach park are snatched up as quickly as they become available.

Here, in the heart of the winter season, a prestigious invitational big-wave riding contest, "The Quik-silver in Memory of Eddie Aikau," goes into a wave-waiting period. Conditions have to be just right, meaning solid Waimea lines of 20-foot plus swell coming through with pleasant wind and weather patterns. If these contest require-ments are met, then the Eddie goes ahead. If not, the whole show is put on hold until the next sea-son. Competitors in the event are all fully-certified hellman/charg-ers, and they push the limits in this event for a first place check of fifty grand, one of the highest prize purses around. Eddie Aikau was a well-known Hawaiian waterman who took off fearlessly on some of the biggest waves at Waimea dur-ing his time. He was also a respect-ed lifeguard on the North Shore, but was tragically lost at sea in 1978 while attempting to swim to shore for help while serving on the crew of an experimental ancient Hawaiian sailing canoe named the *Hokulea*. The *Hokulea* had been damaged and was threatening to go under in rough seas. Eddie's body was never recovered. When the waves are huge and local surfers are scared, they will often look at each other and say, hopefully, that if he were still here, well, "Eddie would go."

The surf coming in from Waimea Bay to Haleiwa is a considerable downshift from the heaving action around Sunset Beach. The waves are still excellent, however, and reek of 100 percent pure North Shore juice. For those looking for a fun and not-too-threatening peak to surf, **Leftovers** is a good option. The lefts coming in here are nice and wally, providing ample space to boogie on. The odd tube will make a guest appearance at times.

Rightovers are the rights that roll off just up from the lefts; they get fun and give you sufficient room to play. Take heed of the shallow inside that pops up on lower tides. It sounds good, but take into consideration that a boogeyboarder once disappeared from this lineup during an early session, and all that was recovered later was his sponge with a good-sized shark bite taken out of it. A much-visited memorial to him was put up next to the bushes near the checkout spot here.

Across the narrow channel from Leftovers lies **Alligator Rock**. Gator's is a sometimes happening right and short left that stands up and does its thing before going impotent in the channel. Easily checked from the beach, or from out at Leftovers.

Before arriving at the wide-open view of Laniakea, you'll come to another open beach clearly visible from the road. There are two waves here—a left and a right—which break towards each other, and on small to medium size swell days, they can send any sane surfer mad in trying to decide which way to go. A channel in the center of the two separates the movement on both sides and provides a safe paddle-out spot. The rights are known to the world as **Chun's Reef**, and are some of the easiest and fun waves to ride. A myriad of peaks makes up Chun's, and they all turn off and on, depending on local swell, tide and surf-god conditions. The peak by the channel offers a short, fun ride before withering away into the deep water. The outside peak can be the best bet, with good rides pushing all the way through to the other side, baby. Chun's features a fine performance-tuned wall that is great for any maneuver you may have lingering in your mind. It all sounds good, except when you see

Below: Looking lines at Lani's. It looks majestic, but now, if you could only snag one for yourself . . .
Photo: Jeff Divine

the packed water crew that is sure to be there on any respectable day. The odd left is up for grabs, and it's a good way to sneak one away from the pack. A shower is strategically placed on the beach for those wishing to rid their body of saltwater essence. It is regularly put to use, in appreciation of its donor, Rick "Crazy Shirts" Ralston.

The lefts on the opposite side are also great places to hunt for quality breakers. Jock Sutherland, one of the original surfers who defined hotdogging from the late '60s into the early '70s, was one of the first to put in time at this reef, which isn't much of a surprise given that he grew up in a house right on the beach. Along with Jeff Hakman and some of his other neighbors, Jock was a member of the Chun's Reef Surfing Society, an informal and little-known group of North Shore surfers who made up what was probably the NS's first surfing club. Unable to persuade his buddies to paddle out with him because they wussed-out at the thought of having to deal with the gnarly rocks protruding on the inside (remember, those were pre-leggie days, mate), Jock would constantly solo it and reap all the spoils. That's the local tale behind the naming of **Jocko's**, which also goes by the name **Jock's Reef**.

The wave itself is a winding left that can churn out quite a mean barrel on its day. Lipsmacking areas are abundant, and should be taken advantage of whenever possible. When good, Jocko's can be the ultimate and dreamy left. Be wary of the aforementioned rocks that line the inside. They have a weird habit of making themselves known when one is caught in their vicinity while ducking whitewater. Crowds are once again a pesky factor at this surf spot.

One of the more sought after rights in The Country is **Laniakea**. When on, Lani's exhibits a long and roping ride that can challenge the hardest of the hardcore. An inside bowl near the channel is a great place to hook into wedging wonders, while the outside peak can hand out long on-down-the-line speed tracks leading to the inside. Under 6 feet, Lani's remains playful and can be enjoyed by the majority of surfers on hand. The story changes when the sets start rumbling at 8 feet and up. Heavy lines of waves possess plenty of push-start and are best attempted by more advanced waveriders. Big barrels followed by a rushing wall of waves twist down a long right line, and on good swells from the north, these walls can thread their way all the way across the reef, causing jelly legs at the finish line.

Swells incoming from the west, meanwhile, make for fast-dumping sections and are best passed up for a different spot. Lefts occasionally roll off the outside peak, but hold

Above: Is this view enticing enough to inspire the long paddle out? We think so. Welcome to a place called Avalanche. *Photo: Mana*

out the threat of being caught inside. Getting snared by a freak set on a sizey day means taking serious poundings that may pose the specter of seeing yourself paddle all the way back out from the channel again. You can tell if the surf's happening without even looking at the water by applying the surfer's rule of counting the number of cars in the parking lot. If the lot is empty, it's a good sign that the surf probably stinks.

The peak between Laniakea and Jocko's, called **Holton's**, can dish up some tasty rights. Nice drops followed by a big wall are on the menu and can satisfy any surfer's appetite for adrenaline on bigger, holding days. It is easily checked from the Lani's carpark.

To the left of Lani's and about a mile out to sea is **Himalayas**, a mountainous peak that holds monster swells. Not a place for surfing alone, so if you feel like going for it, take at least one buddy (if not several) and a big board. Rarely surfed due to the beastly nature of the place. Towing-in is usually a better riding strategy.

When the buoys hit the 20 feet/20 second mark and most of

the North Shore is macking and closing out, your list of rideable wave venues starts to really get limited. You could go for it at a maxing outside reef Pipeline or Sunset if they are holding up, or go for the guts and glory of Waimea. If the big stuff isn't on your agenda, then give **Puaena Point** a look-see. There are actually two spots to surf that show their stuff when the swell starts getting serious. The first place of refuge is the bowly peak at the edge of the channel that forms a fast-breaking right driving into the deep water. Wave sizes here are usually only a fraction of the surrounding swell. You can tell if it's going off or not by looking at it from the beach. If it looks good from land, it's probably better in the water.

For those looking for more of an adrenaline boost, the outside is the call. Thick long rights come in from way out the back, and if you should snag a good one, it will take you for a lengthy shoot to the inside. Beware of fast wide ones that will work you and leave you helpless to the brutality of the rest of the set. Some of the size of the swell is reserved for this outside

break, and it can get big. Keep your eyes peeled for those notorious sneaker sets.

Homely Haleiwa

Haleiwa could possiby be one of the trickiest waves to surf on the North Shore. From the beach, the nicely-shaped rights are deceptively inviting, but from the water it's a whole different story. A super-solid rip that could tire out a shark runs through the break, causing a constant paddling to keep up with it and to maintain your position. The waves themselves tend to section off, crushing those waveriders who have the tenacity to try their luck on them.

A deathly shallow end section called the **Toilet Bowl** borders the end of the right, and at times can suck straight out to near dry reef, as if someone had just flushed a bowlful. The local boys who call Haleiwa home are among the stingiest around when it comes to sharing waves, and they are out nearly every rideable day in an attempt to make sure that their wave quotas are met—and then

some. Sneaker sets that send you propeller-arming for the horizon are more than common, particularly on solid days when getting spanked-drilled is an uncomfortable consequence. For those who "no can handle" and feel that they have to tap out, lifeguards are almost always on duty to make sure that things don't get out of hand. If you can deal with all of this, then you may just have a fun sesh out here. When on, Haleiwa can produce some of the top performance waves around. High-speed rights beg for a lipbash, and even the odd left that can be jumped on fills the reef. Indeed, on good mood days, everyone has fun.

On bigger and decidedly more intimidating days, beginners and minigroms can amuse themselves by frolicking on an inside reform section that rolls through before dissipating. And for those who don't surf, the beach park is definitely user-friendly and the perfect place to have a picnic, soak in the rays and observe the action at sea. At the surf center, if you're polite enough, Uncle Lee may even lend you the paddles and ball for da ping-pong table.

Above: Haleiwa always looks way easier from the beach than it actually is. Add the racing rip currents, shifty peaks, clean-up sets and anxious locals and it very suddenly becomes much less alluring.
Photo: Jeff Divine

OAHU

THE NORTH SHORE

Left: A straight-up schnapp by Australian Shane Wehner. Hey, it got our attention, didn't it?

Top right: The innovative Kalani Robb turning heads with some new-school surf trickery.

Bottom right: L.A. local Strider "Raspberry" Wasilewski makes like a bird and soars through the sky.

Photos: Jason Childs

When a wave has an intimidating name such as **Avalanche**, you sort of lose interest in doing anything other than observing. And that's exactly what 99 percent of the people checking out the waves at Haleiwa do. For the 1 percent who choose to make the long paddle out to this lonesome peak, we say, "have a grand time," as there won't be many others in hot pursuit of this particular bombie-curl.

What you'll find upon arrival is a deepwater peak that tends to shift around a bit. The lefts lead to a mean inside bowl section that will either give you the barrel—or the beating—of your life. More often than not, you'll get the latter.

This sounds, of course, like about a hundred other waves at Oahu, but the one thing that separates Avalanche from the rest of the wave pack is that it handles the big stuff with ease. By big we're not talking just a solid 10 to 15 "Hawaiian feet," but more like 15 to 20 feet (meaning perhaps 50 feet anywhere else in the world). Smaller, and perhaps non-life-threatening days can be enjoyed here, but again, think before you buy. Just try not to bust your board or leash, as it is a very lengthy swim back to shore.

Moseying around Mokes

The Mokuleia stretch of coastline can be described as a part-time playfield. That's because the angle of the beach causes the blasting northeasterly trade winds to blow in a displeasing side/onshore flow. For those intent on surfing these parts, what this means is that you have to wait for the weather forecasts to read *kona* or variable winds. This produces quality surfing conditions between the stretches of ravaging onshore chop. Note: There's more out here than meets the eye, but our lips will remain sealed out of respect for the locals who were willing to share a lot of surfy *aloha* with us.

Just in front of **Mokuleia Beach Park** at the east side of Dillingham Airfield, a condition-pending right can be found. This wave isn't always good as it only accepts certain small swells from an appropriate angle (and preferably on a higher tide), but if these factors happen to align as the planets rarely do (what's that happening called?), then you may luck into some shreddable right-hand action. Winds need to be dead for this spot to come alive.

At the west end of the Dillingham Airfield strip is a pleasurable left and right peak affectionately known as **Army Beach**, probably after the military types who were once found on this beach. The left is the best bet, and you can pull into some clean, green rooms when it's good. Army Beach is normally blown to bits by the prevailing trade winds (as is the rest of the Mokuleia coastline), and it needs a *kona* or dead wind day to even be remotely considered worth surfing.

If you've only encountered bad surf luck along the Farrington Highway part of Oahu's North Shore, we suggest you cross over to the *mauka* side of the highway and take up the other big sport practiced out here. We're talking about polo, the so-called "Sport of Kings," which has been played for years at the old Mokuleia Polo Field. Along with Pipeline Beach back up the coast, these two places are probably Hawaii's most exclusive athletic arenas.

And if, by days end, you've only caught no-surf luck and found no waves whatsoever, the sunset show going down Kaena Point is always a great way to end your day and to soothe the soul. Just pray for clear skies.

—Lorca Lueras

Opposite: The North Shore has always been the proving ground for cutting-edge performance surfing. Christian Fletcher, one of surfing's early aerial pioneers, rises to well above the roar.
Photo: Jason Childs

Left: On the waves, women are stepping it up as always. Megan Abubo exhibits hot form. *Photo: Jason Childs*

Above: On any given sunny day, you can be sure that there will be, uh, cuties on the beach. *Photos: Jason Childs; except for bottom right by Jeff Divine*

Left: Whenever you're out surfing and there are cute girls on the beach, it always inspires you want to push the pedal to the metal. *Photo: Jason Childs*

Below: Of course, when you just can't seem to get that rhythm going, it makes you wish you'd never gotten out of bed.that morning. *Photo: Joe Carini*

Haleiwa

HALEIWA SURF MUSEUM

Hawaii's "Surf City" Town

Every surfing country has its social epicenter. For California it's got to be Huntington Beach. In France it would probably be Biarritz or Hossegor. In exotic Japan, they bow to the honorable Shonan. In Hawaii, though, it is the little sugarcane town known as Haleiwa.

Haleiwa has always been a crossroads kind of country village. It was originally created by Hawaii's sugarcane and pineapple industries at the base of Oahu's central agricultural plain. In later years, Haleiwa became better known as the gateway to what would one day be called Oahu's North Shore.

For many years, the town of Haleiwa endured little change, but this ended in the late 1950s, when a new breed of tourists began spending their money here and staying in small homes that could be rented for the entire winter surfing season. These first arrivals were big-wave riders, and most of them came from the mainland US and Australia.

Initially, these surfers were a new and curious sight for local farmers and store owners to behold, but soon enough they had become part of an annual migration of surfers who would drive out from Town to Country to ride the reefs around Haleiwa.

A few would even head on up to Sunset Beach, especially if the surf there was big. It was thrilling enough then just to watch Sunset and Waimea break.

For probably the next 10 years or so, little changed in Haleiwa, except perhaps for the addition of a new diner, gas station or maybe a tourist shop that catered to the people who drove through on their way to the North Shore's sandy and isolated beaches. At that time, Haleiwa was gateway to the vacation homes that people from Honolulu stayed in on weekends and holiday breaks. Then, as the mystique surrounding the area's surf spots began to grow, and as the sport of surfing became more popular, larger groups of local and international surfers began living in some of these old homes and cabins on Oahu's North Shore. Many of them stayed for the entire winter surfing season, and as a result of their presence, a new lifestyle evolved in and about Haleiwa town.

While Haleiwa is only an hour away from Waikiki's famous and crowded beaches, physically and psychologically, it exists in an unrushed and sleepy world of its own. To observe a bit of how Haleiwa has evolved over the years, let's take a drive through Haleiwa town—then and now.

If you were a surfer visiting the North Shore in the '70s, you would probably have eaten breakfast at a small diner known as **Yama's**. Years later, Yama's became **Shima's**, which was sold and is now gone forever. In the early '80s, the most popular breakfast place was the **Wizard of Eggs**, a very modern cafe with big plates of rice and eggs and American-style pancakes.

For lunch, you would have bought hamburgers or *saimin* noodles in a cafe near Haleiwa Beach Park known to all as **Jerry's**. That shop is also no longer there, but local surfers remember stopping in at Jerry's to order lunch and then taking it with them to the beach. For dinner, you would have gone to where all the surfers went: the old **Seaview Inn**, which later became the trendy **Chart House** restaurant, and which just recently became reincarnated again as a new hangout called **Aloha Joe's**.

The old and popular Seaview Inn had it all: cheap meals, cold beer, delicious fresh fish caught by local fishing boats, plus a clientele that consisted of surfers from around the world. For many years it was far and away the most popular restaurant for surfers in Hawaii. For Triple Crown surfers who didn't start frequenting Hawaii until the early '80s, places like the Seaview Inn were on their last legs.

After the devastation wrought on the North Shore by Hurricane Iwa in 1982, life in Haleiwa went through some dramatic changes. For one thing, business slowed down considerably due to the emergency repairs that had to be made to buildings and general town infrastructure. This in turn forced the local economy to shift away from recreation and an easy-going lifestyle and, well, "get serious." People found that they had less $ to spend on the fun things in life, and even in sleepy Haleiwa by the sea, where a charming little-town lifestyle had prevailed for many years, people were forced to change their habits.

As a result, much commercialization of Haleiwa and its environs has taken place, even in surfing. For example, in the mid-'70s, there were only two or three surf shops in and about Haleiwa Town. In those days, North Shore surfers didn't need many more shops than that. A small shop up at Sunset Beach took care of most of what people needed, and for more than that, well, people usually just drove to Honolulu.

Within 10 years, the number of surf shops in Haleiwa had tripled. Today, there are at least 15 shops in town selling surfing-related products. Given the ever-increasing number of tourists from around the world who come here and want to return home with a piece of our lifestyle, all of these shops somehow manage to survive, even during the off-season and long after Hawaii's big winter waves have left the North Shore.

Above: A Haleiwa sign of sometimes difficult surfing times. *Photo: Brett Uprichard*

Despite these changes, Haleiwa has managed to retain an old Hawaii allure reminiscent of years past. For the most part, Haleiwa's charming old buildings have been repaired and repainted, and like faithful sentinels they survive and stand strong against the trade winds and the North Shore's fickle weather and surf spray. Even a new highway that bypasses the town and gets you to the surf quicker really hasn't diminished the old magic of the place. Here, in what is arguably the only true "Surf City" in Hawaii, you can still find bits of what you might call Old Polynesia-style. Wander through Haleiwa's old shops and you'll be treated with the rare opportunity to share in the best of the past and the brightest of the present.

Come, *hele* on (move along) and join me as I take a bicycle ride through an old north Oahu cane town that the surfing world rediscovered and brought back to life more than 40 years ago. Get a sense of both the Hawaii of yesteryear and the foreseeable and trendy future.

On a typical cruise of this Surf City—known since ancient times as *haleiwa,* literally the *hale* (home) of the *iwa* (frigate bird)—I usually head into town just before the lunch hour and enter Haleiwa near the **Xcel Surf Shop**, driving down Haleiwa's main road and past the **Cafe Haleiwa**, where all surfers have breakfast. From there I check my mail and dispatch letters at the **post office**, where many of us usually meet to talk story with one another.

From the post office it's on down to the **local surf shops** for wax (or anything else that's necessary to maintain the surfing lifestyle). Later, I might just stop off at the **Raging Isle Shop** for mountain bike gear and more surf talk with famous surfboard shaper/cycle store owner Billy Barnfield.

Further down the road, and especially if it's lunchtime, I will check out the little sandwich shop known as **Storto's**, next door to the **BK Surf Shop**, a place that's owned by the famous '70s surfer, Barry Kanaiaupuni. With the energy to surf the rest of the day, I will drive on down the road, past the **H. Miura Store**, where surfer-style board shorts were first invented for North Shore surfers of the '60s, and where they are still being made for the surfers of today. In this historic shop, you can have shirts, pants and boardshorts custom-made, no matter how B-I-G or s-m-a-l-l you might be!

From here it's back across the **Old Haleiwa Bridge**—alongside the venerable **Surf N' Sea** shop's yellow walls, and then a slow pedal past the big country park where everyone plays soccer on winter weekends. Eventually I'm back on Kam Highway, cruising past Laniakea and the rest of the North Shore until I'm back home at Sunset Beach.

Yup, that's it, folks—a slow and easy cruise to "Surf Town" Haleiwa and back home again. Now, I just have to think about where I'll be surfing and make sure that I didn't forget to buy that bar of wax I'll need before I can paddle out!

—*Bernie Baker, reporting nostalgically from somewhere on the North Shore*

Left: Any male surfer worth his ding-repair kit would love to have a, uh, woodie, especially when he is about to get married. This classic woodie wagon is decked out in style and about to take the plunge.
Photo: Art Brewer

PRO SURFING
and
THE TRIPLE CROWN

BUCK$, BARRELS and GLORY

ntil the Triple Crown of Surfing was created in 1982–83, there had been very little for surfers in Hawaii to be involved in when it came to competitive challenges. There was the early and classic Duke Kahanamoku Invitational Surfing Championships (which had debuted in 1965 and was held sporadically for a few years) and the great Makaha International Surfing Championships, but there wasn't an overall trophy for the best surfer in Hawaii, only individual contest awards. With the creation of the Triple Crown, however, three separate events—The Sunset Beach Pro, The Pipeline Masters and a Haleiwa open meet—became to competitive surfing what the Super Bowl is to football. The Triple Crown now represents the highest laurel in international professional surfing.

Beginning with the Makaha Championships of the '60s and continuing on through to the era of the International Professional Surfing (IPS), competition on the North Shore had always pitted the world's best surfers (meaning the best in Hawaii) against one another. While the Association of Surfing Professionals (ASP) World Championship may be the year-round award for surfing events around the world, ask any surfer—especially one from Hawaii—and he or she will tell you that to win the Triple Crown is to be at the top of the surfing game. Year after year, the three events of the Triple Crown have continued to elicit awe-inspiring performances from surfers. This has always been its purpose, to spotlight the best surfers in the world. But the Triple Crown is also important to Hawaiian surfers for its spirit because it is an award achieved on home reefs and beaches.

In the beginning, forming the Triple Crown was as simple a process as enjoining three friends to start a rock n' roll band. We had our lead guitar (Pipeline), the bass

Kelly Slater and sweet victory at the ASP Men's Pipeline Masters in '94.
Photo: Jason Childs

88

(Sunset) and the drums (Haleiwa), all making great music. These three had been playing their individual songs, and their spirit was strong on the North Shore and in the world of professional surfing. Pipeline and Sunset were already established competition venues, and Haleiwa joined them soon after to form the Triple Crown of surfing.

Former world surfing champion Fred Hemmings, the father of modern professional surfing, was the original founder of the Triple Crown. In 1971, Hemmings started the Pipeline Masters contest, the oldest professional surf meet in the world. In 1975, he founded the IPS to determine a world champion for surfing. Hemmings chose established Hawaiian surfer/promoter and pro veteran Randy Rarick to be his competition director. I was brought in as the technical director to put the pieces together and to keep things tight through the many weeks of competition.

As a loosely-knit collection of surfing tournaments—from California to Hawaii and South Africa and back—the IPS circuit was all that professional surfers had from the '70s into the early '80s. In those early days when competitive surfing first emerged from the surfing lifestyle, international contest placings were often tallied casually, then, at the end of the year, surfers and foreign competitors would venture to Hawaii to compete in the North Shore's three contests.

Then came 1982. That year, surfers got together to form the ASP as a union for professional competitors. In those days, it was obvious that Hawaii would have to lead the world in the direction and organisation of competitive surfing, not only because the IPS was based here, but also because the Islands have what are arguably the most spectacular competition conditions on the planet. The epitome of this was the Triple Crown, an event that offered all the challenges and excitement needed to help launch a modern and professional era of competition. The Crown would also provide worldwide viewers with the opportunity to watch the very best surfing action, no matter where they lived. Satellite television could guarantee a new audience for the sport by putting it on an equal visual level as other major sports.

In those early days, there were slight misgivings about joining a new governing body that would impose a new set of rules on the sport in Hawaii, which was after all the birthplace of surfing. This feeling remained for the first year of competition while Hawaii officials watched and wondered as to what extent the ASP would attempt to control the events. Ultimately, the ASP has come to be recognized as an asset for the global growth of the sport.

Victor Ribas, cashing it in in '99.
Photo: Jason Childs

1982: The Year Before The Birth of the Crown

1982 was exciting and historic for many reasons: first, it was the maiden year of the *El Nino* weather disturbance which by then had been identified and monitored by scientists. Hurricane Iwa swept over Hawaii, causing devastation for two months, but great surf remained for the rest of that winter season.

Days after the hurricane had shut down electrical power on Kauai and the North Shore of Oahu, Michael Ho beat out Hans Hedemann at the Pipeline Masters. Even with a broken hand in a full cast, local boy Ho used all of his big-wave surfing know-how to take control of the event.

This was also the debut Hawaii season for the 16-year-old Australian Martin Potter. For fellow Aussie Tom Carroll, it was a big win for him at Sunset Beach's World Cup, despite his backside disadvantage. 1982 was also historic for Mark Richards as he handily won his Fourth World Championship title.

1983: The Crown's Debut

In 1983, an organizational struggle broke out between the ASP and the emerging Triple Crown of Surfing. Not yet members of the ASP, the Triple Crown's best Hawaiian surfers elected to surf their home events and accept no rating points from the ASP.

Dane Kealoha and fellow islander Michael Ho won the opening events, and Kealoha also handily took the prestigious Duke Kahanamoku Classic. Michael Ho, however, emerged as the first official Triple Crown of Surfing Champion. The future of the sport was, for the moment, firmly placed in homegrown Hawaiian hands.

1984

There's no way to tell who will win what in sports, but this winter season started out strong for Californian Joey Buran. Surfing better than anyone in an 8- to 12-foot BIG Pipeline, Buran beat the likes of Tom Carroll and Derek Ho to win. But Ho did a turn-around on everyone by beating out the rest of the surfers for 1984's Triple Crown.

1985

Mark Occhilupo won the Pipe Masters in windblown, stormy Pipe while past World Champ Mark Richards won the Hawaiian Pro at Waimea in surf that had most of the pros wondering just what their limits really were. Michael Ho tested his and went on to win the Triple Crown in great surf.

1986

Pipeline was very consistent throughout the '80s, and for the Marui Pipeline Masters that year, Derek Ho showed that he was in effect the next-generation Gerry Lopez in both style and aggression. Mark Richards took the Hawaiian Pro one more time in giant Waimea, but for Derek it was his year to win his second Triple Crown title, tying him with his brother Michael at two Crowns each.

1987

Australian Gary Elkerton had just gotten married when he flew in for the Triple Crown. In honor of his new bride, Elkerton won the crown with first places at the Hard Rock World Cup and the Hawaiian Pro.

1988

Yes, it was bound to happen—a winter of up-and-down surf conditions. Still, the Pipeline Masters came through with some of the best surf ever seen, and Tom Carroll was there to steal the show. Barton Lynch won

Pipe: The ultimate wave arena. *Photo: Jason Childs*

the ASP World Title but Derek Ho fired back with his third win of the Triple Crown.

1989

This was the year the senior surfers came back to beat the young guys. At the age of 29, Cheyne Horan won big at the Hawaiian Pro, taking US$50,000 at perfect Sunset Beach. But the big winner was Gary Elkerton, taking the year's Triple Crown title.

1990

Hawaiian pro and Pipeline specialist Ronnie Burns (RIP) had passed away only months earlier, and as the winter contest season began, surfers were dedicating their victories to his memory. The early surf itself was something we could all forget about, but it finally cleaned up and came back around for the Pipeline Masters. Tom Curren won the ASP World Title, but it was a fighting Derek Ho who proved stronger than all others when he convincingly reclaimed the Triple Crown (his fourth) for Hawaiians.

1991

Probably the most exciting finals ever to be held at Haleiwa during the Hawaiian Pro, Tom Carroll, Tom Curren, Martin Potter and Johnny Gomes battled it out in a perfect exhibition of competitive surfing. This time,

it would be Curren who prevailed, finally winning an event in Hawaii. However, it was the other Tom (Carroll) who won the Pipe Masters from Derek Ho, going on to take the Triple Crown in fabulous surf on the North Shore.

1992

This would become the first of a 3-year winning run for Hawaii's favorite son, Sunny Garcia, in his domination of the Triple Crown. In his quest for the year's first crown, Sunny took the Hawaiian Pro while Martin Potter stole away the World Cup. Kelly Slater snared his first big Pipe Masters win, the first of many for the impressive young surfer from Florida.

1993

Sunny Garcia's name popped up again and again in 1993, first for his win at the Hawaiian Pro. While Johnny Gomes captured the World Cup and Derek Ho returned to win at Pipe, based on total points across the board, it was Sunny's world as he took his second Triple Crown.

1994

A new name won big in Hawaii as California's Chris Brown surfed beyond his stature to win at the Hawaiian Pro. Kelly

Slater walked away with the Pipe Masters again, but Sunny Garcia's win at the World Cup racked up the points total for his third big Triple Crown award.

1995

Halfway through the final decade of the 20th century, surfboards *still* had three fins and a kid named Kelly Slater finally took control of Hawaii with his first Triple Crown win. Australian Richard Lovett won at Haleiwa's Hawaiian Pro and his fellow countryman Shane Powell won his first in Hawaii with the World Cup at Sunset Beach. Slater's win at the Pipeline now gave him three championship victories at the world's most breathtaking barrel ride.

1996

Australian Paul Patterson paddled out in the stormiest of conditions for the World Cup of Surfing at Sunset Beach, and, through the rip and chop of the ugly swell, saw an inside section that opened up with a rideable tube IF he just had the perfect timing. If he didn't, he'd be spending the rest of his heat trying to make it back outside. For Patterson, it was his day. He rode one great wave after another and let the other three surfers in his heat spend their entire time in the line-up trying to put together a decent ride.

For five-time world champion Kelly Slater, it was just another day at the office with his win at Pipeline. Then it was time for another local Hawaiian son, Kaipo Jaquias, to turn up the gas and go for broke. That he did by capturing the OP Hawaiian Pro and racking up enough points to take the Triple Crown, his first ever and a long overdue one for the native of Kauai.

1997

It started out as the worst of times but ended up as the best of times, marking a season of competitive surfing that will never be forgotten in the history of the sport. Rough weather started coming through the Hawaiian islands as the *El Nino* weather curtain began to cover the entire North Pacific weather map. The opener of the Triple Crown, the OP Hawaiian Pro at Haleiwa, had to deal with the first wave of bad weather as stormy winds moved in on Oahu. Australian Tony Ray, a veteran of competition surfing, had the perfect answer

to a final set in high winds and sloppy waves: sit outside, ride the biggest waves and don't even think about the smaller sets. Ray played this plan right up to the final second of the heat to win his first major event at Haleiwa.

The next contest in the Triple Crown, the Rip Curl World Cup of Surfing, held up a little bit better for waves, but the strong trade winds pulled in days of rain and thick clouds. Still, another smart Australian figured out the key to winning while way out in deep water. Michael Rommelse quickly took charge of the event, capturing his first ever win at Sunset Beach.

Next in the cards was the WCT thriller at the Banzai Pipeline. In these two events, two Hawaiians—Michael Ho and Johnny Boy Gomes—made ASP history by becoming the only two trialists to meet in an ASP final anywhere in the world. At age 40, Ho became the oldest shortboard competitor to make the final of an event of such prestige. The winner, Johnny Boy Gomes, proved that he was equal to all-star Kelly Slater by beating him twice in a barrel-riding standoff to get into the finals. Gomes' mastery of tube-riding during those last two days will be talked about 'round beachside bonfires for many years to come.

Meanwhile, it was World Cup winner Michael Rommelse who held on to enough points to take the 1997 G-Shock Triple Crown of Surfing award.

And let's not forget Layne Beachley. The Australian showed the world that there was finally a new heroine to take over Margo Oberg's mantle in big Island surf. Capturing the first-ever Women's Kahlua Triple Crown of Surfing award by winning two of the three events, Lady Beachley would soon become the dominant professional in women's surfing.

1998

Kauai youngblood Bruce Irons made surfing headlines worldwide by blowing down the doors from the trials to the finals of the Mountain Dew Pipeline Masters, leaving the crowd in awe after each hair-raising pit at good-sized gnarly Pipeline. The Masters could have been his had Australian surfer Jake "The Snake" Patterson not snagged the winning bomb at Backdoor in the dwindling seconds of the finals. Nevertheless,

Kelly Slater, putting 10s on the board. *Photo: Jeff Divine*

Irons' reputation and Pipe spot had been cemented, all at the tender age of 19.

Mick Campbell and Danny Wills were all in the running for the World Title, but after a disappointing show at the Banzai Pipeline for Campbell and Wills, Kelly showed everyone what was really going on and walked away with the World Title once again.

1999

This was another big year for junior competitors with Aussie Zane Harrison, aged 19, surfing beyond his years at Sunset, taking out the likes of Sunny Garcia and other veterans to capture the Rip Curl World Cup. Harrison also raged through the trials at the Pipeline, eventually losing to Mark "Occy" Occhilupo in the main event. Kelly Slater came out of "retirement" to negotiate yet another win at Pipeline, defeating World Title contender Occhilupo. While it was Occy who won the World Title that day, the attention on the beach was, as usual, intensely concentrated on Slater.

The Quiksilver/Eddie Aikau big-wave event came out of hibernation in 1999, and Noah Johnson emerged $50,000 richer on New Year's Day and at the beginning of a new surfing millennium.

From 2000 and Into the Future

So now, True Believers, let's look into our crystal ball and ponder the evolution of professional surfing in the Third Millennium. Of the new breed of talented young surfers, both male and female, who shall overcome? Where will they come from?

As we think about such things, the professional surfers are already aggressively on tour and competing throughout the world. Judges are judging, points are being tallied on ASP computers, and we will soon avidly witness yet another Triple Crown shootout in Hawaii. By the time the surfers have packed their quivers and as the final three events of the new winter season begin to unfold on the thundering beaches of the North Shore, there will be a list of new "names"—and maybe even a few older ones—posted at the very top of the official world rankings.

As usual, it will be every pro surfer's dream to arrive in Hawaii with enough aggression and competitive focus to become the next Triple Crown of Surfing Champion. There's no telling whose name will be on the trophy, but whoever becomes the "headline hero" in the coming day's newspapers will be heir to more than just a dream. That surfer will be honored by all the other great athletes in the world as a champion of his/her sport, and will have earned an indelible position in the history of surfing.

—*Bernie Baker, from the South Shore*

Preceding pages: Sunset as a surging south swell fans into Honolulu, keeping the "Townies" occupied. The question is, where to surf? *Photo: Steve Wilkings*

Top right: A crisp Kewalo peak enduring a hefty top-to-bottom threesome. *Photo: Steve Wilkings*

Center right: Dwayne Scharsh showing 'em how it's done with a clean green shack at Bowls. *Photo: Mana*

Bottom right: Point Panic cringes beneath the rumble of a monster Town swell. To the delight of the boogeyboarders and bodysurfers, stand-up surfing here is a no-no. *Photo: Brett Uprichard*

Opposite: Wonderful Waikiki never ceases to please the masses. It's all about fun in the sun around here. *Photo: Brett Uprichard*

The South Shore

Hot Time, Summer in "Town"

Summertime, May to September

Can be tricky without a road map

Most breaks are over reefs, some shallow, some not

Whatever you need to rip small waves

Crowds, no parking

Reef cuts, sunburn and sore necks from watching the bodies

Some of the best small waves in the world and scenic Diamond Head

98

OAHU

THE SOUTH SHORE

Right: It's summertime and the surfing is, as they say in Hawaii, "easy, brah." In this photograph, we get a bird's-eye view of surfers from decades past enjoying a surf-filled afternoon at Queen's Beach on what was known as a rare First Break Day. *Photo: from the archives of Grady Timmons*

Ask any locals about the South Shore and they'll instantly inform you that the area of Oahu you're referring to is called "Town." And "Town" it truly is, with its traffic, commuters, highrise buildings and shopping centers. Easy for one to lose track here, forgetting that this is really Hawaii and not the US mainland.

But amidst the hustle and bustle of Honolulu's city life lies a treasure chest of superb waves. Although the swells hitting Oahu's South Shore are generally the smallest on the island, what they lack in size is compensated for with maximum fun. Big-wave lunatic Brock Little once added fuel to Town's rep of only having vertically challenged waves by saying, "I'd be embarrassed to call anything in Town over 8 feet." Remember though, it's not size that counts. With the north/northeast trade winds blowing offshore, Town is consistently rideable, even when small. Reef after reef stretching from Ewa Beach to the end of Diamond Head produce just about every kind of wave imaginable. Depending on your preference, you can pick and choose from long wally rights, grinding barreling lefts, short bowly rights, rippable peaks going both ways, and just about everything else in between. The choice is all yours.

Town's various breaks attract the masses as well. Each surf spot often has its own crew of "A" and "B" team riders making up the pecking order who surf religiously every day the waves are half decent. These surfers have their spots completely wired; they know exactly where to sit on the reef and are absolute pros at working the crowd. This can lead to an extremely frustrating surf session for the rest of the world, who are forced to squabble over the leftover crumbs of the pie.

What this means for most of the surfing population is that they have to get in the water at odd hours in order to meet their wave quota. During precious days of Town swell, it's not uncommon to find surfers already loosened and waxed up riding waves way before the first light of day begins to peek over Diamond Head. Then there are the hardy souls waiting for the last set of the day long after the sun has disappeared, along with your hopes of seeing the mythical "green flash." Night-surfing is almost routine at select spots during a full moon. On a good day of surf, you can be sure that very few waves on the South Shore of Oahu will go to waste.

For many surfers, Town is their special part of Hawaii. Others disagree, dreading even the mention of the place. Still others are indifferent, choosing Honolulu as their home base yet venturing out to explore other spots on the isle. Whatever your mood is, there's always a fun wave breaking somewhere in this concrete jungle, and this fact alone can make all the development, gridlocked traffic and urban stress disappear from your mind, reminding you that this is still Hawaii.

The Kewalo Korner

As you paddle out to the right side of the Kewalo Basin channel, you may happen to see the exclusive break of **Point Panic**. On its day, Point Panic can produce some of the sickest right-hand barrels over its shallow arc of reef. It may look perfect and spitting, but this is an exclusive area and out of bounds to all boardriders; by law, the lineup is reserved for bodysurfers only. Sneaking in a session here might just land you a ticket.

Kewalos is the main spot surfed legally in these parts. Facing the Kewalo Basin Beach Park on the edge of the boat channel is a shifty left/right peak that can get really, really good on its day. The lefts are the call, and can pitch nicely-shaped barrels with stretches of wall reserved for slash-and-burn action, while the right tends to be more sectiony, but can also offer clean hollow sections. On some days, Kewalos is almost a mirror image of nearby Kaisers. Often rideable, but beware of the reef and the odd shark.

Not too far from the Kewalos reef is an open-ocean **Concession** stand offering nice peak waves. Just jump in line and you're sure to be a satisfied customer.

On big summer swells, **Big Rights** does justice to its name and pours out perfect rights all day long. They hit the reef and form gaping gems for the tubeseeker. An odd left is also a possibility.

While the landlubbers bounce tennis balls back and forth at one another in the courts working up a sweat under the hot sun, surfers straight outside of land are coolly bouncing off wave lips and tucking into sun-shielding tubes on a different kind of court. The aptly named **Tennis Courts** break is situated directly out to sea in front of its landbound counterpart. Paddle out to the right side of the three rocks sticking out in the lagoon

and you might save yourself a sketchy rockdance. The wave itself is a winding right-hander that can whip out unreal double-up barrels along the way. Best at around 4 to 6 feet. Practically all of the crowd condenses on the rights, but the left can sometimes be a good choice if just to get away from the pack. Of course, if the waves just aren't happening, you can always go for a quick sesh at the tennis courts on land.

Over the reef from Courts is a spot called **Big Lefts** for obvious reasons. Further towards Magic Island is the inconsistent right, **Baby Haleiwa**.

Ala Moana Bowls is definitely a contender for Best Wave on the South Shore. Long, perfect lefts reel off along the rock-jetty fronting the Ala Wai yacht harbor. The shallowness of the reef makes for gaping green rooms produced

on any sizeable swell. While surfing Bowls (as it is more formally known) you can act on several waveriding options in order to distance yourself from the tight, overwhelming and invariably aggro crowd guaranteed to be out on any good day. Jockeying for position among the grom rats, longboarders, boogeyboarders and pros at the outside takeoff point could earn you a savored longshot wave all the way through to the inside (providing you don't get burned by one or all of the above), and even possibly a grinding tube to top it off. But you can also stake out the inside bowl and hope for someone to get crunched by a wide racing set, leaving you the leftover portion to munch on. The right here, albeit short, can also show good form, though it doesn't quite match that of the left.

Good ol' Bowls is rideable almost every day that the trades blow offshore, and even on some days when they don't. On maxing swells, you will encounter the infamous pole sets, which are crunching, bigger set waves that rise up to the height of Ala Mo's famous channel-marker poles. This is how the term "pole sets." used to describe big days out here, was first coined. Remember to exercise caution over the reef.

The next break over from Bowls, **Rockpiles**, can also be satisfying. A fun left peels off toward Bowls on one side while a wedging right does its thing on the other. Definitely a fun place to check out, especially if the madness down at Bowls becomes too hot to handle. During lower tides, Rockpiles lives up to its name. The inside reef dries out drastically, and ding-generating coral heads wait intently for their next victim.

Above: Ala Moana is definitely the cream of the wave crop on Oahu's busy South Shore. On any day, given decent swell, Bowls can pump out screaming sections that can drive you to return your air ticket to Indo in a heartbeat. Here Michael Ho styles beneath a vibrant barrel of snapping Ala Mo water. *Photo: Steve Wilkings*

Between Rockpiles and Kaisers, you will find the fittingly named **Inbetweens**. In-B's is usually surfed as a place of refuge as it is set conveniently away from the packs dominating the nearby reefs. Although more of a right, lefts are also an option.

Kaisers is present-day proof that manmade waves do go off. When Kaiser Hospital contractors bombed a boat-channel in the middle of the reef opposite the Hilton Hawaiian Village, they inadvertently created one of the most insane waves in Town. The skeletal remnants of a shipwreck lie directly underneath the shockingly shallow takeoff zone (which adds to the mystique of the break), though the real treasures are to be found above the wreck. Short grinding rights over an inside bowl can jack and throw into crystalline shacks before petering out in the channel. The outside peak can section quickly, but in every set, a wave or two twists right on through to the channel. The lefts are also worthy and can offer long, performance-oriented walls. Be careful over the reef and shipwreck as a bent and crusty metal pole sticks out of the wreck directly under the takeoff zone. You can actually' stand on this pole between wave sets. More than a few sessions (and ribs) have been bruised by this protruding obstacle, so take care.

Also worth a proper mention is **4's**, aka **Number Fours**, just over this channel. Fast, sectiony rights and fun lefts going into the channel are the call here, but 4's is often lacking the kind of slash-and-burn energy one finds at Kaisers.

Way out to sea in front of the US Army museum is the much-revered break known fondly as **3's**, or **Number Threes**. Local lore has it that the locals who used to surf here stashed their boards around the *hau* and monkeypod trees on the beach, and had actually named the spot "Trees". In Hawaiian pidgin, the number 3 is pronounced "tree", so this may have something to do with the name of the place. Whatever the call, on a 6-foot plus south swell, 3's

Below: Same idea as the photo on the opposite page, except during the 1930s. A tandem couple share a Waikiki waveriding moment. *Photo: from the archives of the Associated Press*

can pump out some of the most perfect, ruler-edged right-handers around. Long spinning rides complete with barrel and drawn-out speed sections can start you thinking you've found the perfect wave. And you have, except that it draws one of the rowdiest dawn-to-dusk crowds around. The lefts can offer some relief from the rowdies, but they are nowhere on par with the rest of the wave.

Fun, crowded rights are what make the peaks at **Populars** (named after a public bath house on the beachfront here), well, popular, and the crowd makes sure that little at Pops goes to waste.

Canoes is a fave wave frequented by beginners, "recreational surfers" and, for centuries probably, outrigger canoes. Easygoing peaks that rise over sloping sand-covered reefs make this spot what it is, and a longboard can make it even more cruisy and satisfying.

Set amidst the buildings and city life of Waikiki, **Queens** lives up to its regal name, producing

Royal Hawaiian waves. It was named in honor of Queen Liliuokalani, the last monarch of Hawaii, who had a beach house named *Pualeilani* that once fronted the break. Queens is a high-performance right that peels off and rolls toward an inside seawall. Sections can reform over the inside, providing extra lip-bashing opportunities, or, if you cruise it on a longboard, more area to hang 10. Shorter lefts can also be jumped on. Waves here are usually smaller than at nearby Ala Moana. The highrise buildings and apartments can act as buffers against the intense trade winds and smooth out the bumps a bit. Perfect, fun waves in the heart of Waikiki. Queens doesn't handle much size, and can become a frothing mass of whitewater soup during big swells. If surf is not happening, plop yourself on the beach on any sunny day and check out the beauties on shore making waves of their own.

Publics is the last wave in Waikiki before Diamond Head.

Above: Whenever Queens in the heart of Waikiki works, the result can be fun for all sorts of waveriders. Here a tandem duo giving a demonstration of beauty and grace. *Photo: Steve Wilkings*

When on, a spinning left can peel off neatly. Low tides bring the reef bottom closer to the surface, and the paddle out can sometimes be more of a walk. Named after some old public baths that used to line this world-famous beach.

The fabled wave **Castles** is about as ancient as its namesake, and it breaks only on the grandest of swells (the "First Break" ones that oldtime beachboys made legendary). It is a long and meandering left-hander that takes form on an outer reef off Waikiki. Castles is a rare South Shore big-wave usually surfed only by able watermen.

Windy Diamond Head

Surfing at the foot of the dormant volcano, the famous Diamond Head, offers more than just a tourist attraction. Waves below this volcano can be just as explosive as an intense eruption when the con-

ditions are right. Reefs here are at a more exposed angle due to the protrusion of the volcanic headland into the sea; as such, they tend to catch at least a foot more swell than most of Town. Swells face more of an easterly direction, and so trades blow more sideshore than off. Diamond Head is particularly popular with the local windsurfing society, a group that delights in hitting the water during windlashed conditions. Surfers sit onshore, meanwhile, and pray for dead-wind glassiness.

Suicides is the first stop on our Diamond Head tour. Located a short paddle away from the Diamond Head Beach Park, Suicides is actually more fun than the name suggests. A perfect, long left can peel into the channel, with a shorter right doing it's thing on the other side. Not much of a suicide until the tide drops out, making the eager reef just a bit too close to the surface than is comfortable.

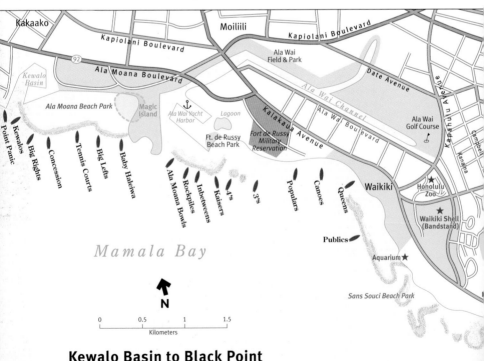

Kewalo Basin to Black Point

The wave also starts to hollow out more, and can throw grinding barrels at you. Inside blocks of rock can also make the paddle in (or out) treacherous.

Also outside of the Suicides right is a sometimes long, lined-up left called **Sleepy Hollows**. Needs a bit of swell to work, but a longboard can make it more exciting.

Driving along the cliff road below Diamond Head, you eventually encounter a pretty Coast Guard lighthouse. This white lighthouse isn't the only attraction here. Surfers' attentions are fixed on the **Lighthouse** break in the water. On good days, swells here leap over the reef and wedge into perfect right-hand and double-upped barrels. Carving sections can also be had, but the barrel's the go. Local boys always know when it's on, so be prepared for hassle if Lighthouse is happening.

This is a Diamond Head spot, and trades blow the place to bits.

Best to wait for calm wind days. A bit of north can be good, too. Make your way out through the convenient channel just inside of the right, and be wary of protruding rocks on the inside, particularly during low tides.

Cliffs is usually a better bet for an average, everyday sesh. Cliffs tends to be consistent, featuring left/right peaks that roll over the reef. Unlike Lighthouse across the channel, waves here are more open-faced and less barrely. They can throw, but more often than not, you'll find yourself flying on down the line instead of pulling in.

But remember to check the wind. Once again, prevailing trade winds blow Cliffs to smithereens, so it is a fave spot amongst the windsurfing crowd. If they are out, it's a good idea to check out a more wind-friendly spot elsewhere. Paddle out just inside of the lefts, opposite the rights rolling towards the Lighthouse.

Town's End

At the end of our Town surfari, we end up at a cutoff point where the last stretch of beach starts turning in towards the southeast shore. The waves found in this vicinity, namely between and around the Niu Valley and Aina Haina areas, are created by distant offshore reefs that generate breaking waves which are usually disappointing and chopped out by the trade winds. Surfing around these parts is generally reserved for those in the know of the flow of the motion in the ocean. Translated into English, this means *local knowledge*. **China Walls** is the one exception. This spot can come to consistent and fun life on big south swells. Long left-handers here can bowl bigtime, breaking right off the wall at Portlock Point, just at the foot of sleepy Koko Head.

—*Lorca Lueras*

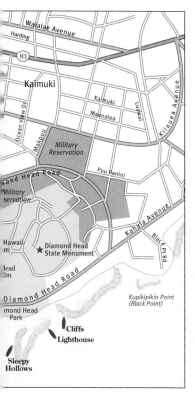

"Far out to the opalescent horizon stretches the ocean in broad
bands of jeweled color—turquoise, sapphire, emerald, amethyst;
and curving around it like a tawny topaz girdle presses the
hard, firm sand of the shore. The pearly surf, diamond
crested, sweeps in with a swift, strong surging unlike
any sound I have ever heard before; and balanced
in superb symmetry on their surfboards, the
beach boys come riding in toward land."

—*Frances Parkinson Keyes, from*
Paradise of the Pacific, *1926*

hboys

Beachboy

The word shares a common history with Waikiki. It conjures up images of a romantic past: of cruise ships and stateroom parties, a luxurious pink hotel, and a strip of sand once described as "curving in a gentle, flesh-covered arc toward Diamond Head." The word brings back memories of tandem surfing on giant redwood boards, baritone ukuleles, and nicknames like Splash Lyons, Laughing John, and Turkey Love. Although the beachboy tradition survives to this day in Waikiki, real beachboys are relics of an earlier age. Legend portrays them as bronzed watermen with good humor, enormous charm and musical genius—carefree partying fools, and ardent womanizers. The legend is surprisingly close to the truth.

History does not tell us who the first beachboy was, only that he probably appeared at Waikiki soon after the first major resort, the Moana Hotel, opened in 1901. Likewise, because of the maverick nature of the profession, there has never been much agreement on what exactly is a beachboy. In his 1996 master's thesis "The Waikiki Beachboy: Changing Attitudes and Behavior," University of Hawaii sociology student Henry Kim noted that contemporary writers have portrayed the beachboy in, "schizo-

Beachboys, Diamond Head and a Waikiki wave, ca. 1920s.

phrenic terms: at one moment he is a throwback to ancient Hawaii; at the next, a social parasite."

The dictionary defines a beachboy as someone whose livelihood is derived from surfing instruction and outrigger canoe rides, but even this is a limited definition.

tle of beer with his thumb. Joseph "Scooter Boy" Kaopuiki had a "*poi* dog" or mongrel that he taught to surf. John "Hawkshaw" Paia could paddle out to sea with a surfboard, a chair and a ukulele, then catch a wave, sit on the chair, and play the ukulele as he rode in towards the beach.

American silent film star Betty Compson with beachboys.

There is a larger sense to the word "beachboy", one that suggests a complete way of life. Men like Duke Kahanamoku, who was not a professional, were beachboys in the truest sense. They lived for the ocean and for a lifestyle centered around its beaches.

Waikiki's beachboys were a fascinating collection of men. They were predominantly Hawaiians and part-Hawaiians, ruled spiritually by the great swimmer-surfer, Duke Kahanamoku, and led officially by William "Chick" Daniels, a strapping six-footer with a personality as wide as the beach. Charles "Panama Dave" Baptiste, his comic sidekick, was the designated clown prince.

Beachboys often had improbable names and nicknames that were a bit, well, different. George "Tough Bill" Keaweamahi was so tough that he could pop the cap off a bot-

These nicknames contributed significantly to the allure and charm of the beachboys. Sarah Park, the beachside reporter for *The Honolulu Star-Bulletin* during the 1950s, once imagined what it would be like to introduce them at a party. "Of course, you've met Dad," she imagined herself saying, "and this is Turkey. And on your right we have another man from the beach, Sally. And have you met Steamboat? And this is Steamboat Jr. And these are Steamboat's relatives: Tugboat, Sailboat, Lifeboat, and Rowboat."

The beachboys provided the world with much needed comic relief ("What characters!" everyone said). They took anxious, overachieving executives and taught them to relax. They took their children and taught them how to surf. They took women who were recently divorced and taught them how to laugh and love again. In return, movie moguls took the beachboys to Hollywood, and entertainers such as Arthur Godfrey took them to New York. Ed Bennecke, whose family partly owned Schlitz Beer, took them to the World Series. It's hard to imagine another group of men in any period of history who led a similarly ideal existence. In the eyes of the world, beachboys did not work for a living. They played for a living. They belonged to life's greatest profession.

"What's important to remember about the beachboys," former world surfing champion Fred Hemmings recalled, "is that it wasn't really a business for these men. It was a lifestyle. Working and taking tourists canoe surfing was incidental to the fact that they were men who had a lifelong love affair with the ocean." Of course, not all of the beach-

Western-style rowing regattas. Writing in *The Journal of American Folklore* in 1891, H.C. Bolton noted that he had not witnessed surfing until he visited the remote island of Niihau. In 1892, anthropologist Nathaniel B. Emerson wrote disparagingly that, "The royal sport of surf riding possessed a grand fascination, and for a time, it seemed as if it had a vitality all its own as a national pastime. Today it is hard to find a surfboard outside our museums and private collections."

That a sport of such beauty and grace could fall so far is as dismaying as its revival was unlikely. This revival began in 1907, when Alexander Hume Ford, an eccentric promoter and former newsman from Chicago, stepped off a boat in Honolulu and began a crusade to revive "the royal sport of surfing". Ford observed that the beaches of

In the eyes of the world, beachboys did not work for a living. They played for a living. They belonged to life's greatest profession.

boys were Hawaiian, but they embodied the Hawaiian spirit. "These men were all little boys at heart," Hemmings added. "There was a glow in their faces that manifested itself in everything they did. They appreciated the values of a beautiful environment, a clean ocean, sharing with their friends. Everybody now seems to be trying to measure their happiness in dollars and cents. These men never had that bottom-line mentality. They had a true appreciation for what I consider to be the finer things in life."

The beachboy first emerged at the turn of the 20th century in Waikiki as part of the revival in Hawaiian watersports. At that time, surfing and canoeing were at their nadir; indeed, both sports had been in decline since the onset of contact with the West in 1778. During the 19th century, outrigger canoe racing had been all but displaced by

Waikiki were becoming closed to the "small boy of limited means." Private villas and a posh new hotel were choking off access to what was an already small strip of sand between two protruding seawalls. Ford decided to do something about it.

First, he first enlisted the support of the writer Jack London, whom he had introduced to surfing, and who was at the time enjoying a sojourn in Waikiki. Next, Ford negotiated a 20-year lease on a small plot of land adjoining the Moana Hotel, relocating two grass shacks there and founding the Outrigger Canoe Club. Membership fees for boys were set at five dollars a year. "Such dues," wrote Ford, "made it possible for every kid with guts to live at least half the day fighting the surf."

Ford then tried to enlist as the club's first captain the noted Honolulu waterman

George "Dad" Center (who later coached the 1920 US Olympic swim team). "He scorned the surf," Ford wrote. "It took me two years to persuade Dad to come to Waikiki to take a look-see."

When "Dad" finally came, he stayed. Indeed, he was part of a growing 20th-century phenomenon: the discovery of surfing by *haoles* (Causasians). Ford, who by then had started *Mid-Pacific Magazine*, was on hand to chronicle surfing's growing popularity. When it was fairly demonstrated that outsiders could learn the secrets of the Hawaiian-born, the beach at Waikiki took on a new aspect as the people of Honolulu turned their attention to reviving the oldtime water sports. Hundreds learned to ride the surfboard. During visits by the fleet, surfing carnivals were often held, and, to the astonishment of the jackies, boys and men would come in upon their surfboards while standing on their heads. At night, expert surfers would fit contrivances with red lights onto the bows of their boards and put matches in the caps on their heads before they caught some monster wave, treating those on the beach to the sight of radiant sea gods outlined against the darkness, standing upon the white crests of the waves, which they rode erect and elated.

Ford's attempt to revive the ancient Hawaiian watersport was successful, but his surfing club had a curious flaw: it was almost exclusively Caucasian in membership. A rival club was formed in 1911, one composed almost exclusively of Hawaiians or part-Hawaiians. Called Hui Nalu, or "Club of the Waves," it had as one its founders the 21-year-old Duke Kahanamoku, who was beginning to make a name for himself as a surfer and swimmer. Unlike the Outrigger Canoe Club, Hui Nalu had no clubhouse. Members met beneath a *hau* tree on the lawn of the Moana Hotel. The Moana Bathhouse, located in the hotel basement, served as the locker room. Dues were only a dollar a year.

The two clubs were friendly rivals, with some members belonging to both. A certain ethnic pride, however, lay at the heart of

Waikiki beachboys at Diamond Head, 1921, with a playful member of royalty in the ranks.

their competition: *haoles* vied with Hawaiians in a sport deemed the domain of the latter. Contests between the two clubs would eventually contribute to a modern-day renaissance of the sport of canoe racing.

The two clubs were also integral to the revival of surfing. Tourists in Waikiki during the early 1900s were entranced by the sport: to stand on a board and be hurled towards shore by a set of waves was to experience the rarest of thrills. The men of Outrigger and Hui Nalu had the proper skills and equipment to teach the public how to perform these feats, and they were to become the very first beachboys.

Thanks to the efforts of these early watermen, surfing began to spread to the mainland US and further abroad. In 1907, a Hawaiian-Irish beachboy named George Freeth was invited to California to demonstrate the art of surfing. Billed as "the man who can walk on water," Freeth was a well-known Waikiki waterman of whom Jack London once wrote, "He is Mercury—

a brown Mercury. His heels are winged, and in them is the swiftness of the sea." As a result of his exhibition in California, Freeth became known as "the first surfer in the United States".

In 1915, Duke Kahanamoku took surfing to Australia, and a year later he became the first man to surf on both the east and west coasts of the United States, giving demonstrations at Atlantic City, New Jersey, and Nassau, New York. In 1939, Kahanamoku and a coterie of Waikiki beachboys became the first modern-day surfers to tackle the big winter surf at Sunset Beach and Makaha on Oahu's North and West Shores. In 1954, Waikiki waterman Wally Froiseth organized the Makaha Surfing Championships, which soon became one of the world's top big-wave surfing events. Among the first winners of this tournament were beachboys George Downing, Rabbit and Jama Kekai, and Froiseth himself.

And yet, despite their abilities, most Waikiki beachboys were not big-wave riders.

They were fun-loving exhibitionists, and their giant surfboards were their stage. It was far more common to see a beachboy on a small wave, riding in while standing on his head or carrying a woman in his arms, looking as though he was carrying her across a threshold.

Indeed, the old-style surfboards were well suited for such antics. They were big as beds, at least 10 feet in length and weighing well over a 100 pounds. Just carrying such

When you were a beachboy, the ocean was your mother. The beach was your life.

a board took enormous strength. To ease the strain, a beachboy would shoulder it like a rifle. From the beach, he would then run into the water, drop the board, jump on it standing up and glide out into the surf. Buffalo Kealana, the 1960 Makaha surfing champion who started his own surfing contest— Buffalo's Big Board Classic—to revive the dying art of longboard surfing, explained that one basic difference between riding the boards of yesterday and the modern surfboards is that, "on a small board, you have to make the board perform. On a big board, *you* perform."

On a big board, it was possible to sit, lie down, carry a girl on your shoulder, stand on one foot, face backwards, do spinners or walk the board. A good surfer could improvise endlessly, and many did. Few were better than Scooter Boy Kaopuiki. Even his nickname was derived from one of his many tricks: paddling his surfboard with one foot to catch a wave.

When beachboys talk about Scooter Boy, they often have trouble finding words to adequately describe him. Coming up short, they will suddenly jump up on a picnic table or

The KAHANAMOKU SURF-BOARD POLO Champions 1930

run up and down their living room, demonstrating how Scooter Boy rode his 15-foot hollow board. "Scooter Boy had that board flying all over the wave," said Buffalo as he snapped into his surfer's stance one day at Makaha Beach. "He would run to the front of the board, jump up in the air and land on the nose, kicking the water from the nose so that the board would spin right around. And then he'd run to the back of the board. He was really a classic surfer."

"For sheer skill, natural know-how and athletic talent, that guy was fabulous," remembers Wally Froiseth. "He did whatever he felt like doing, whenever he felt like

112

Group portrait and a remembrance of things past.

doing it. That's how all the beachboys were. They wanted that free feeling, that free type of ocean living. Surfing was the expression of a lifestyle."

Scooter Boy was 8 years old when he began surfing at Waikiki. The call of the ocean was like a siren, and it quickly led to his expulsion from school. Like so many other local kids, Scooter Boy realized early on that the beach was his favorite classroom. There were so many things to do at the beach, so many things to learn.

There was also a camaraderie that you couldn't find on a street corner. The older boys looked after you. Duke and the others started you surfing at the easy spots and then guided you to the more difficult breaks when you were ready. They steered you toward a canoe and away from trouble.

There was a certain code that was observed on the beach. You learned to keep the beach clean, and as a result you felt clean. There was respect for the ocean. When you went to the ocean, you took from it only what you needed. When you were a beachboy, the ocean was your mother. The beach was your life.

—*Grady Timmons*

Child actress Shirley Temple and beachboys, 1935.

~ MEMORIES ~
OF
THE DUKE

Most year-long blocks of time are much like waves. They arrive blue, new, unridden and pure every January 1st, then, by the end of December, crash into a whitish blur of improbable encounters, memories and experiences with the known and unknown.

That seems to be true of most years, but now and then you experience a particular 12-month cycle that is so memorable it literally whacks you in the face and remains forever alive and in prime time at the back of your mind. 1963 was just such a year for me because of two surfing-related experiences. One incident had to do with US President John F. Kennedy, and the other involved the great Hawaiian surf legend Duke Kahanamoku. President Kennedy and The Duke may sound like an odd combination of characters to group together here, but if you will allow me the literary license to do so, I will attempt to explain in surferese what this oblique surf story is all about.

I remember, for example, crystal clear (perhaps like everybody else in America or even the world at that time), what I was doing on that day in September 1963 when I first learned that President Kennedy had been shot. That year, I was a freshman at California Western University in San Diego (the ultimate surfers' school of higher learning in those days), and early that morning a fellow freshman and surfer, Bill Tucker, and I had left our Point Loma campus to surf a jetty-protected beachbreak at nearby Ocean Beach. Following a fun morning surf session, we paddled into shore, and as we trudged across the beach with boards under our arms, we saw a black man running maniacally across the beach in front of us. He had a transistor radio (remember those?) pressed against his left ear, and as he raced

past us he looked at us with big and wild eyes and yelled: "The President's been shot! The President's been shot!" Tucker and I figured this guy was a nutcase, so we gave him lots of room for his morning run and made our way to Tucker's pickup truck to go back to campus in time for late-morning classes. Once in the pickup—we were wet, salty and cold—we clicked the truck's sound system on to our favorite San Diego radio station, but what was usually loud with early-'60s rock music was instead replaced by a somber reporter's voice breaking news about President Kennedy's tragic motorcade ride through Dallas.

When we got back to campus, we saw professors and students gathered in somber groups, listening to loud radio transmissions. Some students were already hanging black bunting over doorways and windows, and others were crying together in strange little clusters. What a bummer scene, I recall, and as I threw my surfboard into our dorm's longboard locker, I remember thinking that America would never be the same again. What had began as a decade of hope and optimism had in seconds become a modern Greek tragedy of the highest order.

Now the reason I mention President Kennedy is that only a few weeks before, at the end of a great first summer spent working and surfing in Hawaii, I had visited the newsroom of *The Honolulu Advertiser*, Hawaii's morning newspaper, and was shown a press photo taken only a year or so

The Duke in his prime—as a swimmer, surfer and the most famous person in Hawaii.

earlier of President Kennedy at Honolulu International Airport. In the photo, our young and immensely popular President was surrounded by a crowd of important civilian dignitaries and military personnel (Hawaiian and otherwise) who were all on hand to greet him. He was amiable to all, but upon stepping off *Air Force One*, Kennedy had checked out the important politicos on hand to greet him, voiced a cursory "hello" to all, then, improbably, impulsively, had abandoned protocol and spent most of his time at the airport chatting with the one person there that he had instantly recognized as one of his childhood heroes. This man was, of course, every swimmer's and surfer's hero, the world-famous waterman known as The Duke. Kennedy, as some oldtimers/historians might recall, was a keen all-around waterman-swimmer-sailor during his life (and indeed, even during his presidential years), and so, when he saw the great Duke of Hawaii at the end of that Hawaii receiving line, looking especially striking in a white linen suit and a big Hawaiian flower *lei*, Kennedy was as excited as any of us would be to meet one of aquatic history's greatest and most-storied characters. The politicians in that same receiving line—which included the governor of Hawaii as well as US senators, House representatives and other assorted fat cats—were visibly miffed, but for President Kennedy, this was an important moment in his life for sure. The same sort of thing happened four years later in May of 1966 when Britain's Queen Mother paid a royal visit to Hawaii. But on that occasion, the Queen Mum didn't just bid the Duke a special *aloha* at the airport. Rather, after accepting a white flower *lei* from him, she totally shed proper English decorum and

The Duke in his middle years, leaving the water following a swim at Waikiki Beach.

joined him for an impromptu *hula* dance. The next morning, pictures of Hawaii's Duke and Britain's Queen Mother dancing were featured on the front pages of newspapers around the world.

So now my story is even more complicated, involving as it does President Kennedy, the Queen Mother and, again, The Duke. All of which, if you will allow me yet another digression, reminds me of the first time I met the great Duke of Hawaii.

At that time, in early June of 1963, I had gone to Hawaii "to surf," fulfilling a youthful ambition that began at the age of 13 after I'd ridden my first wave in the old Boneyard surfing break at Southern California's Doheny Beach State Park. Like many another teenager in the late 1950s and early '60s, I had been hooked by the surfing bug, and I spent all of my extra time surfing to live, or, perhaps more accurately, living to surf. Nothing was cooler or more bitchin' to do at that time, and I was deeply into it, despite objections from family, school and the assorted "greasers," "ho-dads" and "kooks" that I had to deal with at that time in history. They were sure that I was wasting my time in a frivolous search for waves.

One of the journeys that was important to any surfer in the early 1960s was the obligation—perhaps akin to the Haj—that at least once in your life you had to go to Hawaii and ride the waves there. Yes, California was "boss" back then, but Hawaii was where surfing—and the true surfing lifestyle—were really at. In keeping with this dogma, as espoused in Volume I, Issue 1, of our Bible (*Surfer* magazine), in early June of 1963, I went to Hawaii with a high school friend, a naturally peroxided chap named Frank Sydow.

Both Frank and I were naive, idealistic, invincible and silly, but we knew what we wanted, which was to go to Hawaii and spend a carefree summer between high school and university, riding, what we had been told, were the world's finest waves. With that in mind, we each scraped up enough money to buy a one-way Pan Am ticket to Honolulu, but after doing this and boarding a flight to Hawaii in Los Angeles, all we had, besides our enthusiasm, were some odd clothes, one longboard each and a very small amount of cash. I recall that when I arrived in Honolulu with Sydow on a late afternoon, my possessions consisted of a satchel of clothes, a well-used Wardy surfboard and 50 dollars. Not much (though 50 dollars went a lot farther in those days), but we figured that we would somehow survive and have a lot of good summertime fun. As it turned out, we were right on target and about to embark on one of the great summers of our young lives (I was only 17 at the time).

While we were on that Pan Am flight, we met two fellow Californians who were in the same sort of boat as us, and together we figured out how to pool our resources and make things work out to our advantage. Together we talked a guy in a pickup truck into taking us and our boards into Waikiki. There we found out about a rooming house in the old "Waikiki Jungle," where we could rent a simply-appointed, crabs-infested apartment for 65 dollars a month (split four ways). It was a block from Waikiki's world-famous Kalakaua Avenue and from the surf, and in that party-prone apartment house we met a number of other waveriders, both local and Californian. We settled in by stringing ropes from wall to wall to create a temporary surfboard rack, and immediately began looking in the classified sections of local newspapers for job opportunities. Lots of jobs seemed to be available, so on our first night we strode haughtily into the unknown for

A rare 1965 Duke surfing trophy, one of waveriding's most coveted honors.

the first of what would be many sunset walks along Waikiki Beach. That night, we stumbled across a great drunken gathering of Waikiki beachboys beer-deep into cha-lang-a-lang Hawaiian music, but we wanted to go surfing the next morning, so we went back home to sleep.

The following morning, as recounted in another book I wrote about surfing, we experienced the following:

At dawn the next morning we carried our boards nearly the length of Waikiki Beach and paddled out to the famous Ala Moana surfing break under the grey-pink of first light. The waves didn't look very big from the breakwater, but as we made our way out through the Ala Wai Harbor's boat channel, we watched big-eyed as a long-haired Hawaiian in red baggy trunks dropped into a swell that had lifted above Ala Moana's outside marker poles. We coast haole were honestly terrified by the beauty, motion and power of an overhead Hawaiian wave. As that local boy casually disappeared into a warm aqua tunnel, another Hawaiian yelled loudly: "Go Hawaii! Go!" "Hawaii" went, and a moment later he emerged from a crushing but pure Ala Moana tube. As his ride ended, he kicked out in a neat standing-up position, tore at his dark hair with both hands, and screamed a primeval scream. In approving response, a chorus of surfer hoots [Frank's and mine included] filled the balmy air. "Hawaii" was stoked, our minds were blown, and nothing else in the world mattered during that moment of pure, euphoric rebirth. Except, perhaps, the next, outside wave . . .

We figured the going would be tough, but seeing waves like that made survival a matter of secondary importance. We would overcome, we vowed, and indeed within a few days we had all landed summertime jobs in and about the Waikiki area. I scored gainful employment as a counterman/pizza maker at a place called Chic's Pizza Hut in a then-new Waikiki tourist attraction by the name of The International Marketplace. It wasn't a great job, but I worked evenings and so was able to surf all day in what were then relatively uncrowded waves. 1963 was also a good year to be in Waikiki because highrise buildings were still a rarity and tourism had not yet reached the monster proportions that were to become the norm during the '70s and after. It was in this pleasant Waikiki milieu that I one day accidentally met Duke Kahanamoku, Hawaii's contemporary "Father of Surfing," for the very first time.

This meeting happened about a week after I had arrived in Waikiki. While I was working at the pizza place, I had befriended a feisty old local beachboy whom everybody called Joe. Old Joe used to drink coffee every morning at the International Marketplace and would regale anybody with an open ear with his stories about early 20th-century days in Hawaii. Sometimes he was boring, but sometimes his stories were fun to listen to. One morning while I was small-talking with Joe, a big smile crossed his face and he yelled out loudly: "Eh, Paoa. Howzit?!"

Joe's hand reached out to the object of his greeting, an elderly Hawaiian man with long and neatly combed-back white hair who was strolling by. Joe's pidgin greeting was returned with a warm handshake and the answer, "Eh, Joe. Howzit to you too." Joe turned to me and said proudly, "Leonard, dis is my old friend, Paoa. And bruddah Paoa, dis is my new friend, Leonard." Joe was always introducing me to passersby so I simply shook Mr. Paoa's hand and said, "Nice to meet you, sir." I remember that his right hand was huge, dark and strong, and that his eyes were big, glassy and shot with blood in the manner of some Hawaiians. Most of all, I remember him smiling a great big and winning smile and saying softly, "Hello, bruddah. Nice to meet you too." I also remember that he was wearing white pants, white buck shoes, and a dark blue *aloha* shirt that was cinched at the collar with a local-style cowboy bolo tie.

After greeting us, Mr. Paoa continued on his slow way to the back of the International Marketplace, and as he walked away from us I noticed that people were murmuring and talking about him. "Who was that nice old man?" I asked Joe, and Joe, who at his age was nearly toothless, smiled through a big gap in his front teeth and said, "To me his name is Paoa, but to everybody else in the world, he is the great Duke of Hawaii."

I said to Joe, "Not *The* Duke," and he said, smiling again, "Yes, little bruddah, *Da Duke*." It took a few seconds for the reality of what Joe had said to sink into my adolescent pea brain, but when I finally realized that I had just met Duke Kahanamoku himself, I felt truly honored. Later that day, I recounted this story to my surfing friends at our Waikiki Jungle apartment house and they thought I was hallucinating—or simply namedropping a lie.

That night, I read a history book about Hawaii, in which the author explained that the Duke's full name was Duke Paoa Kahinu Mokoe Hulikohola Kahanamoku. "Duke" was part of his name because he was named after his father, who had also been called

The Duke during his later years, admiring a silver surfer hood-ornament that adorned his "Duke"-plated automobiles.

Duke because he was born in 1869, shortly after a visit to the Hawaiian Kingdom by England's then-popular Duke of Edinburgh. The Duke himself was born on the 24th of August, 1890.

Whatever the origins of his name, I was honored to meet the man himself, the so-called "Surfer of the Century." Life has few true heroes, and for me, the Duke was indeed a special kind of hero. His was not just the most famous and revered name in surfing, but it was also one of the great historic "names" in the sport of swimming. Hawaii's "Bronze Duke" was the greatest swimmer of the 1910s, 1920s and early 1930s. During that period, Duke competed in four Olympic Games from 1912 to 1932, winning five major medals. He was the fastest swimmer in the world for a long time, and during his life helped to popularize surfing all over the world. While on a goodwill visit to Australia in 1915, for example, the Duke made his way to a Sydney-area hardware store, bought some wood, handmade a surfboard, and then, at Freshwater Beach, demonstrated surfing to the people Down Under for the very first time. All this he did while serving as Hawaii's unofficial ambassador, as Hollywood actor, the owner of a string of gasoline filling stations in Honolulu (which he ran while he was sheriff of Honolulu), and, during his later years, as the "official greeter" for the State of Hawaii. The Duke was a kind and gentle man who was perhaps too kind and gentle, given his international stature.

As fate would have it, I was to meet the Duke many times in 1963 following my initial encounter with him. The next year, I was hired to work full-time with him as an assistant and public relations type for Kimo Wilder McVay, the president of what was then called the Duke Kahanamoku Corporation. While working at that job for a few years during summers and winters between my university studies in California, I found myself spending a lot of time with Duke, his wife Nadine, and many of the people who made up his social world. I traveled with him extensively (both in Hawaii and on the US mainland), and while in Honolulu, the Duke, his sidekick Henry Ayau and I would cruise around Oahu in either one of his two white Rolls Royces or in his Lincoln Continental (all of which were emblazoned with Hawaiian license plates that said "DUKE").

We also shared many quiet moments before his death in January 1968. On these occasions, Duke just wanted to "talk story" and be himself, and the stories he told then were charming to the extreme. One of the high points of this period was when The Duke, McVay, Fred Van Dyke and I joined forces to produce the first great big-wave surfing contest, the Duke Kahanamoku Invitational Surfing Championships, held during the winter of 1965 in huge and perfect waves at Sunset Beach on the North Shore of Oahu.

There are many other great stories to tell about the Duke, and perhaps they will be the subject of a separate book one day. My purpose here is to simply pay a personal and overdue tribute to surfing's *Main Man* and to ask surfers the world over to honor the great heritage that he so nobly established for us.

—*Leonard Lueras*

THE 25 MOST INFLUENTIAL SURFERS OF ALL TIME

SURFER

40th anniversary collector's issue

SURFER OF THE CENTURY

In a special Summer, 1999, issue of *Surfer* magazine, The Duke was posthumously honored as surfing's "Surfer of the Century."

The Duke Kahanomoku statue at Waikiki Beach Center.
Photo: Brett Uprichard

At Night When the Shadows are Falling

One of my fondest memories is of the early 1960s when I was surfing the breaks at Waikiki during the summer months. My early morning adventures would usually begin with the unlocking of my 9'6" Hobie from the surf rack next to the Reef Hotel. The Reef was one of the first Outrigger Hotels on Waikiki Beach, and it competed with the Royal Hawaiian and the Moana. Waikiki didn't have as many lights back then, so I would paddle out to a break called Number Threes while it was still very dark. When it is working, Threes is probably the finest right-slide wave on Oahu's beautiful South Shore.

I recall paddling out in the oily-smooth glassiness of the pre-dawn as tiny water ripples fanned away from the nose of my board and the smell of saltwater was clean and strong. Since there were no commercially available specialty waxes back then, we used common paraffin wax which smelled of a soft, neutral vanilla. In the darkness of 5 am, the only way to navigate the long distance out to the surf break was to follow the sound of waves cracking as they hit the reef. Sometimes they sounded like a rifle shot, and at other times they were more of a roar, but never was there any doubt in the dark about how to find one's way to the break.

Within a few minutes, the familiar lightening of the morning sky would start its daily rise up behind the black silhouette of Diamond Head crater. You could then enjoy an early sunrise orange glow that reflected off the whitewater, even though the wall of the wave was still very dark. The surreal colors of mango sherbet and licorice on the waves were a visual treat, especially when you knew that the ocean would soon return to its familiar turquoise and sea-green once the sun was fully up.

While waiting between sets, I always enjoyed watching and hearing Waikiki wake up. Delivery trucks, refuse collectors and the previous evening's empty bottles all made rude and clanging noises that signaled the start of another tourist day. Nobody could ever sleep through a city-wide alarm clock like that one.

If there was a gentle offshore breeze, however, you could smell the sweet scent of plumeria, and on extremely still mornings, even from far out on the reef, you would sometimes hear mynah birds waking up and singing their morning song from the *hau* tree. Later each morning, the Hawaiian beachboys would set up shop under the shade of that same *hau* tree to play ukulele, flirt with pretty tourist girls, rent surfboards and take sunburned *haoles* out for surfing canoe rides on the easy, rolling, inside breaks.

I used to cherish how special it was to leave both land and its stresses behind. Many times I was the only one out until around 7 am, when, gleefully exhausted, I would paddle past latecomers and prepare to start my own work day.

I Hear Your Rolling Surf Calling

Today, some 40 years later, I still find myself paddling around in the dark. But these days I'm at Queens, a right break much closer to shore than the Number Threes of my youth. Queens now has, as does Number Threes, a small "Dawn Patrol" crowd, but these sunrise regulars all range in age from 45 to 80 years old. We're all riding long boards again, and us "Oldtimers" still never tire of a good bottom turn, a ride along a nice long wall, and maybe even a little nosework before a kickout.

Still a lot of fun, but the Waikiki of today is a very different place. Now there is the difficulty of locating a nearly nonexistent parking space, then having to wend your way through ladies of the evening and drunks trying to sleep the previous evening off. Maneuvering through a dense and unnatural growth of highrise hotels to get to the beach is not the short jaunt I remember it being long ago. The famous *hau* tree and its beachboys have been uprooted, we rarely see big waves during the summer, and some of the breaks have even shifted location due to sand accretion. In fact, our Mayor has even proposed dredging offshore sand to help restore Kuhio Beach. This idea has a lot of us worried because our favorite Queens break may shift yet again.

Surf etiquette with the morning regulars, however, is still intact. We make sure the eldest get whatever wave they want or are able to take, and we make sure that newcomers learn their manners, too.

It seems these days that mental health is as important as physical health, and I still marvel at my body's physical response to the familiar process of paddling a surfboard, leaping to my feet to make a turn, and then smiling from the pure joy that remains after all these years. The mental health attained by my continued surfing for four decades is as magical and stress-relieving as it was when I was very young.

I look forward to continuing to drive over the Pali Highway at 5 am and I grin when I think of how lucky I am to not be in traffic jams with all the commuters on my way back home. Mornings like this are special. I plan to be a member of the "Dawn Patrol" for at least another 20 good summers that'll be filled with climbing, dropping and sliding towards the shores of Waikiki.

Lucky I live Hawaii.

—Carey Smoot

The magic of Waikiki—sun, sand, palms and all—at the Diamond Head side of the Queen's Beach surfing beach-break.
Photo: Brett Uprichard

Above: Magical Makaha Point is the gem of Oahu's Wild West Side.
Here it's colors radiate in the ultraviolet range. *Photo: Jeff Divine*

Following pages: West Side surfer-celeb Rusty Keaulana knows his local reefs like the back of his hand. That's pretty useful knowledge when one confronts a sucking Klausmeyers bowl like this one.

Ewa and Da West

Neva Eva Go Ewa

Year-round wave action, though winter is bigger

The Farrington Highway hugs the coast

Reef, some flat, some sharp

Big-wave boards for winter

Heavy local crowds and theft

Reef hits are your biggest worry here

Year-round surf and a Hawaiian aura

Ewa Beach begins at the west bank of Pearl Harbor, at a military housing area called Iroquois Point. Fortified during the Second World War, the reef was planted with railroad ties and strung with barbed wire. These obstacles, without the wire, were surfed through, around, and into occasionally for massive dings. Known as Tank Traps during the '60s and surfed by military brats on glassy days with 2- to 4-foot waves. Trade winds or east winds chop this area up. The iron has been removed by the military. Access is limited to those with military IDs.

Across the harbor lie Hickam Air Force Base and outside surf spots. Back across the harbor and further down this nice sandy shoreline is Marine Beach, right next to and in front of a military rifle range. Time to paddle in when the popping starts.

Leaving the military behind, we come to **Ewa Beach Park**. A long paddle out to a sandbar with glassy conditions will give you waves that are bigger than you thought. Rights and lefts, 2 to 4 feet, fast and fun. The Ewa Beach coast is at the same angle as the Diamond Head to Aina Haina coast and will take the same swells. Southeast, south, southwest and even big west wraps during winter push along this long coastline. North winds are ideal but glassy water is a blast. The water is seldom clear due to the current sweeping the bottom from Pearl Harbor and flowing west to Barbers Point. A lot of seaweed (*limu*) is found in this area; har-

vested by hand, certain varieties are local favorites for *kau kau*.

Turning off Fort Weaver Road to Ewa Beach Road and driving halfway down it is a public right-of-way to the beach. This takes you to **Empty Lot** (or **Lots**). No more empty lots anywhere nowadays. A surprisingly good spot, primarily a right with lefts, with long rides through sections and double-ups. Johnny Stadowski, the Makaha International junior champ, came from this spot. Herbert Pruse would hang 10, turn around and hang heels, then walk straight to the tail to turn around and do a cut back, super smooth on his John Kelly Jr. Inter-Island Surf Shop Hydro, ca. 1965.

Off Pupu Street is **Dud's Reef**, a backyard surf spot that requires a leash due to the jagged rocks that the surf slams into. Fun at 1 to 3 feet, a good imagination helps the ride. Home to the occasional beer drinking surf contest, by invitation only.

Entering "Shark Country"

At Pupu Place you can check out an area not affectionately called "Shark Country." A big left that can hold a 10-foot wave peels outside a rock point into a small bay. Murky water and stories of hits and misses by the men in gray keep you wary, but, hey, we came to surf! Good fun at 2 to 4 feet; you can have long rides with plenty of turns and cutbacks. Ewa Beach offers surf spots with really long stand-up experience, which is

130

Right: Westsider Brian Pacheco has been making quite a name for himself as the Waianae Coast's most promising talent. Here he picks off fine wave energy at the closely-guarded Third Dip surfing station.
Photo: Mana

quite refreshing compared to some quick bowl action spots. Let's see, how did Shark Country get its name? Early morning sessions with 4-foot glassy waves make you a believer.

Haubush is right next door and can connect with Shark Country when big. A left with rights, many locals started surfing right here, even yours truly. One to 3 feet and rides to the small beach. Good fishing too!

At the end of Papipi Street is the road to a public beach park that is littered with every kind of household appliance, car part and whatever, a shame. Next to the not-so-safe park is **Sandtracks**. At 2 to 4 feet, this is a spot to work the rights. Not always friendly, get a few waves and perhaps move on. Newcomer cars left unattended are subject to random inspection by the hungry. Outside reefs along this area will reveal good surf on really big days. Wind is the factor that makes it worthwhile to paddle out or not. Of course, there is nothing quite like being way, way outside in big choppy surf, just to give yourself a test.

The Barber's Shop

Four-wheeling from Sandtracks up the shoreline towards **Barbers Point** for surfing and fishing is fun to do. The *kiawe* (mesquite) forest comes right up to the car path along the beach. The thorns from this tree will break off in your rubber slippers and surprise you later. You will swear they are coated with a hurtful potion. Great firewood.

Passing a small point with a World War Two concrete bunker we find **The Cove**. A nifty little left with bowls and sections. A little tide helps out. Rocky shoreline. Fun and usually not crowded.

The next thousand yards of coastline is classic Ewa Beach. No one around except a few fishermen

and maybe a surfer or two riding simple little closeout double-ups. Looking at Diamond Head from here lets you see just how big the crater actually is. Sunrise and moonrise, this is a tranquil spot.

The military lets you know you have approached their territory with a 10-foot-high steel fence that goes out across the sand into the water. Welcome to Barbers Point Officers Beach (the old name). The army has surrendered the property to the State of Hawaii and now it's open to the public and known as **White Plains Beach**. Previously the Barbers Point Naval Air Station (and still home to a Coast Guard unit at the end of Nimitz Beach), the area has assumed its ancient name of Kalaeloa. Access is through two gates, the Makakilo main gate off the freeway and the other at Ewa Beach at the end of Geiger Road. But us guys like da backroad an' we go paddle roun da fence to surf.

The parking lot at White Plains Beach is large and gets filled to capacity. This is a family beach if there ever was one: simple parking, beach pavilions, barbeque pits, shade trees, a bandstand, bath houses, a snack bar and outside showers. The surf rolls in with rights and lefts that double up over and over again, providing the occasional hundred yard ride or more to the beach. The bottom is sandy with flat rock. Two to 3 feet is about it for this area, but the outside reef can handle much larger surf if you want to paddle out for it. Just like all of Ewa Beach, glassy is great and north winds are better, but side chop is the norm.

Standing on the beach and looking outside to the right is **Tankers**. A thousand yard paddle may reward you with an exceptionally explosive wave that can be a smoker of a right at 4 to 6 feet. It's there if you want it, but remember: big gray things roam the waters around here.

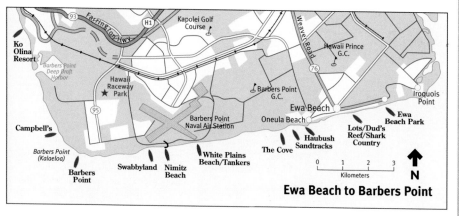

Ewa Beach to Barbers Point

From the fenceline, you can walk for several miles on beautiful beach that was litter free under the military but which is now being sprinkled here and there by the carefree public, auwe!

Winding along the shoreline road past permitted campsites, we break out of the *kiawe* trees to the road next to the airstrip. Following this we arrive at **Nimitz Beach** (Enlisted Men's Beach in the old days). This is an outside break that sections and closes out. It can be good, but you have to catch it, uh, just about right.

Just beyond Nimitz Beach, the Coast Guard has a presence *mauka* of the beach. Oceanside of this is a treeless beach area with a jetty on the right. **Swabbyland** is straight out a good thousand yards. What a spot. Good from 4 to 12 feet with thick juicy rights, this spot requires your attention. Getting caught inside is very memorable. Very similar to a big-wave spot at Diamond Head named Browns, with a touch of Laniakea, and there you have it.

An interesting aspect to this spot is that when you're forced to prone out and you're rocketing toward shore, the whitewater backs off very quickly as you pass over a trench and you're left skittering over deep water. Cool! Swabbyland is no secret and can get crowded. Too many surfers—everywhere. You know what a

swabby is, right? Just a Navy enlisted man, that's all.

It will be interesting to see how the State of Hawaii will manage this newly acquired land. Keep it clean, folks. This is the end of the beaten path for Barbers Point. Beyond is yet another great fence, and, on the other side, Campbell Industrial Park.

A freeway exit to Campbell Industrial Park is coming up. We go. Past the depressing concrete and metal warehouses lies the southwestern tip of Oahu, and the glorious West Side begins. Not surprisingly, the name of the spot is **Campbell's**. It's actually a fairly wide area with different spots showing when the surf height changes. Access to the water is over a coral shelf that is not really user-friendly when the surf is big. Once you've determined your launching point and jump in (in the hope that your leash won't snag on a rock), all is well. A hollow left with a shifting peak is straight ahead; 3 to 4 feet is good. A big right just west of this can handle 10 feet, but it gets spooky.

In the early '70s, a helicopter survey of the shark population was conducted around here and this area had more sharks than they could count. Sounds good? Perhaps this was just a phenomenon of the time. Still, keep your eyes open. Trade winds blow straight offshore and north winds are good

Above: Johnny Boy Gomes, one of Hawaii's surfing heavyweights, slams one home at Yokohama Bay. *Photo: Mana*

too, except they carry odors from the industrial plants. No worries, no known—or unknown—mutants running around.

The industrial zone ends at the Barbers Point Deep Draft Harbor (Malakole Harbor). Big west and northwest swells have impact on either side of the harbor mouth.

The **Ko Olina Resort** lies west of the deep draft harbor and has outside waves for the brave. Access is through a public right-of-way to the ocean, with free parking provided at a side lot of the hotel. The hotel is luxurious but has a fair-priced bar. An aquatic attraction is the shallow shark pond with small blacktips cruising along. Now where did they find those fine specimens? The swimming lagoons have heavy-duty black nets across the openings in the break wall where the ocean flows through. How come?

Westside Wave Action

The leeward side of Oahu stretching from Kaena Point to Nanakuli

is yet another wave-rich area of the island that, like every other shore, has it's own unique characteristics. In order to more clearly understand the general area, take into consideration the following points. Upon first inspection, one will find the land to be considerably more arid and barren than the rest of Oahu. The vibe here is very family-oriented, and there are more local, dark-skinned bruddah types than Caucasians. The west side is also one of the rougher parts of the island, where stinkeye and theft are as commonplace as swells in the heart of winter.

With all that said and done, let's move on to the surf. The west shores of Oahu are the best bet for year-round surf on the whole island. The constantly switching wind that batters most parts of the island with chop always seems to take pity on the west, and with regards to a variety of wind directions (except for *konas*), west coast conditions will range from crisp offshore to sideshore (at worst). Swells march onto the reefs here on a year-round basis as well.

During the winter, big swells wrap around Kaena Point and generate substantial wave action. West swells angle right in and are the best bet for winter surfing. During the summer months, south to southwest swells push up lines of waves that hit the reefs from a different angle, giving them a different feel. With this dual combo of year-round swell and wind patterns, the Waianae neighborhood produces enough wave action to keep da boyz happily at home.

One of the prime playground waves on the west side is located in Nanakuli, just north of the Kahe Power Plant. **Tracks** is the first break of significance as you delve into the western coast, and it consists of several sand/reef peaks around the Hawaiian Electric Beach Park. Tracks earned its name from the railroad that used to run past the beach, ferrying beachgoers intent on scoring some juicy wave action. Though the railroad is but a distant memory, the alluring waves of decades past show no signs of ageing, and still come through as fun as ever.

Tracks is a year-round surfing spot as it works on a multitude of swell angles, stretching from the northwest to southwest. It is also usually the most vertically challenged wave (we won't say small) breaking on this portion of the island during vertically enhanced swells, which provides a perfect refuge for those not seeking out enormous drops. As long as it's not too big and closing out, the performance peaks will continually roll in and produce what they are best known for. A little south along the beach is a reef peak that can give hollow short rights and fun lefts.

Due to the playful, easygoing nature of Tracks, the everpresent crowd of locals is eminent, so hitting it early (and especially not on weekends and holidays) is the wisest choice. Actually, you could also say that for just about every other popular surf spot in Hawaii.

Entering Nanakuli, you will encounter Hawaiian Homestead Land right on the ocean. In this neighborhood is a local spot named **Keaulana's**, a fun right at 2 to 4 feet. A very beautiful setting in a

Above: Da boys checking out the West Side action from a parking lot conference room. *Photo: Mana*

OAHU

EWA AND DA WEST

small bay with comfortable old houses full of Hawaiians who surf. Howzit Gannigan! Moving on.

Maili Point is another of those pumping left-handers that you used to draw sketches of in your textbook when you were still in school. When everything clicks, Maili can churn out some of the most crisp lefts around. Waves hit the reef and pitch, making for nice tubing sections, and when conditions are right, you can score nice, lengthy rides. Big winter west or summer southwest swells usually do Maili the most justice, and once again make for year-round surfing pleasure. Avoid bringing valuables with you as the beach/parking area is known to be sketchy. The local surfers have Maili wired, so be sure to give them space.

Maili Breakwall (or Green Lanterns) is famous for the huge waves that feather and break super far out in the blue water. Known as **Maili Cloudbreak**, it is beautiful to watch even when no one is riding. On the inside, waves wrap around a small point and present a straight wall that moves fast to the right. It is a bit difficult to paddle out through continuous whitewater, but you can do it. This spot was

a bummer before leashes because of the rock point and the break wall. You should not push your luck here even with the convenience of a medical clinic across the street. The outside can be ridden from 15 to 20 feet and bigger. Are you ready?

A few hundred feet up the road is **Sewers**. An aromatic surf spot across from, you guessed it, a wastewater treatment plant. So many surfing areas have come to life thanks to the leash. Borrowing your pal's board and riding here without a leash could bring an end to your friendship. A beautiful wave that smokes right or left is just a short distance off the ledge; 3 to 6 feet and you're grooving—or you would be, if there was any room at this tight little spot. A strong northwest makes the rights open up at 6 feet.

At the far end of Waianae town is Army Street. Turn here and park outside the gates of this military reservation. Limited parking available with military ID. Say hello to the guard and walk on through to this oasis known as Rest Camp due to the many bungalows and recreational facilities. Looking out from the shower area near the steps that

lead down to the beach, you will see **Pokai Bay**. When Makaha is 6 to 10 feet and up, this area gets a strong push but at half the size. You can see the sets coming from this side of the horizon. A long right slide with a left that shoots toward a raised shelf. It gets crowded real fast with good local surfers and some novice military guys checking out the real Hawaii.

Up the road a bit you will see a small mountain that is oceanside of Farrington Highway. This is **Lahilahi Point**. An apartment building comes into view quickly so get ready to pull over and park. This surf spot is not visible from the road, nor can you see the good-sized bay and wide beach. Looking toward the point, the setup is evident; lefts wrap and push to the beach. South swells find a home here. The middle of the bay takes the west and northwest swells, with shifting peaks. This place can easily handle big waves.

"Savage" Makaha

Pulling up to Makaha Beach, we see outside on the Waianae side of the bay a big thick left with not even one surfer out. Welcome to **Klausmeyers**, a somewhat treacherous and unforgiving wave where getting caught inside is the norm. Expect to take serious gas here at any working size.

The epicenter of surfing on the western shores is focused around one special point named **Makaha**. Makaha is a family wave and has followers ranging from the tiniest of *keikis* just learning to stand up, to grandpas who are still charging 'em like Buffalo. For these people, Makaha is their playground, and they treat it as their home. Aside from surfing, this is a prime spot for diving, fishing, bodysurfing, canoe surfing, tandem surfing, and other recreational water sports. Makaha works around the calendar to keep its devotees satisfied.

Makaha's outside break is a freight train of a wave when the swell hits life-threatening proportions. Waimea seems to get the bulk of the attention as *the* big-wave spot, but those in the know and who are intent on surfing some serious juice keep their eyes set on Makaha's outside. Of interest is the fact that when Waimea Bay is 25 feet with 60 surfers in the water, Makaha may be just as big with only a handful of people out. Brian Keaulana, u da best.

Why don't the big-wave riders of the North Shore ride huge Makaha? Not enough cameras? The drive too far? How about a 200-yard-long 20-foot wave? I think I'll go buy groceries instead.

While Waimea features an intense hair-raising drop, Makaha does just the same, and then stands up and peels along the reef into an inside bowl that sucks up those with lesser ability and bad karma. The waves hitting this bowl take one of two paths, either a sketchy, thick barrel or a hideous closeout. Of course, add the fact that you're riding on a 15-foot-plus monster and you may consider surfing here a life or death situation.

Makaha is also the site of Greg Noll's infamous wipeout on what was (and very possibly still is) the hugest paddle-in wave ever attempted. Back in the winter of '69, the North Shore was being bombed by one of the biggest swells in memory, easily closing out Waimea and drowning it in whitewater. Noll made his way westward to Makaha, where thick lines of ocean were peaking and peeling off perfectly at who knows how big. After muscling his way out the back, he waited for what he figured was "a good one" and started stroking for it. As he got into the wave and went into the drop, his board reached it's maximum speed and skipped out like a stone skimming over water. Noll took some serious beating, amazingly without drowning, and legend has it that after this experience he hung up his boardshorts and took a long break from surfing.

Not all of Makaha is as ferocious or scary as it's hyped up to be. Further inside over the reef towards the beach is another peak that is perfectly suited for high-level tricks and cruising. On 6-foot and under days, you can ride along all the way to the beach, going through both reform sections as well as board-whomping back-wash. Crowds by the droves line the water, and often you will find yourself simply floating while everyone else is riding.

The Makaha International Surf Meet was a big venue here in the '60s. Collect the money, send them out, no matter what the size or conditions, and enjoy the swim. It was a fantastic surfing exhibition with worldwide talent on view for all of us. Heroes have confirmed their

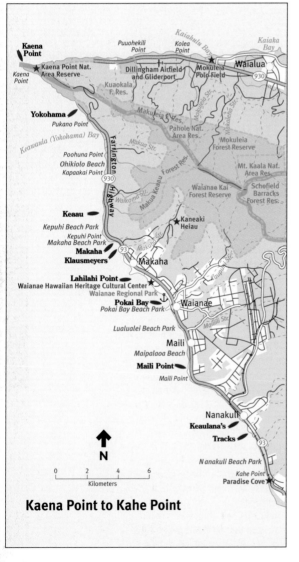

Kaena Point to Kahe Point

worth at Makaha. Rell Sunn is gone, but not her spirit. What a babe, she could outsurf most men, anywhere. Surfboards Makaha is alive and well, with Jay Richardson and son at the helm.

A funny note on the word *makaha*: in Hawaiian it means "savage" or "fierce," in reference to a group of bandits who were based deep in the surrounding valley. They would hide out and wait for unsuspecting passerbys to show up, and then pillage and plunder before making their getaway. The banditos have been absent for a good many years now, but one should still be cautious, especially about leaving valuables in the car.

Just past a residential area at the point lies **Keaau** (Free Hawaii) Beach Park. Pull in and there it is: a left on a big south swell in front of a ledge that peels into a little inlet. A serious wave that works well in the 4- to 5-foot range. Make sure your leash has no cracks or stresses; these rocks are unforgiving. Northwest swells during the winter will entertain you with 8-foot waves.

The Ranch is a roadside attraction just ahead. A northwest swell will let the wave here open up for a longer ride. **Pray for Sex Beach** is also at hand, so bring a friend and bodysurf. Down the way and far outside the Makua Cave (when it is 15 to 20 feet), you will find Brian Keaulana and his tow-in crew taking on the challenge of a very fast breaking wall. The ultimate breakfast club.

Yokohama, meanwhile, lies dead ahead. It gets blazingly hot out here, so it's a good idea to have a cooler along to help out. This spot catches a south swell too. The takeoff is awesome as it jacks up from deep water, hits a flat shelf and grinds down the beach. A left peak, very intense and thick. Good for home movies of your friends eating it. Yokohama can take 10-foot waves, easy.

Third Dip is next. A spot perfected by Johnny Boy Gomes and others with their intense commitment and "no scared of nothing" approach. Yikes, take my wave too. Great area to just watch the show when the bruddahs are rippin'. Watch the tide, swell direction and whether or not the swell is increasing. These factors will impact your day as 4 to 6 feet is a lot to handle here. PS: if the fishermen are here before you, tough luck; baited hooks on long lines have been cast. Do you really think they'll stop what they are doing so you can surf? Goodbye.

The road continues to **Kaena Point**. The road around the point is protected from motor traffic for environmental reasons, so this is the end of the line out here. This is also, you will see, where the West side of Oahu meets the North. Tremendous surf, strong currents and deep water have inspired some of the new breed of tow-in surfers to approach this desolate endzone. More power to them (and maybe you), but when heading here, don't forget to bring along a harpoon to fend off any territorial beasts. Walk around and get a sense of this desolate place, but don't leave your surfboard in or on your car. As with the entire West Side, the mountains are close, dry, and always beautiful.

—Barry Morrison, with additional text by Lorca Lueras

Above: Yokohama Bay and a surfer from the barrel's point of view. *Photo: Art Brewer*

Following pages: The guy on the beach must be surfed out, because there's no way anyone in their right mind could just sit and watch a tantalizing A-frame peak such as this one bombing into pretty little Yokohama Bay. *Photo: Mana*

Rell Sunn

1950 – 1998

Above: A mass of surfers gathers at Makaha Beach during a service held to honor
the memory of the late Rell Sunn, surfing's beloved and undisputed Queen of the West Side.
Photo: Dana Edmunds; inset portrait: Brett Uprichard

Windward Waves

Sometimes Surf

Year-round, but best whenever the winds die

The highway goes right past all the breaks

Reef and sand

Boogeyboards for the shorebreaks and maybe a helmet

Neck-breaking shorebreaks

Getting hammered by the shorebreaks

Hanauma Bay and other tourist attractions; insane but deadly shorepounds

OAHU

WINDWARD WAVES

Opposite: Underground ripper Dwayne Scharsh takes a clean slice out of a Sandy Beach section. *Photo: Mana*

So, as we depart Honolulu and travel east, leaving behind that last safe haven of Henry Kaiser known as Hawaii Kai, we begin the glorious ascent from the neighborhood of convenience to the true East End of Oahu's windward coast.

The 4-minute trip initiated at the pedestrian bridge at Lunalilo Home Road brings us to Hanauma Bay, a significant geological sight to take in, but leave your surfboard at home. There is no one here to watch your boards. Beyond the bay we come to Bamboo Ridge, a barren outcrop of lava flow from Koko Head Crater. Bamboo Ridge gets its name from the fishermen who fished from the cliffs in the deep, blue-purple water. Even though fishing poles have evolved greatly, the area is still remembered for those bamboo poles and the men who used them.

The short drive is stunning as the geology of the region is right on you. Check it out; the push from this caldera (Koko Head Crater) is here. The coast road cuts through the stratification of the lava, revealing a rich spectrum of colors that any surfer on any substance can appreciate. Primordial rock on the *mauka* side and the blue of the channel on the *makai* side. On a clear morning, rounding the bend, you can see the islands of Molokai, Lanai, and beyond, Maui.

All of a sudden, we are at the Halona Blowhole, a tourist stop, but one well worth a visit. Abrupt cliffs, deep water, strong swells, a hole in the shelf, and, bingo, we are getting big spray.

Alas, from the Blow Hole we look further east to the Sandy Beach area. Very desolate and remote in the '50s and early '60s, this straightaway between the Blowhole and the rise to Makapuu was *the* place to drag race your Heavy Chevy against the Fast Fords and anything else that showed up. No drinking allowed, yeah, right.

The Sandy's Scene

Well, here we are, at **Sandy's**. The ultimate roadside attraction beckons, and we succumb. Hey, this is beautiful, the people look friendly, the ocean is pristine, and did you spot those girls back there? Quick, see if you can find parking. Sandy's has been (and will continue to be) the destination for high school and college kids as a place to do your thing with your friends.

Welcome to Sandy's shorebreak. You are standing on the eastern corner of Oahu and looking at an area that is wind driven with a swell backing it. The prevailing trade winds or strong east winds produce continuous action on this corner of the island. Taking an east swell plus a south, southeast or even an ideal north wind, you will find this surf spot packed with brand name surfers. The shore break is but one facet of this region. A word of caution to the novice and the skilled: Sandy's will maim and hurt you. There are many recorded incidents of broken necks, spines, wrists, knees, el-

bows, and even total anatomy mishaps. But, hey, we go! The lifeguards are strong and truthful. If you have any doubts, ask about conditions and tell them your ability. Talk to them. By the way, I hope you changed clothes and stashed all your valuables in the car while you were back at the Blowhole, because you are not advised to make these arrangements in full view of the needy public down the road. Waves from 1 to 8 feet can move into this zone. An attraction is the wave action upon women's bathing tops and bottoms that are displaced at random from unsuspecting ocean participants. Yaahoo! Sandy Beach is probably best between 2 and 4 feet. Bodysurfing and bodyboarding are both allowed here.

Outside the shorebreak as the swell increases in size, **Middles** or **Chambers** will start to show. It's a deep beach right that can be bodysurfed or bodyboarded. Outside of this is **Generals**, a deep water spot that is boardsurfed, bodyboarded, and bodysurfed. Keep in mind that this area can hold 300 or more people in the water. Elbows and bums. I know someone who broke another guy's jaw with the left side of his face while on a wave. Both guys apologized to each other and went in to swell up and get medication. Remember, Sandy's means impact: with sand, loose coral chunks, other people, and even banging against yourself, all for free.

Moving down the beach where the black volcanic rock becomes visible and the point projects, we come to **Pipelittle**. This spot is good up to 4 feet and will then start to connect with Middles (Chambers) as its size increases. Primarily a left break for bodyboarders and surfers (for boardsurfers, before and after lifeguard duty). The knowing waterperson can take the occasional right that peels over the sashimi rocks that protrude everywhere, right and left. Outside of Pipelittle is **Halfpoint**. This spot is rights and lefts and can connect through Pipelittle, producing a screaming left with boils and barely submerged rocks to greet you as you fly past. Surfers who know their stuff will take off at the Halfpoint end of Pipelittle, ride to the shore, walk back up the beach near lifeguard tower #4B and weave their way through the rocks out to the lineup for more action. Further out we come to **Fullpoint**, another left of some merit. On an exceptionally great day, the surf will connect from Fullpoint right on through Halfpoint and Pipelittle.

Just behind us *mauka* of the beach is a large grassy area that in years past was used for rock concerts. People were having way too much fun so the city put an end to it. Nowadays, kite flying has taken over the grassy plain, offering visual excitement with colors and movement. Check out the lunch

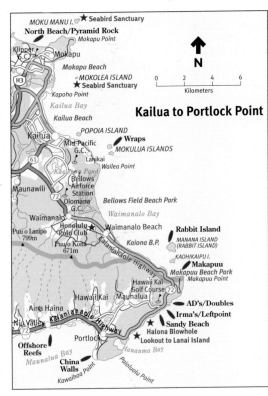

Kailua to Portlock Point

wagon that pulls up daily for that surfer food that gets gravy over everything. Solid.

Up the road a bit we come to **Irma's**, a spot for the not so hardcore, but very challenging with plenty of rocks. Best at 3 feet and better at 5 feet, Irma's is a left with a right if you are ready for doom and a beating. Next, we come to **Leftpoint**, which maxes out at 4 feet unless you catch it at a super high tide. The next spot up the coast is **Alan Davis** or **AD's**. Rocks and concrete pilings block the way for car entry so you need to take a short walk to this right slide. Good up to 5 feet with an inside spot called **Doubles**.

The whole Sandy Beach area has strong currents and you will always find yourself paddling to stay in the lineup. Due to the many rocks, timing is everything when paddling out at all spots. There are stories from the early '60s about 15- to 20-foot waves from a big east swell that were surfed from way outside Fullpoint almost to the Blowhole. Yikes, and no leashes either. The important thing to remember is: "All the chicks go to Sandy's."

Leaving Sandy Beach and winding our way around the corner to **Makapuu**, don't forget to pull over at the tourist lookout for a fantastic view of the Windward coast. Sheer green cliffs, blue ocean and islands in the stream is what you will see. Makapuu has a long, wide beach that ends at the cliffs of a huge point that wraps back around to Alan Davis at the end of the Sandy Beach area. Bodysurfing and bodyboarding are practiced here, and inflatable rubber mats are also used. For people with no equipment, the McDonald's food tray is a favorite both here and at Sandy's. The number of swim fins lost from being sucked over the falls and the explosive impact is great. A local entrepreneur searches the shoreline and dives for single swim fins, selling them from the trunk of his car to those in need. Makapuu can get 10 feet in the middle of the bay, but the average is in the 2- to 4-foot range. With glassy conditions; southwest or west winds are best.

There is a boardsurfing spot on the Rabbit Island side of the parking lot called **Suicides** for some reason. A right break situated in front of rocks with the push of a North Shore wave awaits you. There are several ways to paddle out, depending on tide and swell

Above: These signs aren't a joke. Many a beachgoer has been maimed by the notorious Sandy's shorebreak, a mere 10 feet from the waterline. May the buyer beware.
Photo: Brett Uprichard

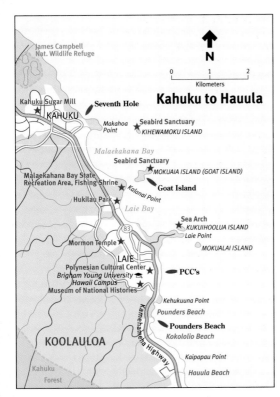

James Campbell
Nat. Wildlife Refuge

Kahuku to Hauula

0 1 2
Kilometers

N

Kahuku Sugar Mill
KAHUKU

Seventh Hole

Makahoa
Point

Seabird Sanctuary
KIHEWAMOKU ISLAND

Malaekahana Bay

Seabird Sanctuary

MOKUAIA ISLAND (GOAT ISLAND)

Malaekahana Bay State
Recreation Area, Fishing Shrine

Kalanai Point

Goat Island

Hukilau Park

Laie Bay

Sea Arch
KUKUIHOOLUA ISLAND
Laie Point

MOKUALAI ISLAND

Mormon Temple

83

LAIE

Polynesian Cultural Center
Brigham Young University
Hawaii Campus
Museum of National Histories

PCC's

Kehukuuna Point
Pounders Beach

KOOLAULOA

Pounders Beach
Kokololio Beach

Kaipapau Point

Kahuku
Forest

Hauula Beach

Kamehameha Highway

direction. Beyond this we come to Kumu Cove, or Cockroach Bay, just before the marine laboratory pier. A sandy beach with rollers that come in and break and reform again. Lots of family action here, with small kids and grownups surfing side by side.

Rabbit Island, or **Manana Island**, is directly offshore from Kumu Cove. The paddle out is an easy 30 minutes nonstop over a pretty deep trench that is dark blue, making the mind very alert. The reward for making it to this fabulous right is the beauty of the surroundings and waves that come from the north and northeast at 2 to 10 feet. The takeoff is near a large suck-out ledge that boils. A submerged rock confronts you on your first turn, then a green wall that fans and bends around the corner. Looking in toward the distant shore you left 3 hours ago, you realize that it may take you longer to go in than to come out. What

doesn't kill you makes you stronger. While paddling in, you find yourself envying the surfers who arrived in their boats with food, water, shade and, no doubt, ice-cold beer.

There are spots on the outside reef of **Waimanalo**, but you've got to live there to know when they are good. All of Waimanalo Beach on through to Bellows Beach is fun shorebreak for bodysurfing, body-boarding and surfing. Beware of the Portuguese man-of-war jelly-fish with its blue bag and blue ten-tacles, blown in by the trade winds.

To get to Lanikai, you travel through Kailua town and go beach-side to the east. Offshore in Lani-kai are the twin islands known as the Mokuluas. Looking out to the island on the left, you see a right-hander peeling. The paddle out is just like the one we did at Rabbit Island, except it isn't as deep. This spot is called **Wraps** and breaks well up to about 6 feet with a north-east swell. West winds are best but very rare. Glassy is great. Some of the local residents paddle out in four-man canoes with their boards strapped on or in tow.

Kailua has an outside reef that holds many secrets. If you live here, they may get told to you.

On the Kaneohe Marine Corps Air Station at the end of Kailua Bay, there are several surf spots, but a military ID card is required for access. The outside reefs in Kaneohe Bay hold secrets too. Pre-viously open to anyone with an ID, **North Beach** is now open to active-duty Marines only. Base command-er decision. North Beach (sandbar city) is similar to Ehukai on the North Shore. The angle of the beach allows a full north swell to march right in. Good at 2 to 4 feet, maybe 5, max. The Kailua side of the beach has sort of a point break that can be ridden up to 8 feet.

Pyramid Rock is on the oppo-site end of the beach. Civilians are

Below: The beach at Sandy's is unreal for a day out. Just remember to avoid storing valuables in your car and exer-cise caution in the thumping shore-pound. *Photo: Brett Uprichard*

Right: Tourists marveling at the Halona Blowhole, a natural wonder found between Haunama Bay and Sandy Beach. *Photo: Joe Carini*

Opposite: Heading up the coast from Sandy Beach, Makapuu is another main attraction on this southeast stretch of Oahu. The lighthouse on the point signifies the easternmost tip of Oahu. When working, Makapuu boasts Hawaii's top bodysurfing conditions. *Photo: Brett Uprichard*

only allowed on this corner of the beach on Sundays. A left/right combo up to 4 to 6 feet as the waves come in and mutate around the rock. Glassy, south, southwest, or west winds are your best bet.

First a Lion, Then a Goat

Way up the coast at Kualoa Point near **Chinaman's Hat** (also known as **Mokolii**), there is an outside left that just waits for southwest or west winds. It picks up the big winter north swell wraps as well as northeasters.

Moving along the coast heading north, we can see the ocean but access is through residential farming areas. More outside reefs that require a boat, glassy conditions, and a big northeast swell. Better to keep moving northward. **Crouching Lion** is visible from the highway where you will park. Very deceptive-looking from shore as to true wave height because it always looks smaller than it really is. A good long paddle takes you to this screaming right that breaks over a shelf. Be prepared for a demanding takeoff and either a pull-in tube ride or a good thrashing. Two to 5 feet is the range, and be sure to keep your eyes on the tide.

Kahana Bay and the points on either side (mainly the right) have a lot to offer, but you have to live

there or drive by at just the right time. More outside reefs require a boat to explore all the way to **Pounders Beach**. Now, how did this beach get its name? Heavy hits while bodysurfing, that's how. Two to 4 feet is fine, but with the right swell direction, bigger waves can be ridden. Fun for a good pounding swim, if you're game.

PCC's across the road from the Polynesian Cultural Center is the freight train smoking left on the Windward side. From 2 to 10 feet, get ready for a fiercely demanding push on your equipment and soul. You'll either make the sections and bowl areas or you won't. When it is big and breaks outside and then doubles up, beware; it is not good to be caught inside. A fair paddle out but not too far. Respect the locals and wait for your turn, it will come when they've had enough or you're obviously in the pit and they hoot. Try not to blow it on your first wave.

Up the road we arrive at Laie Beach. Looking out and to the left, you see **Goat Island** or **Mokuauia**. A walk down the beach to the point and a fair paddle to the lefts can bring some fun. Two to 4 feet, maybe bigger, it all depends on tide and wind. When conditions come together, Goats can turn into one of the bitchiest little lefts, rippable but also bowly. Short rights are also an option, but aren't on the same level as the lefts. We're now near the northeastern tip of Oahu, where the winter swells can wrap to this side of the island.

Driving to Kahuku, we pull over to the public golf course, and, hey, get waves outside. **Seventh Hole** is a nice left with lotsa current. Best when the wind is favorable, or blowing *konas* and the tide not too low. Two to 6 feet is a fairly good range. From here on over, you've entered the North Shore and left the east behind you.

—Barry Morrison

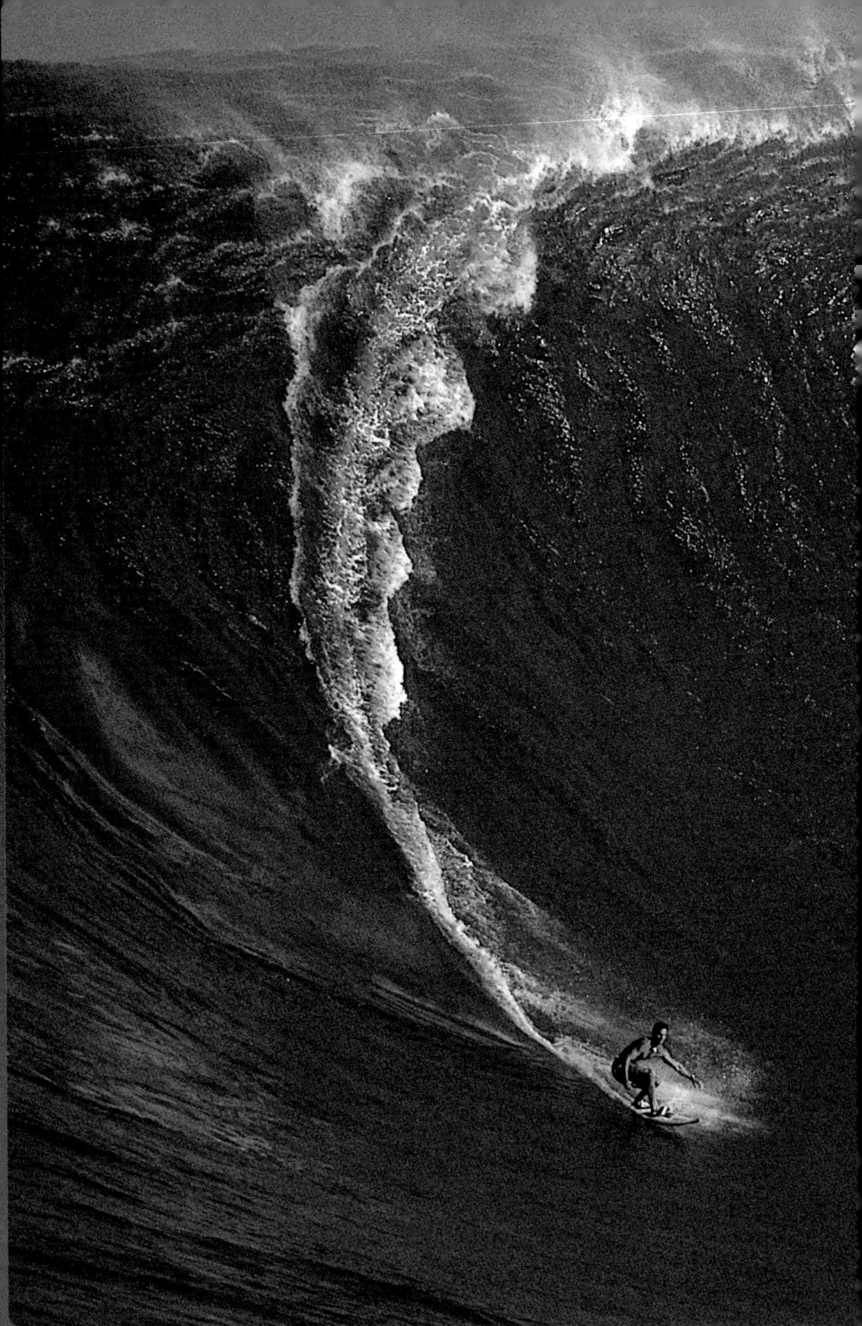

Tow-ins & MONSTER Waves

Pete Cabrinha, heavy positioning at Jaws. *Photo: Erik Aeder*

Surfing in big waves is a whole new dimension in the experience of riding waves. Some wave warriors are addicted to the adrenal-bursting rush you get from racing down the face of a gigantic wave. They are like junkies in desperate need of a fix. Other surfers are content to cringe on solid ground with their leashes between their legs while thinking up excuses for not paddling out. ("Man, I've got the meanest headache . . . ," "I'm waiting for it to get good", etc.) Every surfer, however, has his/her personal limits regarding what he/she will or will not paddle out into and surf, and with each additional 5 feet of wave height, the list of those good-to-go gets shorter and shorter. When waves hit legitimately big heights, say 20 feet and up, there is only a handful of crazies in the surfing world who have what it takes to successfully rope and ride monster waves.

During the past decade, big-wave surfing has evolved radically in appearance and method, and the basic mechanics of riding big waves are in marked contrast to that of shralping small waves. The emphasis in huge surf is not on rail-to-rail maneuvers and trickery—that's child's play. In big-wave surfing, the basic rule can be easily summed up in three steps: Get In, Get Down, and Get Out. If you can do this and look cool, you score extra points. And if you escape a monster session without being drowned beneath a churning cloud of whitewater and foam, or without being broken in two by a cement-like lip, or without blowing a late elevator drop, you are indeed *the man*.

Having the proper equipment is essential. The boards used in such gladiatorial exercises are generally long, thick and reinforced with generous layers of fiberglass cloth to increase their overall strength and prevent snappage. Extra stringers (the wooden strips running down the middle of the board) may also be added for a false sense of comfort and security.

These foam and fiberglass beasts are built for heavy paddling, as well as the ability to push through mid-face chops and to outrun lunging lips in consequential surf. Just feeling the weight of a big-wave board under your arm is enough to send shivers down your spine as you imagine the sort of moving water that it's been crafted for. Indeed, your very life may depend on the make of board you ride. Reputable shapers are not just big names out of talk, but because they design boards that perform. The last thing you want is to be pushing hard off the bottom of the biggest wave you've ever seen when, suddenly, your board stops and skips out at the critical moment in your bottom turn because the tail rocker or rail foil on your board wasn't right.

Tom Curren, stuck in the eye. *Photo: Art Brewer*

Rush Randle stands tall at Peahi. *Photo: Erik Aeder*

But the right equipment can only get you so far. You must be mentally and physically capable of holding your own in a terrifying situation. The actual act of riding a huge wave sounds simple: paddle hard, stand, hold your line and aim for the shoulder. In fact, even lunatic chargers such as Brock Little admit that it takes more skill to land 360 aerials in 2-foot surf than it does to charge a 20-foot drop at Waimea. But it's the big-wave surfers' search for a rush, their thrill-seeking compulsion, that drives them to take risks, sort of like when you were a kid and there were always those in your group who would do the most balls out and gutsiest things for fun, say bombing down steep hills on skateboards, standing up to neighborhood bullies, or launching big airs off ramps on mountain bikes. These are the same fearless kind of people who will go for it on big days.

Aside from being thrill-seekers, big-wave surfers also need to have a knowledge of the ocean and how water moves when massive volumes of it are pushing around. This only comes from years of experience. You need to know how currents run, how to relax when getting pounded, how to pace your breathing, etc. Some notable surfers even swear that it's possible to take in small amounts of air underwater through bubbles produced by the aeration of a huge breaking wave (believe it or not).

Physically, you've got to train for the worst by being in the best condition. Holding your breath in turbulent water without panicking when you don't know which way is up and your leash goes slack—this is a situation you'll be facing in heavy water. According to Darrick Doerner, "You'd better be able to swim 5 miles, hold your breath for more than 2 minutes in churning water, and ride the biggest waves of your life."

Some surfers have taken to more unconventional methods of training such as free-diving in lava caves or running underwater while being weighed down by a rock. Jogging, paddling and swimming laps are also good forms of cross-training, but every surfer has his or her own training regimen. The bigger the wave, the faster it travels through water, which means extra-stiff stroking on your part to keep up with it and to get yourself over the ledge. Pussy paddles are going to get you nowhere but frustrated, whether you are caught inside, outside, or both. Slouches are better off on the couch and out of the way.

Because of the extreme conditions of big-wave surfing, the sport has had its fair share of tragedies, many involving the most prominent names in surfing. During one of the Eddie Aikau big-wave specialty events at Waimea Bay, Titus Kinimaka was halfway through a good-sized late-drop when a wave lip overtook his descent, collapsing on him and instantly breaking one of his legs. Kinimaka was unaware of this until he resurfaced and felt something banging against the back of his head. He assumed it was his board; it turned out to be his leg. On 23 December, 1994, noted big-stuff man Mark Foo drowned after a similar accident on a "small" wave (12 to 15 feet) at Mavericks in California. Exactly a year later (some say to the hour), Californian pro Donnie Solomon passed away at Waimea Bay after taking a bad spill, just after riding what he claimed was, "the best wave of my life!" The best and worst on the same day. The next year, Todd Chesser, one of the main Hawaii players and well respected for his ability in the serious stuff, got caught unexpectedly by a clean-up set while surfing a mysto outside break on the North Shore. Even as well-conditioned an athlete as Chesser met his match against the ocean. Even though fatalities and accidents are rare, safety in such vociferous waters should be emphasized at all times.

There comes a point when a wave gets so powerful and fast-moving that conventional paddling just doesn't work anymore. No matter how hard you scratch and claw your way into one of these monsters, your efforts will be in vain. And even if you do manage to get into one, by the time you stand up and negotiate your drop, the wave will have overtaken you and pounded you like a fart in a windstorm. This wave size is generally accepted as a good 30 feet, a height that some have dubbed "the unridden realm." Consider the example of Greg Noll at Makaha during the raging swells of '69. Even though no photographic records exist of his ride, witnesses say that Noll forced his way down the face of what must have been at least a 30-foot wave (or even bigger), only to confront his worst nightmare as his big-wave gun reached its maximum velocity and skipped out like a stone. It was a miracle that Noll survived. On another occasion, Brock Little stroked into an easy 30-footer at the Eddie Aikau, making it halfway down before he got sucked back up the wave's face as his board got passed up (yes, he took a major licking). This got some of the world's elite surfers thinking about how they could tap into such energy and successfully ride some of these arrogant giants.

In the late '70s, surfing pioneers such as Jeff Johnson, Roger Erickson and Flippy Hoffman paddled into breaks such as Avalanche and Kaena Point to test being towed into huge surf on their 10-foot Brewer guns by small outboard-powered boats. For some reason, these ploys never really

A heartfelt drop at Waimea by Mike Parsons. *Photo: Art Brewer*

Mark Warren jams hard at a good-sized Honolua Bay. *Photo: Dana Edmunds*

took off, and such projects were put on hold for a good decade or so. Fast-forward to the early '90s and to a new crew of big-wave masters/watermen/windsurfers searching for an innovative way to break through the barriers of traditional big-wave surfing. Darrick Doerner, Buzzy Kerbox and Laird Hamilton—three well-respected watermen and surfers—start taking to outer North Shore reefs with Zodiac dinghies, tow ropes and 9- to 10-foot big-wave boards. The result was incredible and radical performance surfing on the faces of waves of unimaginable size and girth. After a cover story in *Surfer* magazine showing the trio styling and trimming like never before seen in solid 20-foot waves, their reputations were cemented. Towing-in was hot, and they were the vanguard. Magazines worldwide proclaimed a new era of big-wave riding, and Hamilton, the pioneer of the whole gig, started appearing in all kinds of publications. Even mainstream magazines like *National Geographic* and *Outside* sent reporters to write about this new surfing sensation.

As with other avant-garde ideas, refinements were essential to smooth out the rough edges of this rapidly-expanding breakthrough. Zodiacs and outboard motorboats were replaced by jet skis (because of their maneuverability and ability to make quick rescues). The absence of the outboard motorboat also reduced the chops in a wave's face and guaranteed smoother rides. Drastic changes in equipment also had an explosive impact on a surfer's ability to handle big waves. Due to the design and length of the modern tow-in board, rippers like Hamilton and company have redefined what performance surfing can be in sizeable waves. Nowadays, instead of the same ol' same ol' drop in and aim for the channel approach, these guys are into fading drops, gouging full-rail carves, pulling in behind 20-foot bowls, and even launching some of the meanest airs ever seen in monster surf. Preconceptions of what was possible in the mean and lean stuff have been blown away, and it is now anyone's guess as to how far big-wave surfing can go. Already, some of the biggest waves that were thought to be unrideable have been challenged and slain.

By traditional big-wave standards, current boards do not make a whole lot of sense. They are generally around 7'6" long, 17" wide and just over 2" thick, compared to average big-wave gun measurements of 9'6" long, 19–20" wide and 3" thick. The difference between the new slivers and traditional log-like big-wave boards is that the paddling factor has been taken out of the equation because of the tow-in variable. The extra foam needed to get surfers in has been stripped away, leaving only what is truly necessary for riding a wave. Foot straps are essential to keep the riders in place as they take the plunge on a huge wave. More often than not, the wind is stiff and blowing, which creates large chops running up the face of the wave. Without the straps, riders would get blown off their board and eat it on every serious chop. Since there is so little foam in the board, under normal glassing they would snap like toothpicks. Therefore, tow boards are laminated super thick with double 10-ounce layers on both sides, making them as solid as a rock. This has the advantage of allowing your board to keep going down the face of a huge wave without being caught in the wind. The extra weight also keeps you on the wave and not stuck on its lip; sometimes, lead weights are fastened to the board's deck to add more mass. Normal tow-in boards are so solid that you can drop them on the ground and they won't even experience a ding.

The last significant big wave day in memory, the legendary *El Nino*-fueled swell of 28 February 1998, was a moment that changed everyone's perspective of big waves. It was a day that saw prominent big-wave venue Waimea Bay so out of control that it was closed to the public by the State of Hawaii. All attention then shifted to the outside Logcabins break, which was peeling as perfectly as a well-formed sandbar, except at gigantic proportions. Wave heights were beyond anyone's estimate, but were best described by Kenny Bradshaw as being, "25 to 40 feet and perfect." The photographic records of the waves and the handful of surfers being towed-in on them that day are incredible, and to this day still evoke hoots and other wondrously surfy remarks.

Meanwhile, there is the attitude and approach that Laird Hamilton, Darrick Doerner and the rest of the strapped-in crew on Maui have taken at the outer break called Peahi on Maui's north shore. Anytime there's even a rumor of it breaking, there are helicopters and boats on standby for photographers determined to document this crew going head-to-head with the ocean's gnarliest foe. Peahi, aka Jaws, is a wave of extraordinary features. It has only ever been paddle-attempted by a few brave souls, and is normally the domain of demented windsurfers looking for cheap thrills. The reef at Jaws barely shows signs of being a surf spot in swells under 10 feet, but is way more than capable of holding waves that, on the right swell, can produce some of the most hair-raising and humongous surf ever witnessed by man. So far, the Maui boys have astonished the surfing media and world with their daredevil, go-for-broke attitude while

Laird Hamilton making it look easy, brah. *Photo: Erik Aeder*

Munga Barry, critical positioning at Sunset. *Photo: Art Brewer*

facing some of the heaviest waves ever seen. In the process, they have created an art form out of riding the place. Anyone wanting proof of this need only ask any surfer in the know, or flip through any recent publication about big-wave surfing in Hawaii. This crew of watermen, windsurfers and surfers are the backbone of the who's, what's, and whoas (!) of the tow-in surf epoch.

As with any trend that takes off, there are always the naysayers. Critics claim that towing-in equals cheating and that there is no soul or challenge in machine-aided surfing. They scorn the thought of waverunners with pumped-up egos whizzing past them into surf that they would never have been able to handle at half the size, had they paddled. They claim that with the amount of new jet skis being purchased by every other pro, legend and wannabe out there, there will surely be a slew of incompetents running around putting lives in jeopardy just for a shot at getting into the mags. They deplore the congesting of rapidly diminishing outer reef spots.

On the other hand, there are just as many surf-watchers who are totally enraptured by this new wave of activity. They have dutifully paid their deposits on personal water-scooter-mobiles, bought towboard quivers, and they now claim that towing-in is the next best thing since the leg rope in the rarefied sport of riding big waves.

Big waves and *towing-in*. These days, the two words are synonymous in any surfer's vocabulary with what is truly going down.

—*Lorca Lueras*

The open-air photo studio at Waimea. *Photo: Bernie Baker*

Above: A laidback Maui scene "on the rocks" at Honolua Bay. Surf? Sun? Whatever you desire.
Photo: Steve Wilkings

Following pages: Victor Lopez, deep in a meditative moment at Honolua Bay.
Photo: Dana Edmunds

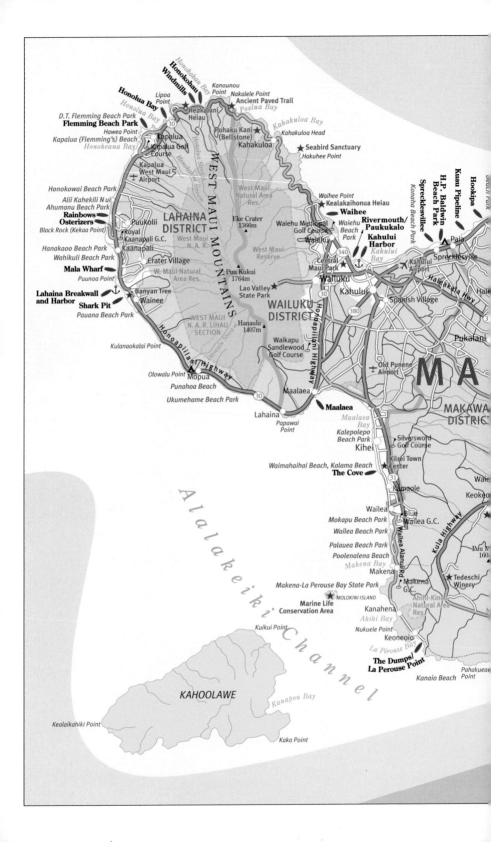

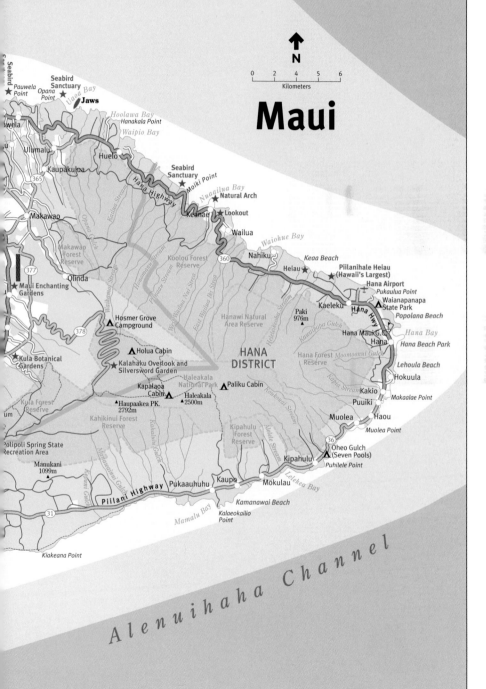

PACIFIC OCEAN

Maui

N

0   2   4   5   6
Kilometers

Seabird
Sanctuary
★ Pauwela   Opana   Jaws
Point   Point   Uaoa Bay

Seabird
Sanctuary ★
Hoolawa Bay
Hanakala Point
Waipio Bay

Ulumalu

Huelo

Kaupakulua

Makawao

Hana Highway

Seabird
Sanctuary
Moiki Point
Nuaailua Bay
★ Natural Arch
Keanae
★ Lookout

Wailua

Waiohue Bay

Nahiku
Keaa Beach

Heiau ★
Piilanihale Heiau
(Hawaii's Largest)
Hana Airport
Pukaulua Point
Waianapanapa
State Park
Popolana Beach

Kaeleku
Hana Hwy

365

377

Makawao
Forest
Reserve

Olinda

★ Maui Enchanting
Gardens

378

★ Kula Botanical
Gardens

Kula Forest
Reserve

Koolou Forest
Reserve

Hosmer Grove
Campground

Holua Cabin

Kalahaku Overlook and
Silversword Garden

Kapalaoa
Cabin

Haleakala
National Park

Haupaakea PK.
2792m

Haleakala
2500m

Paliku Cabin

Hanawi Natural
Area Reserve

Paki
976m

Kawaikapu Gulch

Hana Maui G.C.

Hana

Hana Bay
Hana Beach Park

Lehoula Beach
Hokuula

HANA
DISTRICT

Hana Forest
Reserve

Moomoonui Gulch

Kakio

Puuiki

Makaalae Point

Kahikinui Forest
Reserve

Kipahulu
Forest
Reserve

Kapia Stream

Kaunakaui Stream

Malele Stream

Muolea

Haou

Muolea Point

Polipoli Spring State
Recreation Area

Manukani
1099m

36
Oheo Gulch
(Seven Pools)
Kipahulu
Puhilele Point

31

Piilani Highway

Pukaauhuhu

Kaupo

Mokulau

Lelekea Bay

Kamanawai Beach

Mamalu Bay

Kalaeokailio
Point

Kiakeana Point

Alenuihaha Channel

Maui
On My Mind

The days when a surfer could pull up in front of a spot on Maui and ride perfect waves with just a few friends are long gone. The population of resident surfers has grown off the scale, and in many cases, the children of the early pioneers and even their children's children are now filling up the lineups.

Additionally, the resurrection of longboarding has revived many once dormant older surfers left behind by the shortboard revolution, and the invention and popularity of bodyboarding have also helped to saturate the surf.

And yet, Maui is still a surfer's paradise, less expensive and exhausting than an Indo boat trip, with much more cultural stimulation when the waves are flat than is usually available at a surf resort. The hiking is exceptional, the diving is rewarding and there are excellent restaurants and live music. And, yes, you can drink the local tap water.

Maui boasts one of the world's top point breaks (Honolua Bay) and fastest waves (Maalaea), along with numerous other hollow reef spots in an ocean that is refreshingly cool during hot weather, yet refreshingly warm during colder conditions. When howling winds render the waves unappetizing to surfers, conditions become perfect for sailboarders and kite-sailors. And if you can't afford to rent a car, hitchhiking is legal, although it can be time-consuming. As the state's second largest island, it can take forever to get from one side of the island to another chasing after favorable swell and wind conditions.

Because of its unusual configuration, Maui essentially has two surfable shores, north and west, with the north shore having northerly and easterly components, while the west side has northerly and southerly elements. The north and east parts of the island are lush and wet, with tropical forests extending to the shoreline, while the west side is arid and dry, becoming more moist and green north of Lahaina.

As always, Hawaii's prevailing winds will determine whether the surf will be prime time or wasted time. Trade winds blow offshore on northwest/southwest shores, while *kona* winds (westerlies) turn the usually bumpy waters off northeast/east shores into visions of pristine delight.

Additionally, mornings can be smooth and clean before the trade winds pick up. And during winter especially (and sometimes during summer), the high pressure cell that normally dominates the eastern Pacific breaks down, creating a land breeze/sea breeze regime with light offshore winds around the entire island in the morning, replaced by onshore winds by noon.

Without waves, none of this matters. Each side of the island has the usual wave patterns that show variations from time to time, but which are usually predictable. The northwest/northeast shores enjoy the best swells during winter (October through April) from fierce storms that leave the Asian mainland and rage across the Gulf of Alaska on their way to the US mainland. These booming west/northwest swells can reach all the

Opposite: An image of a perfect cutback with Shane Beschen demonstrating a clean sweep on a Maui shoulder. *Photo: Erik Aeder*

175

MAUI

Year-round surf; winter is biggest

Just a short flight away, "Here today, gone to Maui"

Reef is predominant

Proper boards for surfing prime Hawaiian waves

The swell can be blocked by other nearby islands

Bouncing off reef bottoms, brain damage from Maui Wowie

Some of the top windsurfing in the world

way down the northwest coast to Lahaina, bringing to life spots from Windmills to Hana on the northeast/east coast. The cold fronts from these winter storms that pass over the island are preceded by *kona* (southwesterly to westerly) winds that clean up the waves on the usually onshore windward side of Maui.

During the summer months (April through October), the dominant wave-producing systems of winter storms in the Southern Hemisphere (as well as the cyclones in the South Pacific) bring southwest and south swells that energize the southwest/west coast from La Perouse Bay to Mala Wharf. As a bonus, typhoons rampaging through Micronesia and the Philippines during this period can get caught up in cold fronts coming off of Asia, sending west/northwest swells to Maui. Meanwhile, hurricanes born off South America and Mexico can send swells to Maui's east coast, while hurricanes that form farther west can send south and southwesterly swells. Maui surfers are tormented by the islands of Lanai, Molokai, Kahoolawe and Hawaii, which

Above: Honolua didn't earn its reputation as one of the world's best waves by chance. Perhaps it's the unbelievably round tube sections that give it such credibility. *Photo: Steve Bingham*

Left: Board cemetery at Windmills. *Photo: Erik Aeder*

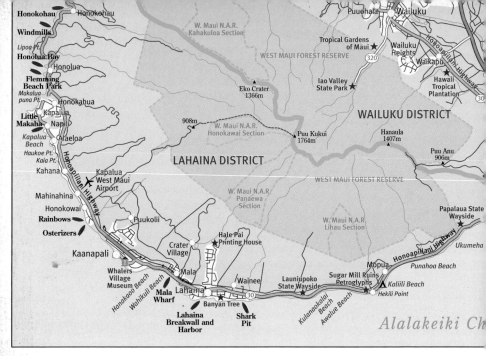

Honokohau — Honokohau
Windmills
Lipoa Pt.
Honolua Bay
Honolua
Flemming Beach Park
Makalua puna Pt.
Honokahua
Little Makaha — Napili — Kapalua
Kapalua Beach
Haukoe Pt.
Kaia Pt.
Kahana
Mahinahina
Honokowai
Rainbows
Osterizers
Kaanapali
Whalers Village Museum
Mala Wharf
Lahaina
Lahaina Breakwall and Harbor
Banyan Tree
Shark Pit
Mala
Wainee
Crater Village
Hale Pai Printing House
Puukolii
Honokoao Beach
Wahikuli Beach
Honoapiilani Highway
Kapalua West Maui Airport
Alaeloa
Puuohala — Wailuku
Tropical Gardens of Maui
Wailuku Heights
Waikapu
Waikapu
320
Hawaii Tropical Plantation
Iao Valley State Park
Eko Crater 1366m
W. MAUI N.A.R. Kahakuloa Section
WEST MAUI FOREST RESERVE
908m
W. MAUI N.A.R. Honokawai Section
Puu Kukui 1764m
Puu Kukui
Hanaula 1407m
Puu Anu 906m
WAILUKU DISTRICT
LAHAINA DISTRICT
W. MAUI N.A.R. Panaewa Section
W. MAUI N.A.R. Lihau Section
WEST MAUI FOREST RESERVE
Papalaua State Wayside
Honoapiilani Highway
Ukumeha
Mopua
Punahoa Beach
Sugar Mill Ruins
Petroglyphs
Kaliili Beach
Hekili Point
Launiupoko State Wayside
Kulanaokalai Beach
Awalue Beach
30
30
Honoapiilani Highway
Alalakeiki Ch

block many south, south-west, west and northwest swells from reaching Maui's shores.

As the rest of this tour of Maui will show, there are still plenty of waves to go around. Unfortunately, there are also plenty of local surfers to compete with for these waves. When frustrated by the crowds, it's easy for the locals to lash out at strangers, so the best way to ensure a good time on Maui is to be low-key, pass out the smiles and, when your turn comes, show everyone you know what to do with a wave. Most people bring along their own troubles when they travel in the form of aggressiveness and selfishness, so put on a friendly, generous traveling face and see if that isn't an improvement.

The West is Da Best

The end of the road on Maui's southwest coast is home to a pair of surf spots that offer as much excitement as anyone can stand. **The Dumps** and **La Perouse Point**, both at La Perouse Bay, deliver gaping left barrels that are compromised by extremely jagged lava rock and sharp coral. These waves come booming out of the south from hurricane swells, giant Southern Hemisphere winter storms or cyclones in the South Pacific. Beware, only expert surfers can expect to challenge these waves with any expectation of success and safety.

There are a few fun surf spots along **South Kihei Road** suitable for surfing, bodyboarding or bodysurfing. Most popular and consistent is **The Cove** at the south end of Kalama Beach Park. West and big south swells provide rights and a few lefts, but this spot breaks best on a west.

Just off the breakwater at **Maalaea Small Boat Harbor** is a series of fun peaks suitable for everyone from beginners to experts. On a few exceptional days every year, super-strong south swells will bring to life an exceptionally fast and exhilarating right that will provide a memorable, if frustrating, ride of a lifetime as you try to beat the wave by violating the laws of hydrodynamics. The

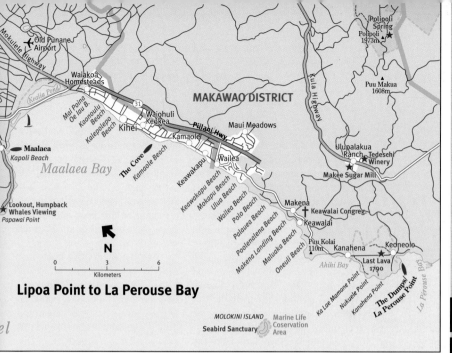

Lipoa Point to La Perouse Bay

waves at **Maalaea** are under siege from boat owners, commercial enterprises and the Army Corps of Engineers, all of whom want to extend the breakwater and increase the size of the marina, which would destroy the waves as well as nearby green sea turtle foraging areas. A letter to county and state legislators could help to save one of the ocean's unique surf spots.

Along the **Honoapiilani Highway** between the tunnel and Lahaina lie a series of fun beach breaks and reef breaks that are easily visible from the road. Depending on swell and wind conditions, the waves can range from fun for longboarders and bodyboarders to exciting for everyone.

At Lahaina's south end is **Shark Pit**, famous for its breathtakingly hollow peaks, fun when small and excitingly dangerous when overhead. Requires a little ingenuity as this is a residential area and ocean access isn't obvious.

In the heart of Lahaina is **Breakwall**, which is just outside the breakwater of Lahaina Harbor. Waves here can be pumping when

the rest of the south shore is small and weak. South swells result in long lefts while north swells can shoot the gap between Maui and Molokai and bring long, peeling rights in the middle of winter.

At the north end of the breakwater is **Lahaina Harbor**, a short, intense right and long, peeling left made more challenging by the constant boat traffic entering and exiting the harbor. At high tide, the lefts are a speed run, while low tide shows shallow coral and sharp *wana* (sea urchins). Lahaina is a very user-friendly and high-performance setup that is seldom uncrowded. The proximity of excellent locations for spectators inspires surfers to outrageous levels of performance.

The last spot in Lahaina is **Mala Wharf**, a long, perfect, peeling wave that has become a haven for longboarders, though it offers an exciting, fast, hollow wave for shortboarders and bodyboarders as well.

All of the spots mentioned so far are best from April through October, which is when the south swells come booming in, though a few receive the big west and north swells of wintertime.

Osterizers and Rainbows

The spots from Osterizers to Honolua Bay are at their prime from October through April, when the winter storms send powerful northwest, north and northeast swells to Maui's shores. At the start of Honokowai is **Osterizers**, which transforms north swells into A-frame peaks. An easy paddle to the north is **Rainbows**, which also comes alive on north swells and provides long, fast right barrels and short but intensely hollow lefts, both over a shallow reef. Definitely worth the risk.

Along Honoapiilani Highway through Honokowai and Kahana are a variety of reef breaks that have become more popular as other places have become more crowded and, well, less fun. The best place to check conditions is at **S-Turns**, where Honokowai and Kahana connect at a sharp turn in the road. Most of these spots fall in the fun rather than epic category, though the lack of crowds compensates for the lack of tubes.

Little Makaha, right in the middle of Napili, is a good facsimile of its namesake, with long walls and good rides. The wave, a right, is swept clean by the predominantly offshore trades.

Bodyboarders and bodysurfers gravitate to **Flemming Beach Park**, a series of beach breaks and reefs that can also be good for board surfers. The showers, restrooms and picnic areas are a rare attraction in this area, and surfers from adjacent spots make good use of them.

The last spot on the northwest side is the toast of the coast, arguably the best wave in the state and certainly the best wave on Maui. During summer, **Honolua Bay** is a great place to dive as it is part of a Marine Preservation District and sealife is abundant. But from October through April, waves are the main attraction. Honolua is a classic right point setup with three distinct areas: **Coconuts**, on the outside edge of the bay; **Outside**, the middle section; and **Caves**, the racy, hollow inside section that ends in the middle of the bay and fronts a board-devouring cave. When the wind (trades are offshore), swell (north,

Below: Sometimes Hookipa is pretty as a picture and deserves to be framed. *Photo: Erik Aeder*

north-northwest or north-north-east) and tide (medium is best) cooperate, the wave is a slice of heaven. It ranges from fun at 2 to 4 feet, to exciting at 5 to 8 feet, to challenging at 10 to 12 feet, and terrifying at 15 to 20 feet. When it gets too big for your level of competence, the cliffs provide the perfect vantage point to watch the big boys perform. Rest assured, it's always crowded here.

The Endless North Shore

The coast from Punalau Bay to south of Hana bends and twists in a variety of directions, ensuring that most swells with any north or east in them will find a receptive reef or sandbar. Though prevailing trades are onshore along this coast, with the help of jetties, breakwaters, cliffs, bays, coves, *kona* winds and land breezes, the surf here can be exceptional.

At the start of the northeast coast is a spot that has broken a lot of boards and shredded a lot of flesh. **Windmills**, at Punalau Bay, has a hollow barrel of a left that breaks over jagged coral, and can handle waves up to 18 feet. The shore is lined with ankle-breaking, slippery rocks, and the whole setup is extremely unforgiving. Give it a go if you think you can

handle the potential beatings. Maui Land & Pine offers camping in the area.

Honokohau is the exact opposite of Windmills—fun, easy and relaxing. The peaks are usually made bumpy by trade winds, but clean up with *kona* winds, land breezes or morning glass.

The rest of the road from Honokohau to Waihee is difficult and mostly devoid of good surf. The next good surf is at **Point North**, at the end of the long, tortuous Highway 30 just past Waihee. This area is well worth exploring for the long, peeling lefts. North and northeast swells are best, though an exceptionally strong north/northwest swell can wrap in. Usually blown out, but glassy mornings, *kona* winds and land breezes can make it prime.

Waihee offers a variety of peaking reef breaks that need juicy north to northeast swells for optimum conditions, and *kona* or absent winds. Take the opportunity to meet the local surfers at **Rivermouth** and **Paukukalo**, the prime surf spots in Wailuku. Rivermouth has a right/left setup over a reef, while Paukukalo features long, peeling lefts and shorter rights, and can handle big north and northeast swells, and huge northwest swells, though the danger factor increases with each

Above: When at Maui, check your rearview mirror. You never know what you might be missing. Photo: Dana Edmunds

increment of size. Trade winds can make the waves here rather messy.

The breakwater of **Kahului Harbor** protects waves from the usual trade winds, and the setup creates glassy rights and hollow lefts on big north or northeast swells. Check this spot when big waves turn other spots into awkward maelstroms of whitewater.

Rights, Lefts, Even Sharks

For sometimes heartstopping wave action, find a way to get out to **Pier One**, an intriguing cloudbreak far offshore of Kahului Harbor that features giant rights and lefts, and a veritable gauntlet of sharks, heavy rip currents and sharp and shallow reefs.

The ever-blowing trade winds usually make **Sprecklesville** a sail-boarding haven, but on *kona* wind days, glassy mornings or with land breezes, the numerous right and left reef breaks suddenly become attractive to anyone looking for a fun time.

Sprecklesville's mysto spot is **King's Reef**, a distant spot that is usually overhead in winter and can handle huge swells, turning them into right and left barrels of im-

mense proportions. Only for the stout-hearted.

Baldwin Beach Park is a fun zone for everyone. Trade winds are no problem, and the park can usually turn any kind of swell into a rewarding experience for an array of longboarders, shortboarders, bodyboarders, bodysurfers, skimboarders, McDonald's tray riders and all of their supporters.

Farther along Hana Highway, **Kuau Pipeline** is a thrill-a-minute adventure with a super-hollow left barrel that is usually ravaged by the trade winds. But with favorable winds, it becomes a tubefest followed only by a dangerous, shallow bottom, a long distance from shore and strong currents. It can handle some size, and the aforementioned rugged conditions help limit the size of the crowd.

H-Reef, aka **H-Poko**, used to be a viable alternative as an escape from the crowds at nearby **Hookipa**. But even the long paddle from Hookipa and limited shoreline access does nothing to keep people away from this reef setup offering long, peeling lefts and short but intense rights. Still, it's guaranteed to be less crowded than Hookipa just next door.

—George Frayne

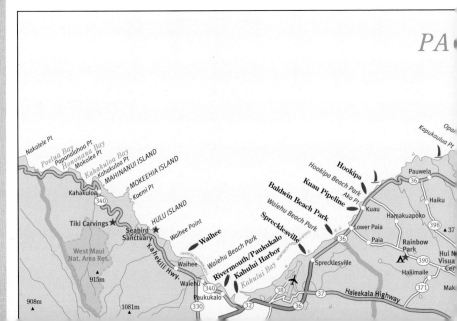

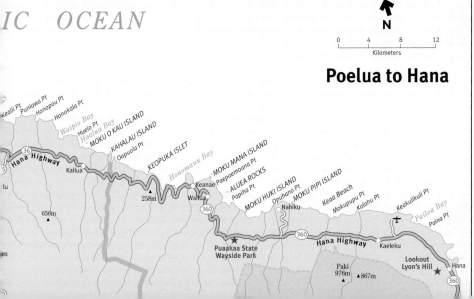

IC OCEAN

N

0 4 8 12
Kilometers

Poelua to Hana

Kealli Pt
Puniawa Pt
Honopou Pt
Honokala Pt
Waipio Bay
Huelo Pt
Hoalua Bay
MOKU O KAU ISLAND
KAHALAU ISLAND
Oopuola Pt
KEOPUKA ISLET

36 Hana Highway
Kailua
5
lu
258m
656m ▲
Waitua

Honomanu Bay
MOKU MANA ISLAND
Keanae Paepaemoana Pt
ALUEA ROCKS
Papiha Pt
MOKU HUKI ISLAND
Opuhano Pt
MOKU PIPI ISLAND
Nahiku
Keaa Beach
Mokupupu Pt
Kalahu Pt
Keakulikuli Pt
Pailoa Bay
Paina Pt

360

360 Hana Highway
Kaeleku

Puaakaa State
Wayside Park

Paki
976m
▲867m

Lookout
Lyon's Hill
★
Hana

360

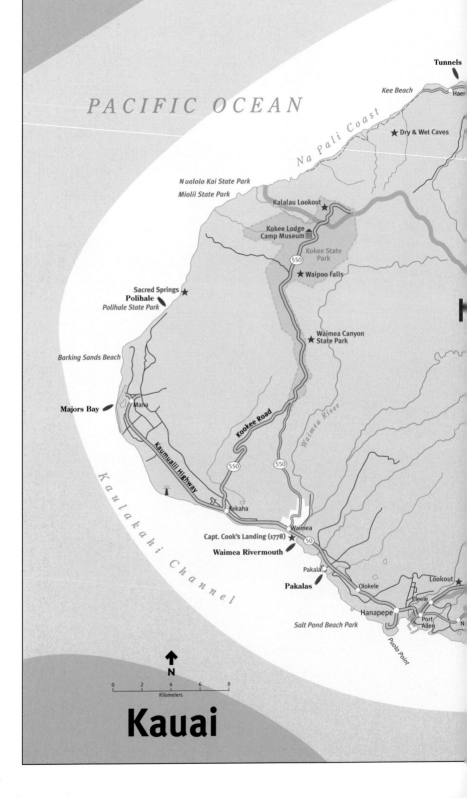

PACIFIC OCEAN

Na Pali Coast

Tunnels

Kee Beach

Haer

Dry & Wet Caves

N ualolo Kai State Park

Miolii State Park

Kalalau Lookout ★

Kokee Lodge
Camp Museum

Kokee State
Park

550

★ Waipoo Falls

Sacred Springs ★
Polihale
Polihale State Park

Waimea Canyon
★ State Park

Barking Sands Beach

Majors Bay

Mana

Kookee Road

Waimea River

Kaumualii Highway

550

550

Kekaha

Capt. Cook's Landing (1778) ★

Waimea

Waimea Rivermouth

50

Pakala

Lookout ★

Pakalas

Olokele

Eleele

Hanapepe

Port
Allen

N

Salt Pond Beach Park

Puolo Point

K a u l a k a h i   C h a n n e l

↑
N

0   2   4   6   8
Kilometers

Kauai

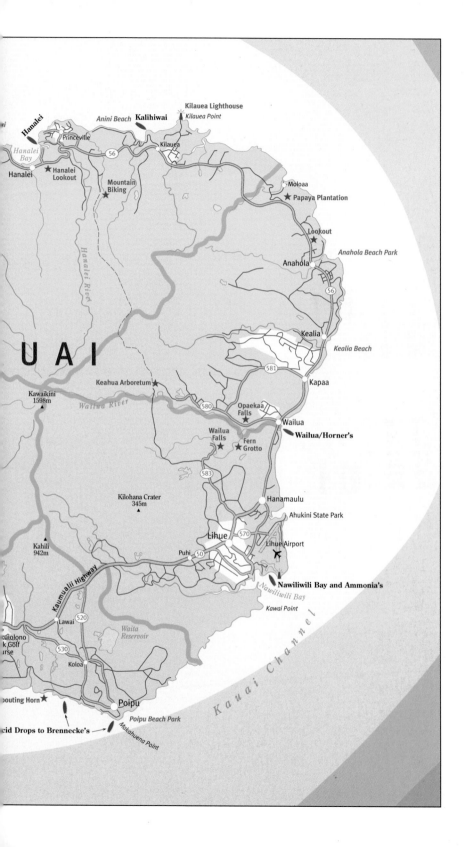

Kauai

Hawaii's Lush "Garden Isle"

A legendary basalt rock located on the coast at Kaena Point on Oahu's northwest tip is said to have once been attached to Kauai. From that landmark, Kauai lies some 70 miles over the horizon, due west-northwest across the Kaieie Waho Channel, in one of the roughest waterways in the Pacific.

This physical separation from the fast-paced world of surfing at Honolulu's town breaks and on the North Shore's winter waves gives Kauai its age-old reputation as "The Separate Kingdom" of the Hawaiian islands, a land located on the other side of a liquid barrier, a 550-square-mile isle where settlers from the Marquesas and other distant points south were able to create a unique Polynesian culture in total isolation.

Kauai is arguably the most lush and picturesque of Hawaii's islands. It is Hollywood's Hawaii movie island, the setting for *Jurassic Park* and the opening scene of *Raiders of the Lost Ark,* and one of the few resort destinations in the world with scenery that far surpasses the hype of travel advertisements. Geologists say the fantastically eroded pinnacles of its main volcanic dome—topped by a peak known as Waialeale that receives over 400 inches of rain per year—took five million years to form. As the oldest main island of the chain, Kauai is ringed by miles of white sand beaches and a minimum of rocky shoreline, with surfing waves breaking through the calendar on all shores.

The island's feel is primitive, wild outside of the narrow strip of modern development that stretches in a horseshoe from Hanalei and Haena on the North Shore to the West Side's northern border at Polihale. In his 1930s study of Hawaiian surfing traditions, the legendary waterman Tom Blake called Kauai surfers the best in the pre-modern era of Hawaiian surfing due to their hardiness gained from riding the waves of this wild environment.

Today, this individualistic spirit of old Kauai lives on in the surfing culture of the bountiful Garden Island. Local surfers are renowned for safeguarding their surf spots to the point of threatening visiting photographers and ungracious surfers who dare attempt to exploit their waves.

But observers of the Kauai surfing scene note that this defensive attitude goes deeper than a simple desire to ride the waves unhindered. At Kauai, being accepted in the water and on the beach takes time and an ongoing commitment towards respecting and understanding the ancient traditions that underlie the world of Kauai surfing. To the descendants of the Kauai surfers of old, this respect is a matter of saving the soul of a unique and precious island that used to be an independent kingdom until the 1820s.

The fact that many modern-day Kauai surfers are on the cutting edge of surfing provides a counterpoint to their respectful attitude towards tradition. This is evidenced by the skill and status of

Preceding pages: Great beauty can be found amidst the misty Na Pali wilderness. Hiking is the best way to take it all in. *Photo: Tim de La Vega*

Opposite: One of the many spectacular sights you'll see while on the Garden Isle of Kauai. *Photo: Tim de La Vega*

Above: Old surfiana leans against the front of the Hanalei Museum. *Photo: Brett Uprichard*

local surfers such as Titus Kinimaka, Terry Chung, Laird and Bill Hamilton, Andy and Bruce Irons, Kaipo Jaquias, Braden Dias, Dick Brewer, Rochelle Ballard, and many other important surfers.

Kauai's surf can be categorized best by island district or *moku*, as the major Hawaiian island land divisions are known. The main wintertime surfing arena is Hanalei Bay, the centerpiece of the Halelea *moku*, which stretches across the central north shore. Halelea, or "House of the Rainbows," is blessed with a backdrop of three main peaks—Hihimanu, Namolokama and Mamalahoa. The half lei-shaped Bay holds point and reef breaks, as well as a long stretch of beach breaks. More isolated breaks lie to the west and east. All can be fickle and unrideable on any given day between September and April, with heavy rains pouring down from Waialeale across verdant taro fields onto Kuhio Highway crossing the main road.

The diminutive Koolau district in the northeast corner of Kauai is generally bypassed by wave explorers zipping past onshore conditions here as they drive between Hanalei and the West Side in the winter, and the South Shore during the summer.

Further down the coast lies Puna, with the ancient Kauai capital of Wailua at its center. Here Hawaiian chants and histories tell of the exploits of mythical Kauai surfers such as the *alii* Moikeha, who rode the waves of Wailua Bay before Columbus sailed in search of the Spice Islands. Generally, onshore wind conditions prevail, pushing trade-wind-driven waves up against the coast and providing surf for local surfers living in Kapaa and Wailua, but nothing that approaches the world-class breaks that Hawaii is known for, except on rare days when *kona* winds clean up the swells.

Makai of Lihue, Kauai's outer island-style political and commercial capital, is Nawiliwili Bay. A breakwater at the mouth of the bay created a safe harbor for inter-island shipping in the late 1920s, but also doomed a stretch of surf spots along its inner shore. Today, waves roll in at Kalapaki offshore of the Marriott Resort, providing tourists on rental boards with a good learning ground and local surfers with a close-to-home break when strong trade winds actively stir up the inside harbor surf.

South of Lihue on the other side of the ancient Haupu Range lies Koloa, home of the first commercial sugar plantation in all Hawaii. Archeologists are finding significant remains of once-thriving fishing villages along the coastline at Koloa, dating back to the arrival of Polynesian settlers ten or more centuries ago. However, unlike Wailua, no significant Hawaiian surfing traditions are associated with this area. Perhaps the shallow reef breaks along the coast at Poipu Beach weren't suited to the riding of heavy *koa* (breadfruit) surfboards. It is known that owners of sugar plantations along the West Side built summer homes along the shore here to launch the stretch of white sand beaches and coves as a getaway. As late as the 1950s, teenage surfer Nick Beck and his brother surfed the area alone, occasionally joined by the traveling surfers of Wailua-based Nalu Alii surf club.

Today, Poipu is a compact Waikiki with lowrise hotels and condos hugging the shore from one end to the other. Summertime waves break in a similar fashion to Kaisers and Threes off Waikiki. Bodyboarding is big here, with the beach break at Brennecke's still recovering from a massive bottom realignment during Hurricane Iniki in 1992.

Searching for surf west of Koloa requires a drive along Kaumualii Highway past wavering green fields of sugarcane and buildings covered in red dirt. The surf east and west of Waimea (a second capital of ancient Kauai) breaks in opaque water tinted by rainwater washed down through Olokele and Waimea canyons. Further down the highway, mirages loom ahead, reflecting the more arid climate. At Kekaha, one of the longest stretches of white sand beach in Hawaii goes on for miles towards Polihale, the site of an ancient *heiau*. Along the way are isolated beach breaks that require a 4-wheel-drive vehicle for easy access, as well as a few well-established point breaks that require a pass to get to because access is controlled by the Navy's Pacific Missile Range Facility.

Between the end of the road at Polihale and the end of the North Shore at Kee Beach is Na Pali, an isolated wilderness lined with breathtaking valleys. The coast is only accessible by kayak or boat, or by hiking in from Kee along the Kalalau Trail. What surfing there is along the coast is mostly limited to bodysurfing or bodyboarding. Conditions are treacherous here, with drownings occurring at easy-to-get-to Hanakapiai even on relatively flat days in the summer.

—*Chris Cook*

Below: A windblown little tube opens up for a lucky taker. *Photo: Tim de La Vega*

KAUAI

'Round Hanalei

The Northernmost Shore

The North Shore of Kauai, arguably the most beautiful region in all Hawaii, was named *Halelea*, or "House of the Rainbows," by native Hawaiians of long ago. Though its beauty outshines that of Oahu's North Shore, the number of surf breaks is limited compared to that other coast, and what Kauai's North Shore offers is an outer island getaway from the fast-paced surfing of Oahu.

Unlike Oahu with its mile after mile of world-class breaks, outside of Hanalei, Kauai's North Shore surf spots are iffy and dependent on the right wind and swell conditions, with hazards such as cliff faces and barrier reefs to the east and shallow reefs and shorepounding shorebreaks to the west. Trade winds turn onshore at Kilauea to the east, and Na Pali peaks bring the coast to an end at Kee Beach, cutting off easy access to over 14 miles of coastline where the surf batters against the base of steep cliffs and washes into a handful of isolated valleys, a place great for kayaking during flat summer days, but lacking in true surf spots and potentially deadly for most winter waveriding.

The Crescent Bay

Set amidst the beauty of the North Shore is the rolling right-hander at Hanalei Point, a fall-winter-spring wave that today is the focus of surfing on the North Shore. Like most breaks in this area, strong paddling skills are a necessity for all major breaks require a fairly long paddle out, and more than a passing knowledge of handling powerful Hawaiian water conditions.

October to April, the winter months

Some breaks are just off the main road, some require lengthy paddles

Gnarly reefs and some sandbars

Big-wave boards and even tow-in boards are used

Heavy locals, damaging reefs, and savage surf

Reef bounces

Surfing against one of the prettiest backdrops in the world

There is no firm historical evidence of the main outside break at Hanalei being surfed in ancient times. During a visit to Kauai by Queen Liliuokalani in the early 1890s, an inside reef break across the bay (known today as Middles) was noted by *kamaiina* myth collector William Hyde Rice as being the main training ground for surfers in Hanalei Bay. It is also said that Hawaiian surfers enjoyed rolling beach break waves near the Hanalei Pier prior to the arrival of fiberglass and foam surfboards in the late 1950s.

Outstanding local surfers who have surfed at Hanalei over the years include Titus Kinimaka, Jimmy Lucas, Carlos Andrade and Nick Beck. Descendents of native Hawaiians who can trace their *ohana* back hundreds of years, such as the family of legendary waterman John Hano Hano Pa, still enjoy riding their ancestral home breaks and are very protective of them. Some of these surfers are members of families who lived in isolation for centuries at Kalalau and other remote Na Pali valleys.

In the late 1990s, the desire of local surfers to protect Hanalei (the "Crescent Bay") was supported by activists, and these groups protested against tour boats that cruised out to Na Pali from Hanalei Bay. This led to the eventual shutting down of most of these operations by the governor of Hawaii.

It goes without saying that the local surfers at Hanalei (as well as those at every other break on Kauai) are very protective of their waves, though the number of surfers in residence has been growing, with a new wave of luxury homes being built along the beach at Hanalei, the Princeville Resort opening up dozens of vacation rentals with a view of the bay, and an expansion in building in adjoining towns.

This increasing exposure has been the trend for the past 50 years. During the '50s and '60s, local surfers were low-key about letting the outside world know about the break. Hanalei was first popularized on the US mainland by big-wave rider and surf filmmaker Greg Noll. Following the filming of the Hollywood musical *South Pacific* at Hanalei in 1957, Noll, Dewey Weber and a crew of fellow Southern California surfers rode push bikes out from Lihue Airport with their longboards in tow.

Below: Hanalei rumbling at an easy 12 to 15 feet. The lines look makeable enough, so why aren't there any takers? *Photo: Sean "Jonah" Thomas*

Camping out at the pier, Noll's crew captured what is perhaps the first modern-day footage of the wave, which Noll then proceeded to show up and down the coast of California.

Then in 1966, Southern California surf filmmakers Greg MacGillivray and Jim Freeman brought Bill Hamilton and Mark Martinson to uncrowded Kauai for the filming of *Free and Easy.* Hamilton recalled the sense of discovery he felt on his first trip to Kauai: "Our destination, Hanalei Bay, was a long, solitary drive over a bumpy patchwork of asphalt and pot holes. I remember the only thing that seemed to be open for business was the old Dairy Queen in Kapaa, a virtual ghost town from beginning to end. Princeville was one big cow pasture."

The filmmakers were almost denied good footage by the typically rainy conditions. In a pictorial spread that appeared in *Surfer* magazine in 1967, they wrote: "Kauai is the rainiest spot on earth and we believed it. There has been nothing but rain, rain, rain for a

week . . . a week of junk surf and no filming." Nevertheless, the film got made, and a classic color photo of the crew's surf cruiser crossing Hanalei Bridge became an icon for surfers worldwide who wished to escape to Paradise.

Hamilton returned to Kauai in the early 1970s where he is today a leading surfboard maker. As for MacGillivray, he returned in 1981 to film scenes for *Behold Hawaii,* an IMAX film shown only in specially equipped theaters. Thanks to the help of Bishop Museum experts, and due to the painstaking research conducted by him and his crew, MacGillivray's production is credited as being the most accurate representation of Hawaii's ancient culture ever filmed, and it features a scene of Hawaiian surfers riding replica oversized wooden surfboards.

Hanalei's isolation truly ended with the building of the Princeville Resort in the early 1970s. The construction of hundreds of hotel rooms, resort homes and condominiums just minutes from the surf provided housing and jobs for

Below: Hanalei again, on a much more manageable surfing day. How's the lucky sap gliding down the line? *Photo: Tim de La Vega*

surfers migrating to Hanalei from California, Oahu and other surfing places east and west.

The Bowl and The Point

At **Hanalei**, the main wave is the speedy right point break that rolls over the edge of a coral reef below and west of the Princeville Hotel, commonly known as Hanalei Bay. Each section of the surf spot has its own protective crew of local surfers, many of whom are transplants from Oahu and the US mainland now living on Kauai's North Shore of Kauai. Some have been surfing the peeling point wave since the '60s and early '70s.

Surfers congregate around **The Bowl** on the inside and **The Point** on the outside. On smaller days, the inside break can be dominated by longboarders and crews of young surfers of high school age and younger, with shortboarders hanging outside, while larger days bring out a fleet of semi-guns and veteran riders. The paddle out is about a quarter-mile from the

shore at the Hanalei Pier. It is a rare event to find the break uncrowded on a good day. The reef can keep its shape up to medium-size waves, but isn't known to handle huge surf. The right has a status in Kauai similar to that of Sunset Beach in Oahu.

Around Puu Poa Point (where the luxurious hotel sits on a hillside; surfers once used to drive up to leisurely check out the surf) to the northeast of Hanalei is a series of reef-bottom peaks commonly known as **Hideaways**. This break got its name in the early '60s, when Nick Beck and crew paddled over to bypass the paddle-out beach there that had been locked off by the cowboys at Princeville Ranch. A young surfer with Beck named Pat Cockett was learning the basics of playing the ukelele, and he strummed out a bit of the song *Hernando's Hideaway*, thus providing the name.

Hideaways is similar to Backyards on Oahu's North Shore as it plays second fiddle to Hanalei, with uncertain wind and wave conditions, holding up to medium-size

waves and offering a lower-quality wave on crowded days at Hanalei.

To the west of the main break at Hanalei, along the lei-shaped white sand beach, is about a mile of beach breaks that are generally inconsistent in shape. Most waves are closeouts with fickle, rideable right and left peaks popping up here and there. On days of surf at Hanalei, waves grow in size from east to west along the beach, with the first rideable waves appearing near the Hanalei Pier at a beginners/intermediate break. The best known peak here is **Pinetrees**, located in front of a parking lot lined with ironwood trees brought from Australia around 1900. Here the annual Pinetrees Longboard Contest has been held for more than 20 years, making it one of the longest running longboard-only contests in the surfing world.

Driving west from Hanalei, you pass incredibly scenic valleys but encounter no good surf breaks until Haena. Offshore of the state camping park there is an outside reef break known as **Tunnels**, named for the underwater caverns

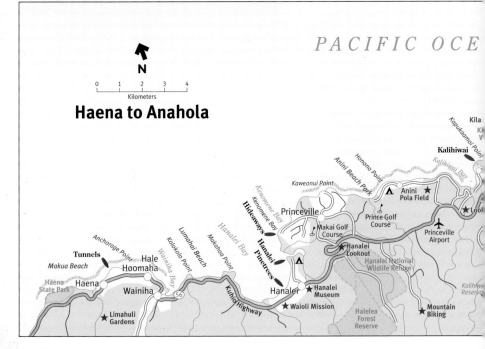

in the barrier reef that form the wave. Tunnels is for experienced surfers: it is one of the longest paddles out on Kauai and highly exposed to trade winds. Its hollow waves break into shallow water. Conditions can be dangerous once the waves are over 4 feet; surfers have been literally pounded into the reef, never to be seen again.

Haena is best known in the surfing world for the days when surfers and hippies helped to cobble together ramshackle homes at a commune called Taylor Camp. Started in the '60s, this hippieville was built on land just off the main beach road that was owned by actress Elizabeth Taylor's brother, Howard. As you neared Taylor's villa, you were confronted by a sign that proclaimed in bold letters: Warning!: Tresspassers Will Be Violated. Visiting Australian surfer Keith Paul captured the spirit of the love child generation that existed here in an article for the Australian magazine *Surfing World*. "Life has its meanings, here framing the Bay lie the peaks. Bathed in morning sunshine, green lush vegetation glistening. Fruit and ferns, exotic flowers all awaiting the adventurer. Searching for truth, being so close to one's self, close to God, with a contentment in a new understanding."

To the west of Hanalei, the coves and cliffs of Princeville fail to hold good surf, with a rocky shoreline and generally onshore conditions when the trades blow. The long barrier reef of Anini is a washout too, though good windsurfing conditions make the beach park there a popular beginner-intermediate spot. **Kalihiwai** provides the only quality surf to the east of Hanalei. The break generally is smaller than Hanalei and takes a larger swell to show. Kalihiwai is known as a locals' break, and the regular crew there is very protective of its pretty much shortboard-only wave. The extraordinarily hardbreaking main peak is a tricky one that pops up in front of an intimidating 200-foot-high cliff face and which requires the skills of an acrobat to truly master. Advanced surfing skills recommended here.

—Chris Cook

Opposite: Spouting Horn, Kaui. One of the many eye-pleasing attractions on the Garden Isle. *Photo: Brett Uprichard*

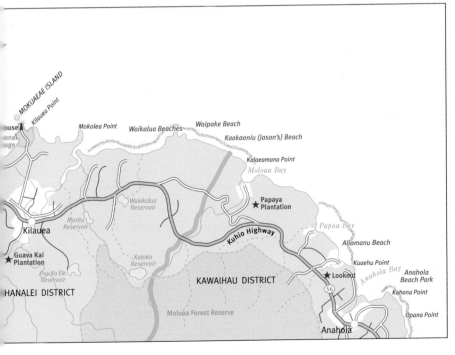

Pioneering Kauai

Words of a *Kamaiina* Surfer

Editor's Note: *Nick Beck, a Kauai kamaaina (oldtime non-Hawaiian local) and surfer, first hit the waves at Poipu in the early 1940s on a mini-mini redwood board. His father was a plantation doctor and veteran sailor. Beck first surfed Hanalei on the tongue of a wooden ironing board found in one of the stately kamaaina beach homes along Hanalei Bay. He surfed Poipu, Hanalei and other Kauai breaks virtually alone in the 1950s and early 1960s, at a time when only a handful of Hawaiian surfers actively surfed the island, most of them hanging at Wailua Beach.*

Beck went all-out to protect Kauai from an invasion of surfers in the early 1960s. During that period, a two-page spread of him surfing appeared in Life *magazine. The photo had been taken with a string-triggered, board-mounted camera, and the caption beneath it obliquely referred to surfing at Waikiki and said nothing about Kauai, though the photograph was obviously taken at the beach break at Hanalei. Beck also had friends who worked at surfing publications play up Kauai's rainy weather and dangerous coral bottoms. One piece tells of a "deadly" reef with a whirlpool sucked into it any surfer unlucky enough to wipe out over it.*

Beck has witnessed the whole modern surfing scene on Kauai evolve and still rides Hanalei when he's not snowboarding at his mainland home on the shores of Lake Tahoe. He served as the principal of Hanalei School

for over three decades and watched Laird Hamilton, the Irons brothers and other top surfers grow up at Hanalei. He is a renowned canoe paddler and canoe sailor, having coached and paddled for the Hanalei Hawaiian Civic Club's canoe team. Today, his sons Hobey and David continue their father's waterman heritage at Hanalei, surfing, paddling and cultivating taro. The following is Beck's view of the Kauai scene.

Surfing at Kauai during the '50s was a total adventure each time I went out. There was either no one else in the water, or just a few guys that we knew.

I cautiously began to ride waves that I had never seen anyone surfing before. It was very different from Oahu, where—even though Oahu was still not crowded by today's standards—there were still lots of surfers.

As kids, we were always looking for "our own breaks." Since I wasn't old enough to have a driver's license, I could only get into the water where we were staying at the time, which was either at Poipu or Hanalei.

On Kauai, it was nice to have someone else in the water with you. There was no use of leashes and this limited some of the places that we would consider paddling to surf. In 1959, I had a summer job working in the pineapple fields with my brother and cousin. We had a house right across from

Brennecke's, which was the best bodysurfing beach at Poipu.

That summer, my brother and I made it a point to surf virtually every wave that broke from Mahaulepu to Lawai Kai. Usually we were completely alone. Our house was taken out by the huge surf that came in from Hurricane Dot in 1959. At that time, there were no hotels and very few homes along the beach front.

When I graduated from USC in '62, I decided to go into teaching so I had to put in a year at UH to get my teaching certificate in order to get into the public school system on Kauai. That year, I got a lot of fantastic big surf on Oahu. Although even then it was relatively uncrowded, the "Hawaiian Surf Frenzy" era was starting and more guys were in the water. Although I'd made enough $ to get myself comfortably through

"That summer, my brother and I made it a point to surf virtually every wave that broke from Mahaulepu to Lawai Kai."

In the late '50s, there were a few more guys living on Kauai and surfing their own home breaks. Whenever friends from Oahu would come to Kauai for a surf adventure, I would really try to swear them to secrecy about the surf . . . to not say anything or that it was junk.

This worked for a while, but the '60s really saw some changes! In the early '60s, it was still a paradise with uncrowded and unsurfed spots. I was away at college at USC and so would come back to Kauai for winter break to stay with Pam Wilcox and her family at Hanalei. I was older, more experienced, had better equipment, and really got some fantastic surf with just a few other guys out in the water.

USC (as well as surf trips to Mexico) by promoting surf films for Grant Rohloff and others during the heyday of high school auditorium surf films, I wasn't stoked to see the influx of surfers and kept looking for out-of-the-way places to find an uncrowded wave.

I was even more determined to get back to Kauai, to surf and try to keep it "quiet." When I started teaching on Kauai the next year, friends would come to surf with me and it was still a joy to have guys in the water with me to surf new places or to go out with on the bigger days. But in the mid '60s, it started changing fast. Friends who had come to surf went back and spread the word. Films and magazine articles exposed and exploited the island. Other surfers from

Opposite top: As a baby, Beck was already a stoked and impressionable beginner.

Above: Beck as a young man, ducking into a stylish and early 1960s Kauai island wave.
Photos: Nick Beck

Oahu and the mainland started coming over and staying. In 1966, I went back to Oahu for a year to get my Masters degree at UH. I was able to get a lot of mid-week surf on the North Shore between classes, but I was so spoiled by what I had on Kauai that I would hardly ever go out on weekends if there were crowds, or else I'd try to get back to Kauai. After I got my degree, I decided that it was time to travel again and maybe find some new spots. I got a job teaching in New Zealand and spent a year there with my wife and two little boys surfing all over both islands. The following year, I took another

also sort of quit surfing for a while the year I returned and really got into sailing my Hobie Cat, even surfing some wild big waves with it, until I broke it up and nearly killed myself.

But one day I looked out at the surf and it was still so beautiful, even with so many guys in a lineup that I'd once had all to myself, that I decided that I wasn't going to get pushed out of something I enjoyed so much.

I surfed with a different attitude. I wasn't aggressive, I took off further out and down the line, and rode bigger days. I also began to look for other spots to ride and not tell anyone about them.

"But one day I looked out at the surf and it was still so beautiful, even with so many guys in a lineup that I'd once had all to myself, that I decided that I wasn't going to get pushed out of something I enjoyed so much."

period of leave from my teaching position on Kauai and hooked up with Gaylord Wilcox and his family, who'd just finished an assignment with the Peace Corps in Malaysia.

We set off on a "family surf safari" around the world and made a surf film about our adventures through New Zealand, Australia, Mauritius, Reunion, South Africa, Europe, England and then back again to Hawaii (among the highlights is a rare scene of Joey Cabell surfing his early downrailer shortboard on Kauai's North Shore).

The film, *World of Waves*, soon paid off our trip around the world. I remember being in South Africa and getting a letter from a friend on Kauai, Jerry Lynn, telling me the surf was getting so crowded with new guys that he was quitting surfing and buying a new beach catamaran that was going to be made by Hobie Alter. I was so upset I immediately wrote him back and told him to also put in an order for me. We had the first two Hobie Cats on Kauai.

When I returned to Hanalei, I couldn't believe the change. So many new faces. I guess what bothered me the most was the drugs, thefts and attitudes that seemed to come along with the new influx. I

Here's some advice for surfers coming to Kauai. Well, I guess surfers are going to travel to new places no matter what we say. I sure did . . . you did . . . we always will. I would plead that surfers just:

Travel with respect to the places you visit. Many local surfers haven't had the opportunity that others have had to be world travelers, so their regular home breaks are their only breaks. Respect them and don't be wave hogs.

Leave the places you visit as clean or cleaner than when you came. It doesn't matter if you see trash that isn't yours; don't be afraid to pick it up yourself.

And when you leave, remember that if you ever want to come back, it will be just that much more crowded when you return if you go home and rave about your "new discovery."

Editor's Note: *As an aside, Beck said: "If you really want a quote from me about Kauai, tell your friends the surf is always ugly, the reefs are gnarly, the natives are restless, the sharks are always very hungry and that it rains all the time. Snowboarding is much more fun . . . and then there are all those mosquitoes and centipedes, sea snakes, seat belt cops, etc, etc, etc."*

Below: Titus Kinimaka and Terry Chung, Kauai royalty and two of the main forerunners of the Kauai scene, pose with a sleekly-crafted tow-in stick. *Photo: Chris Cook*

The Rest of Kauai
From Ammonia's to Acid Drops and on Down to Barking Sands

The lush windward east coast of Kauai runs from the coastal village of Anahola to Kawai Point outside and just southeast of Nawiliwili Harbor, the main port of the island. While year-round trade wind conditions generally blow out waves along this coastline, rare days of light winds and periods of offshore, west-southwest *kona* winds show off this coastline's potential. The scenic beauty is set to a backdrop dominated by the looming figure of 5,000-foot-high cloud-covered Mount Waialeale, one of the wettest spots on Earth.

This section of Kauai is its most populated and made up of the Kawaihau District, which runs from Anahola to the Wailua River, and the Lihue District, centered around the capital of the 555-square-mile island.

While the total population is less than one of Honolulu's urban valleys, east side beaches are well-used recreation centers for its people, including a solid core of local surfers. Though lacking the world-class waves of the North Shore, the East Side is the setting for many of Kauai's ancient Hawaiian legends about surfing.

Heading south from Hanalei, Kuhio Highway begins to hug the coast at **Kealia**, a beach and river mouth fronting a huge valley that runs back to Waialeale. Like most of the East Side beaches, Kealia has been changed considerably by the development of sugarcane plantations in the mid- and late

1800s. The remains of a lava rock walled steamer landing on the north end of the beach provide some protection from the trade winds that produce much of the surf here and at the same time blow onshore. Generally, surf here runs in the 2 to 4 foot range, even on days of large surf on the North Shore, with a sand bottom pocked with outcrops of lava rock. Jagged rusting rails from the days of the sugarcane train stick out at some places along the high tide line.

Peaks on this end of Kealia Beach are wired and well-surfed by crews of local surfers and bodyboarders who live nearby, including students who pour down from Kapaa High School, which is located just *mauka* of the beach. A recent remarkable grassroots cleanup effort here led by local surfer and community leader Kane Pa as well as other surfers has turned a surf spot once heavily littered with rubbish into a beach with pride.

Kapaa is a former plantation town that once boasted a sugar mill, a pineapple cannery and rows of plantation-era buildings erected by Chinese merchants and rice growers known as "rice kings." Tamba Surf Shop (next door to Kojima's Store) and Miura's Store sell surfboards and surf accessories in Kapaa, carrying on the tradition of small local surf shops that began in Kapaa in the late 1960s. The coastline at Kapaa is marked by rock groins and outside

Summertime, some spots work in winter

Generally easy, except in cases of private beach estates

Reef and sand

Small-wave boards, boogeyboards for fun shorebreaks

Shallow reef plus pounding shorebreaks

Reef rash

Once again, the beautiful scenery of Kauai takes the guava cake

reefs. The only quality surf spot situated between Kealia and Nawiliwili is a legendary one.

A Legendary Past

Wailua, along with Waimea, served as the capital(s) of Kauai in the days before Western contact. Known as *Wailua-Nui-A-Hooano* ("Sacred Wailua"), **Wailua** is the site of a surfing *heiau* and a royal surfing spot. It was here that Moikeha, a Polynesian voyager and surfer who existed in the same mythical era as King Arthur, settled down to marry the king of Kauai's daughter and to "live and die" surfing the mythical wave known as **Makaiwa**, offshore of Wailua. The surfing spots at Wailua were renowned throughout the Hawaiian islands; Kamehameha, who took control of Kauai in 1810 and as a teenager surfed at Kona on the Big Island, cited the ownership of these surf breaks as one of his reasons for conquering the leeward island. The waves found at Wailua today may be a shadow of the legendary breaks of the past, due perhaps to a buildup of sand in the bay caused by the sugar plantations diverting water from the Wailua River, the only navigable river in the Hawaiian islands.

The main rolling left breaking wave at Wailua rolls over a reef with some coral heads protruding the surface at low tide. This wave is commonly known as **Horner's**, after the stately beach home of the Horner family, who owned and ran the pineapple plantation in Kapaa. Over 20 years ago, the home was moved *mauka*, up to Wailua Homesteads by the developer of the condos that now line the beach there. Wailua comes on when a large north winter swell breaks and *kona* winds blow, a meteorological juxtaposition that occurs infrequently. The break is mostly surfed by East Side surfers who want to surf near home rather than drive to Hanalei, Poipu or the West

Below: A trio of bystanders checks out reefside wave action from Poipu's famous blowhole tourist attraction known as the Spouting Horn. *Photo:Brett Uprichard*

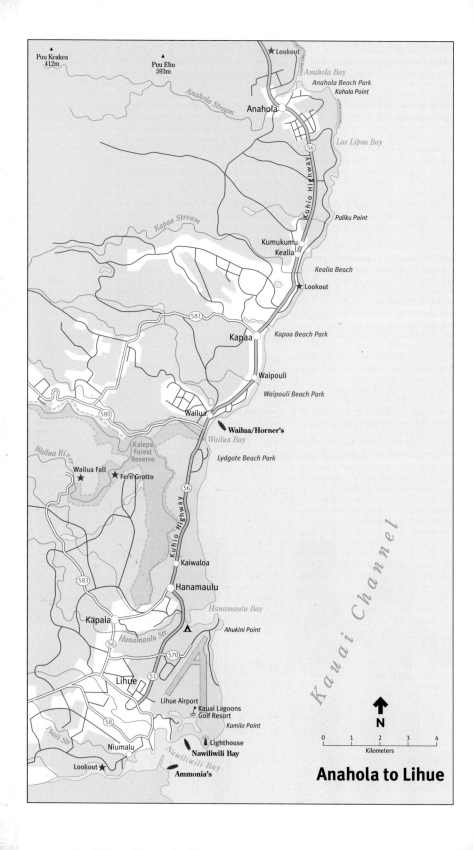

Anahola to Lihue

Side, and who put up with the onshore trade wind conditions in exchange. The beach break south of Horner's has the look found in 19th-century woodcuts of surfing in Hawaii, with its windblown waves and irregular lines of surf, though now it is tourists on bodyboards rather than beautiful Hawaiian maidens who bathe in the break.

Body-Snapping Power

Lihue is Kauai's commercial and political center and home to its inter-island airport. It lies about 5 miles south of Wailua. Down the hill from the town is the curving bay of Nawiliwili. Nawiliwili and Hanamaulu Bay, located just north of the runway at Lihue Airport, have changed considerably since the ancient days of Hawaiian surfing due to the development of deep-water ports. Local lore states that a surfing wave once rolled off the point at Hanamaulu; today, no notable breaks exist. A sizeable breakwater constructed in the 1920s now blocks the swells that once rolled into the beach at Nawiliwili, though surf does still break in the bay.

At **Kalapaki Beach** on the north end of the bay, right and left breaking rollers peak over a shallow reef about 50 yards off the main beach of the Kauai Marriott Resort. The wave is great for beginners and fun for longboarders, but rarely gets over 3 feet. The pack here is a mixture of local surfers and visitors.

Paradoxically, just south of Kalapaki, along the concrete breakwater at Nawiliwili, is one of the hairiest waves on Kauai, aptly named **Ammonia's** for its bodysnapping power. Rideable from about 3 to 5 feet, the right-breaking wave only comes on when high trade winds are blown off the east shore, providing an exciting venue

for local surfing skills as riders either get tubed or slammed close to the unforgiving concrete wall.

From the 1930s into the 1960s, Kalapaki helped to preserve surfing traditions on Kauai. *Kamaaina* Hobey Goodale rode a redwood board built for him by Duke Kahanamoku in the 1930s, along with other local kids who rode roughly hewn planks in the mild waves before going off to World War Two. Inter-Island Resorts built the Kauai Surf at Kalapaki in the late 1950s, and, with the help of Mickey Lake and Bones Johnston, beachboy/waterman Percy Kinimaka introduced fiberglass and foam boards made under the Honolulu-based Inter-Island label (which was launched to provide hotel rental boards). Kinimaka instituted a popular canoe-borne torchlight ceremony that cruised through the surf break at sundown and also taught many personalities how to surf, including moonwalking astronaut Neil Armstrong. In the '60s, Duke Kahanamoku visited the beach and enjoyed the company of Kinimaka and his family,

Below: A local "blahlah" observing the day's waveriding conditions at Nawiliwili Bay. *Photo: Brett Uprichard*

including that of a young Titus Kinimaka, who is today Kauai's leading local surfer.

A significant change in climate occurs as you cross Kauai from Lihue along Kaumualii Highway, past the inland town of Kalaheo and down to the coast at Hanapepe, reaching the island's arid, sunny leeward side. Here surf breaks take on a different face, with perhaps the clearest water on the island as well as the murkiest.

Drops and a Tree Tunnel

Three of the most popular spots on the south and west side are reached by turning off Kaumualii Highway at the Tunnel of Trees and heading for Koloa. On the coast, past the old plantation town (in 1835, the site of the first successful commercial sugar plantation in all Hawaii), along Lawai Beach Road and on the way to Spouting Horn lie a trio of adjoining breaks. The beachside control center for **PK's**, **Centers** and **Acid Drops** is the Beach House Restaurant seawall, with its grassy

lawn and excellent view of the breaks. The left-right reforming wave off the wall is PK's, short for Prince Kuhio, a popular Hawaiian *alii* born in the mid 1800s at a fishing village near the break. Kuhio surfed Santa Cruz, California, in the late 1800s while attending prep school near San Francisco. The pack at PK's is a mix of surfers and bodyboarders. The middle break of the trio breaks both left and right and is aptly named Centers. A few hundred yards west breaks the round, hollow tubes of Acid Drops. The name has a double meaning, describing the hairy takeoff as well as alluding to the period when the wave first gained popularity, the late 1960s. Acid Drops holds the largest rideable wave in the area during the summer surf season, with small south swells breaking in the autumn, winter and early spring. All break in shallow water, with coral heads and rock obstacles along the surface.

A few miles east of the Beach House lies the Poipu Beach Resort. Though "Poipu" is actually the name given to a small beach located at the Poipu Beach Park,

the development of a stretch of good-sized resort hotels here since the early 1960s has become commonly known as Poipu, thanks to the marketeers promoting the resorts. Surfing is banned here at **Brennecke's**, which is located east of Poipu Beach Park and is one of the better bodysurfing spots on Kauai. Brennecke's is still recovering from the massive destruction suffered when huge waves generated by hurricanes in 1982 and 1992 rearranged its sand bottom and the basalt rocks that help form its wave. The coast fronting the resort area has a few near-to-shore reef breaks as well as a few scattered bowling off-shore waves. Seven-time women's world champion surfer Margo Oberg runs a surfing school on the beach at Poipu. Surf shops at Koloa-Poipu include Progressive Expressions (which has been open for more than 25 years in Koloa Town) and the Nukumoi Surf Shop at Poipu.

A gap in surfing spots exists along the coast past the Poipu area all the way to Makaweli, a south-west side valley famous for its rich red dirt soil. Pakala Camp, the home of Gay & Robinson workers here, provides the name for the long, long left point wave. The break is reached by walking from Kaumualii Highway along Aakukui Stream to a small breakwater. **Pakalas** is also known as **Infinities**, a name that aptly describes the long left. It was dreamed up by Randy Weir, a member of the Robinson family who first surfed here in the early 1960s. In his informative book *Beaches of Kaua'i and Ni'ihau,* John Clark describes the break in the following manner: "The waves form on the western end of an extensive, shallow fringing reef fronting Pakala Village . . . the Pakala reef has the exact edge and slope to create the perfect wave." The break will hold a 10-foot plus swell, but generally breaks in the 2- to 6-foot range during the south swell season. A tightknit crew of longtime west side surfers (including County of Kauai head lifeguard Kaleo Hookano as well as newer arrivals from the US mainland) keep a close eye on the break, and the inside section can become congested on good days. The down-side to the break is its murky brown waters which can obscure dangerous marine life. Surfers waiting for a wave have been lifted off their boards by sharks and barracudas that sometimes break the surface; occasionally, some will leap over paddling surfers.

Plans are in the works to build a resort on Gay & Robinson's lands at Kapalawai, next door to Pakalas. Discussions on a tradeoff for surfers—one proposal is for a parking area with a freshwater shower—are part of the planning and negotiations for the resort. One cut of the plans has tent-like cottages on the property up the beach from the break.

A few miles past Pakalas heading northwest is the black sand beach and river mouth at **Waimea**, the site of a once-popular surf spot during the days of riding long wood planks in pre-Western contact Hawaii. Today, the children of Waimea enjoy riding their boogey-boards in the mini-shorebreak here. In 1778, Captain James Cook made his first landing of the Hawaiian islands at the north end of the river mouth (although

Cook's artists did not portray any surfers in their work until they arrived at Kealakekua Bay on the Big Island).

The Protestant missionary Hiram Bingham described surfing at Waimea in his journal during the summer of 1821. The then-youthful missionary also sat on the beach with Kaumualii, the last king of Kauai and a lean, noteworthy surfer in his youth. The pair planned to sail together to Tahiti to meet with Polynesian Christians there; Bingham even carried a note from Kaahumanu, the prime minister of the Hawaiian Kingdom, requesting that they bring her back a gift of a mother-of-pearl embedded surfboard. Instead, the monarch Liholiho (Kamehameha II) sailed in from Oahu and stealthily sent the Kauai king into exile on Oahu after the two kings had made a round-Kauai journey.

Sands that Bark

The 15-mile-long white sand beach known as **Barking Sands** begins at Kekaha, a plantation town a few miles north of Waimea, and

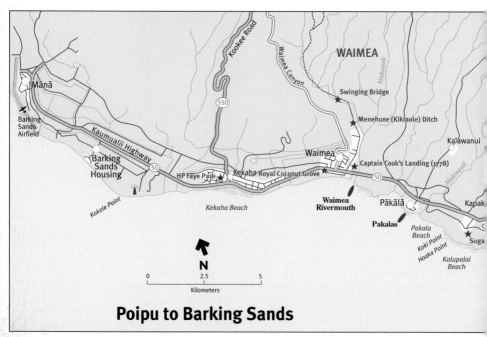

Poipu to Barking Sands

stretches north to a *heiau* and park known as Polihale. Waves break along the isolated shoreline north of Kekaha, producing rideable shorebreak. However, currents and board-snapping shorepounders make this spot dangerous when the surf is happening and up.

The next noteworthy surf breaks are located behind guarded gates along the coast of the US Navy's Pacific Missile Range Facility outside of the now-gone plantation town of Mana. A cluster of several breaks here is highlighted by **Majors Bay**, a right-breaking spot located in a recreation area. The base is used to test the electronics on submarines and to do research on anti-Scud missile systems, in addition to other naval electronics research projects. Military use of the Barking Sands runway at the beach sometimes causes the base to be off-limits to surfers. However, the Navy does its best to keep the breaks open most of the time.

The staging of a professional surfing contest at Majors Bay in 1999 was a landmark event for Kauai, and one carefully coordinated with the ad hoc Kauai Surfing Association. This 12-member nonprofit group includes several leading surfers. Boardmember Bobby Cocke, the owner of Kai Kane surf shops and a top longboarder, says the group works, "to make Kauai a breeding ground for the kids and perpetuate the lifestyle that is here." Cocke adds that the organization also serves to give the surfers of Kauai a voice in surfing-related issues, such as the staging of a pro contest on an island with a strong sense of protectionism.

Majors is named after the home of one of the base's former commanders, which used to be located on the coast here. The wave sweeps right along a sand point, holding its shape up to about 6 to 10 feet. It has some similarities to the waves at Makaha and other breaks in Leeward Oahu. Majors is for intermediate and advanced surfers; a strong current running along the beach can cre-

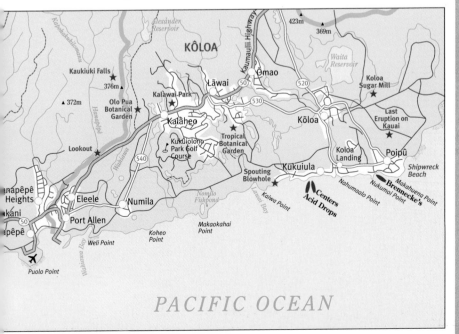

ate heavy Hawaiian water conditions. Having a 4-wheel-drive improves access to the break, located along one of the longest white sand beaches in Hawaii. To access Majors, be prepared to present a valid driver's license, car registration and insurance form to the guard at the gate who issues "recreational" passes.

On the north side of the Barking Sands runway is what's left of the namesake "barking" sand dunes. Old photos show sand surfers plowing down the then-tall dunes on planks of wood. Supposedly, the sand's unique silicon crystals as well as the dampness of the sand helped to create the "bark" when you stepped on the sand, a freak feature found also in the sand dunes of Japan and Saudi Arabia.

Forbidden Niihau

The offshore view here includes a look out to the so-called "Forbidden Island" of **Niihau** 17 miles to the southwest. The island of Niihau, officially part of the County of Kauai, is populated by about 200 native Hawaiians and is strictly off-limits to all but infrequently invited guests of the local Robinson family. The landed Robinsons are *kamaaina* descendants of Scottish immigrants who purchased the island from its Royal Hawaiian owners in 1864. The

Below: Real surfing is banned at Brennecke's, a fact that is received with much stoke by the bodysurfing and boogeyboarding communities.
Photo: Brett Uprichard

island, which measures 18 miles long by 6 miles wide, is one of the few places in Hawaii where the locals actually still keep Hawaiian culture alive and speak fluent Hawaiian.

The white sand beach way out here in nowhere continues north from the Pacific Missile Range Facility (sometimes referred to only by its acronym PMRF) to a sacred and ancient Hawaiian site known as **Polihale**, which in Hawaiian means "House Bosom." Here the remains of a *heiau* lie partly hidden at the base of a rocky cliff, right above the spot where a beach well is marked with the tracks of 4-wheel-drive vehicles. A State Park campsite is reached along a dirt cane road that runs parallel and along the *mauka* side of a long set of sand dunes.

Here also is where the rocky west end of the spectacular Na Pali Cliffs coastline begins doing its awe-inspiring thing. Serious rip currents make the shoreline deceptively dangerous, even on seemingly mellow and low-surf days. Newly installed emergency phones point out the drowning danger here. Fickle swell and wind conditions provide few opportune moments for surfing in this remote and beautiful wilderness area of Kauai.

—*Chris Cook*

Copper tubes reeling around a crescent reef. Coconut palms waving on the point in the trade wind that sweeps over purple hills leading into deep green, red and black canyons.

We had found our perfect wave in our own backyard by following a chance glimpse of whitewater through the *kiawe* trees that covered the quarter mile between the main highway and the ocean. Hawk Kawaihalau, Bobby Kama, Eddie Boy Panui, Kahuku and I waxed up, paddled out and, in 1962, began riding the wave that was to become an unbroken summer tradition for the next 38 years, and which continues to this day.

We were all stoked surfers in our late teens. I had just graduated from high school, the rest were still going. There were probably about 30 active surfers on the island. Most were older guys who rode the old style. The guy who rode the biggest waves was the champ. They rode some big ones. One day at Hanalei, during the winter, waves breaking over the front of the old pier, these older guys paddled out and rode 15- to 20-foot Impossibles, then paddled across the bay to ride Queens onshore and returned to get a few more before paddling in. No specialized guns, just regular boards. From the beach, all you could see were the tracks of the boards streaming up the face as the thick, racing lips ripped down the 200-plus-yard-long line.

Hanalei was well known by this time. Paul Strauch told me that he had been over with George Downing and crew in the late '50s. Early surf films showed Dewey Weber and company riding bicycles and sleeping in hammocks in the shed at the end of the pier. Gaylord Wilcox, Nick Beck and friends had been surfing there since the mid '50s. Hanalei residents such as Ah Fook Tai Hook, Jordan Kahananui, George Kaona and oth-

ers had been bodysurfing and boardsurfing the Bay since they were kids in the late 1940s and early 1950s, 20 years before the Californians Billy Hamilton and Jimmy Irons and Honoluluans Joey Cabell, Jimmy Lucas and others started to arrive. Hanalei had been surfed in contemporary times from a quarter to a half century before young Hawaiians Titus Kinimaka, Kaipo Jaquias and second generation hotties such as Bruce and Andy Irons, the Powers boys and the rest of the Generation X began to make their mark in the surfing world.

But the story of Hanalei's evolution is for another day. This is the story of another wave on the opposite side of the island for a season that happens on the opposite side of winter.

In 1962, we were captured by the magic dream of the new surfing as illustrated by the fledgling surf magazines of the time. Rincon, Malibu and other exotic perfect points filled our imagination. Wave exploration was in its infancy. A drive to the opposite side of the island for us was a major journey, but 18- to 20-something cents a gallon for gasoline made it possible for me to get the family station wagon fueled up for the first run with my tips from busboy work at the Kauai Surf Hotel (one of the three resorts on the island at the time). The other guys didn't have access to a car. Five of us piled in with our five logs sticking out the back of the open window.

It was our first trip west of Poipu, and we were based at Kalapaki. We followed the older guys who rode in an air conditioned "stretch-out" (6-door touring car)

Where the Sun Shines

named Baby Doll to check out Waimea river mouth after checking out Wai Ohai, which wasn't up to the standards of the Baby Doll crew. The manager of Greyline Tours, John Gilruth, sponsored a select group of mostly older guys, so they rode in comfort. We followed in our rusted-out station wagon, eating dust through the canefield roads between Spouting Horn and Hanapepe while they styled it in front of us.

Needless to say, Waimea wasn't happening, but I had glimpsed the edge of a wave as we drove by Makaweli Ranch. Baby Doll and crew blasted back to Poipu and we made history by turning off into the small plantation village with a sign that said "No Trespassing, Private Property." It was the middle of the morning, everyone was at work and the village was deserted. We saw what was perfection for the first time: 4-foot lefts peeling around a gentle curve of reef.

The last section was about 75 yards of machine made for noseriding little grinders that curled around to a white sand beach bordered by a nice channel. However, after years of sugar cultivation and irrigation ditches that dumped topsoil into the sea, the water was a copper brown that got our shark imaginations going full speed ahead. We got chased out on that first surfing day there, and since then, many more have seen the landlord from time to time.

Well, we had surfed our dreams come true. We had our perfect "secret" spot. We called it *Take Five* after the popular Dave Brubeck tune of the time.

It was everything that a young surfer could want in a wave. Insane nose rides, perfection climb, drop and cutback, and thick, board-breaking barrels on the rare 6-foot days and even during rare hurricane swells.

It didn't, however, stay secret for long. Young Kailua surfers came and called it "Infinities." The local Kauai kids such as Liko and Kaleo Hookano were onto it within a year or two. California waveriders such as Herbie Torrens, Jim Beaver and George Weaver settled early in the town of Waimea, and then a younger generation from the village, the Pratt brothers and other sons of the plantation workers, wired the whole reef. Names from Cabell to Occhilupo have slid on these long copper lines as have thousands of others—and they still keep coming.

Well, close to 40 years have passed and I haven't missed a summer. Some of the familiar faces are still out there. The Hookano boys, the Pratts and their contemporaries still hold their ground. I am the only one from that initial crew of surfers who continues to be drawn there, year after year.

On a good south swell, some 40 to 50 cars line the main highway adjacent to the right-of-way that leads to the beach. The parade of surfers never stops from before dawn (there is the usual crew of 15 or more who begin surfing before dawn every day) and well past the setting of the sun over the Niihau and Lehua islands.

There are now plans for a 250-unit tourist resort to be built on this beach beginning in the next year or so. The only real constant, it seems, is change.

—Carlos Andrade

Above: Cruising, Big Island style. You've got to be prepared for all eventualities,
even lava flows, on this volatile island.
Photo: Steve Bingham

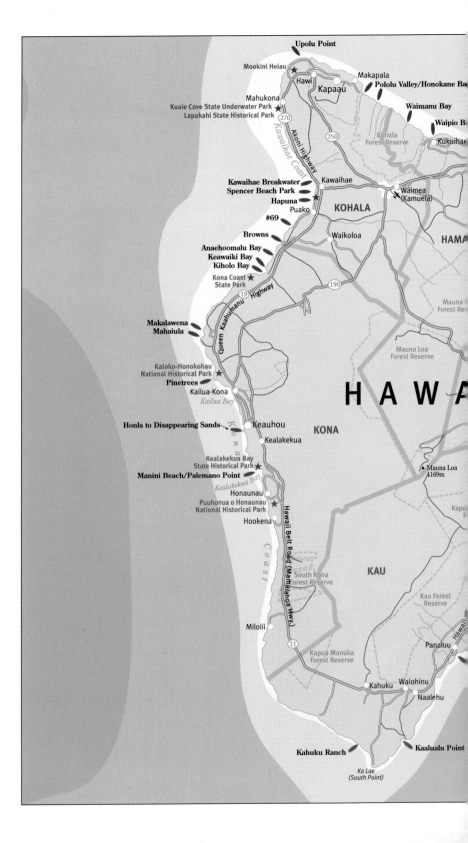

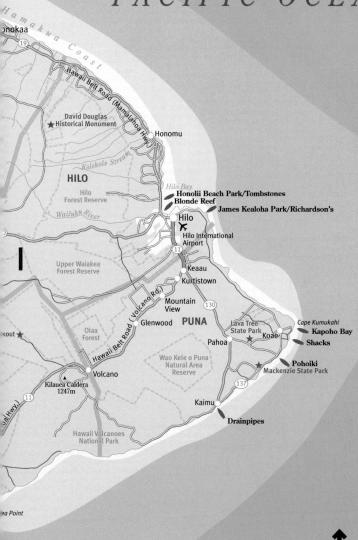

Bay

PACIFIC OCEAN

onokaa

19

Hamakua Coast

Hawaii Belt Road (Mamalahoa Hwy.)

David Douglas
★ Historical Monument

Honomu

Kolekole Stream

HILO

Hilo
Forest Reserve

Hilo Bay

Honolii Beach Park/Tombstones
Blonde Reef

Wailuku River

Hilo ✈

James Kealoha Park/Richardson's

Hilo International
Airport

11

Upper Waiakea
Forest Reserve

Keaau

I

Kurtistown

Olaa
Forest

Volcano Rd.)

Mountain
View

130

out ★

Hawaii Belt Road (Volcano Rd.)

Glenwood

PUNA

Lava Tree
State Park

Cape Kumukahi

Kapoho Bay

Pahoa

Koae ★

Shacks

Wao Kele o Puna
Natural Area
Reserve

Volcano

▲
Kilauea Caldera
1247m

★ Mackenzie State Park

Pohoiki

137

Kaimu

11

Hawaii Volcanoes
National Park

a Point

Drainpipes

↑
N

0   10   20
Kilometers

Hawaii

Hawaii's BIG Island
East Side, West Side, All Around

The island that the State of Hawaii was named after is more commonly known as the Big Island, an appropriate name as it is larger than the rest of the state's islands combined. Thanks to the activities of Madame Pele, the Hawaiian goddess of volcanoes, the Big Island is getting bigger all the time. Kilauea volcano is nearing its second decade of eruption, a process that has added acres to the Big Island's land mass.

Unfortunately for surfers, this means that the Big Island is the state's youngest island, too young for coral reefs and sand to form in sufficient quantities to create a number of quality surf spots. It also means that the surf spots are widely scattered over vast distances, and that surfers have to put in multi-mile car, boat or hiking time in order to reach these spots.

The worst result of Kilauea's output was the destruction of the island's most beloved and powerful surf spot, Drainpipes, which was buried under tons of molten lava at Kalapana, along with several lesser surf spots in Kaimu Bay.

There is a tremendous amount of *mana* (spiritual energy) on the Big Island, and it's easy even for newcomers to sense the power of unseen forces at work in the *moana* (ocean) and *aina* (land). The Big Island was the first glimpse that Polynesian voyagers had of their new home, and it was the site of their first landfall (at South Point). The island is also where Pele makes her home (at Hawaii Volcanoes National Park), and the site of one of the most sacred places of the ancient Hawaiians (Waipio Valley). It also is home to the *heiau* built by King Kamehameha the Great to sanctify his intended conquest of the other islands in order to create a unified Hawaiian kingdom.

The Big Island also has a lot of good surf if you only know where and when to look for it. A car is a necessity, however, for any serious surf exploration. If you intend to hike, it helps to have heaps of patience and faith in people.

It's easiest to divide the island into two main surf zones, the west side and the east side, with sub-regions in each zone that are affected differently by exposure to winds and swells. Unlike the other Hawaiian islands, the huge masses of the ancient volcanoes Mauna Loa and Mauna Kea create their own weather systems. This results in offshore morning wind flows on both sides of the island that become onshore on the east windward side of the island later in the day, blocking the trade winds from blowing out the Kona and Kohala coasts on the west side. Because it is the southernmost island in the chain, any swells with south in them arrive first on the Big Island, and with more power. This also means that swells with any north in them arrive last, and weaker than on the other islands. Additionally, the West side of the Big Island sits in the wave shadow of the other islands for north and northwest winter swells.

During the winter (October through April), west, northwest, north and northeasterly swells

Opposite: Lucky number 69 going off on a smoking day. Looks pretty tasty, huh? *Photo: Steve Bingham*

Year-round; winter is biggest

Can be rough; 4-wheel-drive vehicles or hiking required at some surfing breaks

Reef with some sand bottoms

Smaller boards, though winter can still get big

Rough trails and shallow reefs

Altitude sickness on the mountains, plus jagged lava

Snow, lava flows, and the magnificent scenery and climate

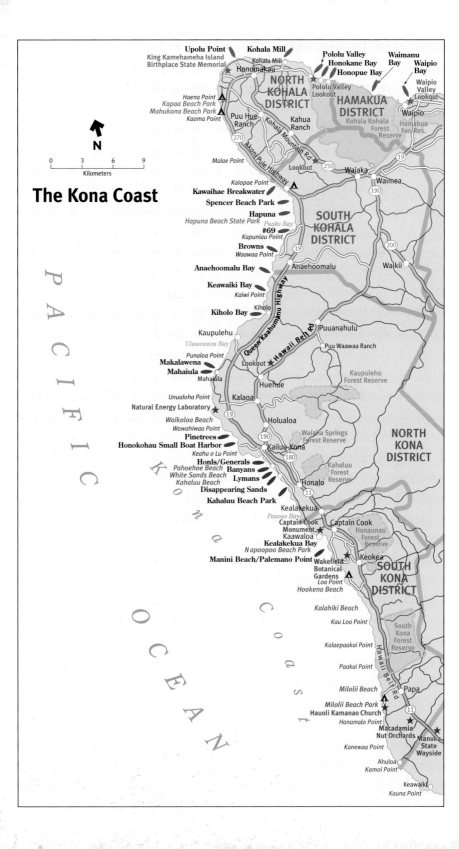

The Kona Coast

N

0   3   6   9
Kilometers

PACIFIC OCEAN

Kona Coast

Upolu Point
King Kamehameha Island
Birthplace State Memorial
Kohala Mill
Kohala Mill
Honomakau
Pololu Valley
Honokane Bay
Honopue Bay
Waimanu
Bay
Waipio
Bay
Waipio
Valley
Lookout

Haena Point
Kapaa Beach Park
Mahukona Beach Park
Kaoma Point

NORTH
KOHALA
DISTRICT

HAMAKUA
DISTRICT

Pololu Valley
Lookout

Waipio

Puu Hue
Ranch

Kahua
Ranch

Kohala Kohala
Forest
Reserve

Hamakua
For./Res.

270

Malae Point

Lookout

250

Wajaka

19

Waimea

190

Kaiopae Point

Kawaihae Breakwater
Spencer Beach Park
Hapuna
Hapuna Beach State Park
#69
Kapuniau Point
Browns
Waawaa Point

Puako Bay

SOUTH
KOHALA
DISTRICT

19

200

Waikii

Anaehoomalu Bay

Anaehoomalu

Keawaiki Bay
Kaiwi Point

Kiholo Bay
Kiholo

Kaupulehu

Uluweuweu Bay

Punaloa Point
Makalawena
Mahaiula
Mahaiula

Puuanahulu
Puu Waawaa Ranch

Lookout

Kaupulehu
Forest
Reserve

Unualoha Point
Natural Energy Laboratory
Kalaoa

Huehue

NORTH
KONA
DISTRICT

Waikoloa Beach
Wawahiwaa Point
Pinetrees
Honokohau Small Boat Harbor
Keahu o Lu Point
Honls/Generals
Pahoehoe Beach   Banyans
White Sands Beach
Kahaluu Beach   Lymans
Disappearing Sands
Kahaluu Beach Park

Holualoa

190

Kailua-Kona

180

Waiaha Springs
Forest Reserve

Kahaluu
Forest
Reserve

Honalo

11

Kealakekua
Paaoao Bay
Captain Cook
Monument
Kaawaloa
Kealakekua Bay
Napoopoo Beach Park
Manini Beach/Palemano Point

Captain Cook

Honaunau
Forest
Reserve

Keokea

Wakefield
Botanical
Gardens
Loa Point
Hookena Beach

SOUTH
KONA
DISTRICT

Kalahiki Beach

Kau Loa Point

South
Kona
Forest
Reserve

Kalaepaakai Point

Paakai Point

Milolii Beach

Papa

Milolii Beach Park
Hauoli Kamanao Church
Hanamalo Point

Macadamia
Nut Orchards

11

Manuka
State
Wayside

Kanewaa Point

Ahuloa
Kamoi Point

Keawaiki
Kauna Point

come booming in from fierce winter storms traveling between Asia and the US mainland, sending waves to surf spots from South Kona on the west side all the way to South Hilo on the east side. Additionally, tropical cyclones near Fiji and Tahiti can send off-season southwest and south swells during Hawaii's winter. The winter months also bring numerous glassy days when the wind vanishes, as well as westerly *kona* winds from passing cold fronts and rogue low-pressure cells called *kona* storms. These conditions turn waves on the usually bumpy windward east side into visions of delight. The summer season (April through September) is usually dominated by trade winds that chop out the waves on the east shore while making the west side clean. However, mornings can be glassy even on the east side, and *kona* storms or approaching hurricanes can bring westerly winds that clean up the waves on the east-facing coastline.

Southern Hemisphere winter storms send southwest and south swells during Hawaii's summer, which tend to hit the Big Island with much greater force and frequency than they do the rest of the islands. Hurricanes that form off Latin America quickly mature as they head west; as a result, they send east and southeast swells, as do hurricanes that form closer to Hawaii and draw a bead on the islands as they proceed westward.

In terms of its geography, the Big Island is a fascinating microcosm of the world's bioregions. As you travel the island chasing the waves, you'll encounter astounding sights wherever you go, such as snowboardable and skiable slopes atop Mauna Kea and Mauna Loa during the winter months.

Because land areas are vast and towns small and scarce, it is easier to refer to most parts of the island according to their districts. Starting on the northwest side, the North Kohala Coast is lush and green, becoming increasingly dry in South Kohala, where desolate ancient lava flows dominate almost all the way to the Kona District. Kona is tropical and lush all the

Below: Indo or Hawaii? Shacks looking very much like some distant Sumatran reef. *Photo: Steve Bingham*

way to the lava fields and forests that cover the shoreline of South Point and the start of the Kau District on the southeast coast. This mix of lava and forest continues north to the Puna District, scene of much volcanic activity at Kalapana. Hilo is rainy and very tropical and carries on throughout Hamakua District on the northeast side of the island and down to the end of the road.

The Sunny West Side

Near the bottom of the North Kohala District is the **Kawaihae Breakwater**, a series of reef breaks that is always fun, and, with the right west or northwest swell, can be wonderful. This is one of the few longboard-friendly breaks on the West side of the island. A few miles to the south, **Spencer Beach Park** has a left/right setup that comes alive with booming winter swells and remains dormant on smaller swells.

Another winter break was inadvertently created by the **Mauna Kea Hotel** when it imported sand for the enjoyment of its guests. Best for bodysurfers or body-

Below: Arjuna Morgan cooling his feet and kicking his heels at A-Bay. *Photo: Steve Bingham*

boarders. A little farther south, **Hapuna Beach State Park** is a great place for a beach picnic when (during winter's west and northwest swells) the main course is good surf. The beach has fun shorebreak waves for bodysurfers, while the cliff area at the south end of the beach has a right/left peak for shortboarders.

When driving south on Queen Kaahumanu Highway, watch closely for telephone pole **#69**. That is your signal to turn *makai* (seaward) for an electrifying session riding barreling lefts and rights on west and northwest winter swells. If you drive past it, turn off at Puako Road and follow it to the end for a series of left/right peaks that close out when serious winter swells get too big.

Follow the signs off Queen Kaahumanu Highway to the Mauna Lani Resort, where a spot called **Browns** awaits with rights and lefts over a manageable reef on winter swells. Farther south off Queen Kaahumanu Highway, is **Anaehoomalu Bay**, or **A-Bay**, a haven for sailboarders and surfers seeking thrills. Two spots just off the Hilton Waikoloa Hotel offer two distinct surfing experiences.

The first closes out over 6 feet and features a performance right-hand point break over a shallow reef. The second is in the middle of the bay and has good, big lefts during powerful winter north and northwest swells.

Take a long hot walk south of Anaehoomalu (or a shorter, more rugged walk from Queen Kaahumanu Highway) and you'll come to beautiful **Keawaiki Bay**, which has a splendid beach and a perfect reef setup with rights and lefts over a shallow reef that is best on winter's west and northwest swells. A bit farther south lies the equally beautiful **Kiholo Bay**, with a right point on bigger west or northwest swells, and a beachbreak in the middle of the bay. Access is provided by the Four Seasons Resort.

The opening of the Kona Coast State Park has allowed ocean lovers access to some of the Big Island's most delightful bays, including **Makalawena**, which features a rippable long, fast right on winter swells, and **Mahaiula**, a powerful right that is best on west and northwest swells. Farther south, Honokohau National Historic Park provides lessons in contemporary history with good waves at **Pinetrees** at nearby Kaloko Point. The trees here are actually mangroves but the wave is the real article, mostly lefts and a few rogue rights that break on any swell, either in summer or winter.

The north side of **Honokohau Small Boat Harbor** is a refuge for winter and summer swells where the lefts come alive on south and southwest swells and the rights are best on west and northwest swells, both of which can handle some size.

Just north of Kailua-Kona town, **Old Kona Airport State Park** has some fin-snapping shallow coral reefs that are manageable at high tide, and will break on any swell with a little west in it, whether it's summer or winter.

In front of the sea wall in downtown Kailua-Kona, you will encounter another test of nerves across from **Hulihee Palace**, a screaming left that barrels on south and southwest swells. The hideously shallow reef has scraped many a hide, but the ride is worth the risk.

In front of a low rock wall along Alii Drive is **Honls**, an ultra-fun reef break that was the training ground for bodyboard legend

Below: Big Island surf smokes. The local boys know that and are on to it anytime it fires. Chris Arruda, meanwhile, walks on Hawaiian fire. *Photo: Steve Bingham*

Following pages: Local Big Islander Frank Pereira cranking a smooth bottom turn a la Occy at Hapuna Point. *Photo: Steve Bingham*

Oppsite top: This engraving detail, believed to be the first known image ever of a surfer, was rendered by John Webber, a ship's artist, to document the arrival of Captain James Cook at Kealakekua, Hawaii, on January 17, 1779.

Opposite bottom: A memorial on a 27-foot white obelisk on the north end of Kealakekua Bay to honor Captain James Cook, who met an untimely end on the very islands he discovered. *Photo: Walter Andreae*

Below: One question: why is everyone standing around and not out there?! The viewing gallery at Kahuku Ranch near South Point. *Photo: Steve Bingham*

Mike Stewart and which is a guaranteed good time year-round, with good rights and lefts until the waves close out over 6 feet.

Generals and Banyans

Farther down Alii Drive is **Generals**, a right that hugs the rocky shore and breaks best on west and northwest swells.

But the prime attraction along Alii Drive is **Banyans**, which breaks in front of a distinctive banyan tree. The numerous surf vehicles are a dead giveaway that this is a spot favored by Kona heavyweights. It is usually packed with locals enjoying the barreling rights and lefts. The rights are best on northwest swells and the lefts are prime on southwest swells, and though you will never surf it uncrowded, it's worth paddling out, if just for the experience.

Just south of Banyans is **Lymans**, a left point wave that can handle size on big summer and winter swells, though it is best on west and northwest swells.

Farther south on Alii Drive is **Disappearing Sands** beach, a good spot for bodyboarding and bodysurfing on smaller days, which has a rocky ledge offering good rights and lefts on big summer and winter swells.

Kahaluu Beach Park is a great place to snorkel and a fun spot for longboarding all year round. Kahaluu can also provide a good shortboard wave on the right swell and tide.

At the *makai* intersection that leads to Kealakekua Bay, go straight to reach **Manini Beach** for a long, fast left that can accommodate big west and northwest swells and huge southwest swells.

Nearby Keei is home to **Palemano Point**, a good left protected by sharp shallow coral. The spot can handle any swell direction, but closes out when the waves get overhead. The last spot that's worth seeking on the West side is **Kahuku Ranch**, a right/left setup

IN MEMORY OF
THE GREAT CIRCUMNAVIGATOR,
CAPTAIN JAMES COOK, R N.,
WHO
DISCOVERED THESE ISLANDS
ON THE 18TH OF JANUARY, A.D 1778
AND FELL NEAR THIS SPOT
ON THE 14TH OF FEBRUARY, A.D. 1779.
THIS MONUMENT WAS ERECTED
IN NOVEMBER A D 1874
BY SOME OF
HIS FELLOW COUNTRYMEN.

next to South Point (*Ka Lae*). Trade winds are offshore here, and it takes swells from the southeast, south and southwest.

The Cruisey East Side

Kaalualu Point offers a good, long left that peels into deep water and takes powerful south, southeast or east swells. You'll find it at the end of a long drive over rough roads northeast of South Point. The bay protects the wave a bit from the trade winds.

Highway 11 offers tantalizing glimpses of rideable waves in southern Kau District. Honuapo Bay is close to the highway and accessible through Whittington Beach Park. **The Point** offers good lefts on big south, southeast or east swells. Trade winds here rip the waves to pieces. Just up the road, **Punaluu** provides an unusual treat, a short right that breaks onto black sand, a remnant of earlier lava flows into the ocean.

Hiking Anyone?

A trio of spots require quite a bit of effort to reach (including seriously long hikes through the Hawaii Volcanoes National Park) in order to take advantage of big south and southeast swells. **Halape** is an A-frame peak that breaks over a shallow reef, while **Keauhou Point** features long lefts. **Apua Point** is a big-wave break with right and left surfriding opportunities. For safety reasons, any plans to hike this area must be reported to the Kilauea Visitor Center, which is the headquarters of the park.

The excellent surf spots in the Kalapana area have been periodically paved over by Pele's fiery lava flows, and the spot long-known to local surfers as **Drainpipes** will be especially missed. **Pohoiki** at Isaac Hale Beach Park, however, is

still intact (at least for the moment), and it features waves at three bays that break all year but can be particularly spectacular and fun during a big enough easterly swell. The first two bays feature small, fast rights over a shallow reef, while the last bay needs big east swells to come alive with long lefts.

Just north of the park is **Shacks**, featuring barreling lefts that zip across shallow reefs, and

which is best on southeast swells. Farther north, **Kapoho Bay** offers some fun waves over shallow reefs on east, southeast and south swells that are best when the trade winds are absent or when the *kona* winds are blowing.

On the east end of Hilo's bay front is a series of surf spots. On the easy end of the scale, **Richardson's** provides fun waves for beginners and longboarders, consisting of rights and lefts that break over a rock reef and close out when the surf gets overhead.

Also in **James Kealoha Beach Park** are some ghastly shallow coral reefs that deliver zippy waves on northwest, north, northeast and east swells.

The outer edge of the Hilo breakwater beckons with the promise of adventure—huge rights

Above: Glassy shorebreak action at the foot of the Waipio Valley. Eddie Lyndsay takes a dip.

Opposite: Picture-perfect Waipio Valley—featuring lines, baby—from a more distant vantage point. *Photos: Peter French*

that reel along **Blonde Reef** (no kidding) when northwest, north and northeast swells get well overhead. Because it's far from shore, your choices are either to take a long paddle out or a boat trip. Whichever you choose, you'll have a memorable session.

At the west entrance to Hilo, the usual weak little peaks along the **Bay Front** come to life on huge north and northeast swells, creating a long, fast, perfect left that peels forever. Very rare, but well worth looking for.

A few miles north of Hilo on the Hawaii Belt Road is a haven that keeps Hilo surfers happy year round. **Honolii Beach Park** has rights and lefts in a beautiful bay with a stream that rearranges the rocky shoal regularly, making each surfing day here a surprise. Longboarding, shortboarding, bodyboarding, bodysurfing—whatever you desire, it's here for the taking.

If the waves at Honolii seem too tame for you, move on during large northwest, north and northeast swells to **Tombstones**, just around the point to the east. Tombstones will provide you with memorable thrills, but experts and adventurers only should apply for the waves here.

The Hamakua Coast along Highway 19 is a surf wasteland

Below: Wayne Bouchain takes the drop on a fine-looking right-hander at Pohoiki in the Kaimu district. *Photo: Steve Bingham*

Following pages: At a secluded beach on a hush-hush neighbor island, a some-times left puts ona show for a jazzed tubeseeker. *Photo: Peter French*

punctuated by cliffs that march down to an ocean devoid of wave-forming reefs or protected bays. At **Waipio Bay**, everything changes for the better. Here, shorebreak waves are rideable year round at the mouth of a beautiful valley.

The next 10 miles of coast harbors four more surf spots, **Waimanu Bay**, **Honopue Bay**, **Honokane Bay**, and **Pololu Valley**, all of which offer good reef and shorebreak waves all year-round. Unfortunately, there is no road, so these spots must be reached by hiking from Waipio to the south or Pololu Overlook to the north, or by boat. However you go, it will be an adventure.

Just north of Pololu and much easier to reach is **Keokea Beach Park**, a spot with fun rights that break during winter's northwest, north and northeasterly swells. Watch out for the many rocks at this surf spot.

The **Kohala Mill** near Kauhola Point has good lefts during the winter month. Right at the line dividing the east and west shores of the Big Island is **Upolu Point**, a powerful point break that is frequently ravaged by the trade winds, but which can be prime on calm mornings or southwest *kona* winds.

—*George Frayne*

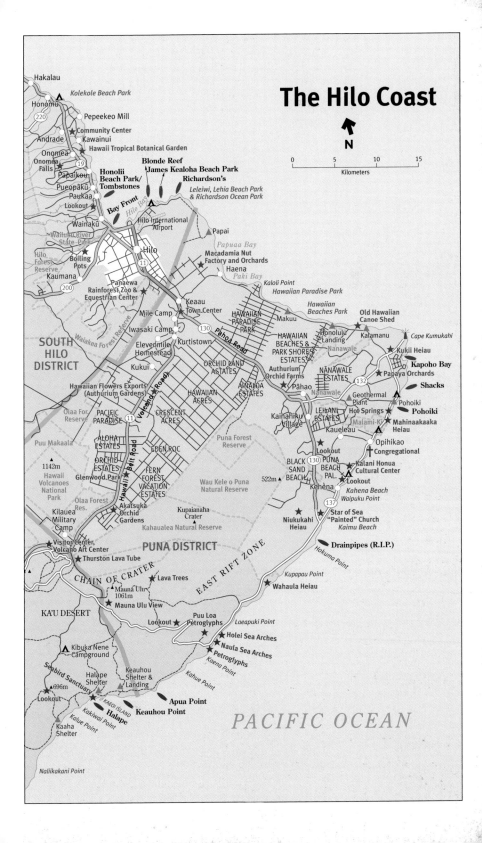

The Hilo Coast

N

0   5   10   15
Kilometers

Hakalau

Kolekole Beach Park

Honomu

220

Pepeekeo Mill

Andrade

Community Center

Kawainui

Hawaii Tropical Botanical Garden

Onomea

Onomea
Falls

19

Papaikou

Pueopaku

Paukaa

Lookout

Wainaku

Honolii
Beach Park/
Tombstones

Blonde Reef

James Kealoha Beach Park

Richardson's

Leleiwi, Lehia Beach Park
& Richardson Ocean Park

Bay Front

Hilo Bay

Hilo International
Airport

Papai

Hilo

Papuaa Bay

Boiling
Pots

Kaumana

200

Panaewa
Rainforest Zoo &
Equestrian Center

11

Macadamia Nut
Factory and Orchards

Haena

Paki Bay

Kaloli Point

Hawaiian Paradise Park

Hilo
Forest
Reserve

Keaau
Town Center

Mile Camp

Iwasaki Camp

130

Pahoa Road

Makuu

HAWAIIAN
PARADISE
PARK

Hawaiian
Beaches Park

Old Hawaiian
Canoe Shed

Cape Kumukahi

SOUTH
HILO
DISTRICT

Waiakea Forest Reserve

Elevenmile
Homestead

Kurtistown

Kukui

ORCHID LAND
ASTATES

HAWAIIAN
ACRES

AINALOA
ESTATES

HAWAIIAN
BEACHES &
PARK SHORES
ESTATES

Authurium
Orchid Farms

Honolulu
Landing

Kalamanu

Nanawale

Kukii Heiau

Kapoho Bay

Papaya Orchards

Shacks

Hawaiian Flowers Exports
(Authurium Gardens)

PACIFIC
PARADISE

11

Volcano Road

CRESCENT
ACRES

Pahoa

NANAWALE
ESTATES

132

Olaa For.
Reserve

Puu Makaala

ALOHA
ESTATES

ORCHID
ESTATES

EDEN ROC

Puna Forest
Reserve

Kainahiku
Village

LEILANI
ESTATES

Geothermal
Plant

Hot Springs

Pohoiki

Pohoiki

1142m
Hawaii
Volcanoes
National
Park

Glenwood Park

FERN
FOREST
VACATION
ESTATES

Wau Kele o Puna
Natural Reserve

522m

Kaueleau

Malami-Ki

Lookout

BLACK
SAND
BEACH

130

PUNA
BEACH
PAL.

Mahinaakaaka
Heiau

Opihikao

Congregational

Kalani Honua
Cultural Center

Olaa Forest
Res.

Akatsuka
Orchid
Gardens

Kahaualea Natural Reserve

Kupaianaha
Crater

Kehena

Lookout

Kahena Beach
Waipuku Point

Kilauea
Military
Camp

Visitor center,
Volcano Art Center

Thurston Lava Tube

PUNA DISTRICT

Niukukahi
Heiau

Star of Sea
"Painted" Church

Kaimu Beach

Lava Trees

EAST RIFT ZONE

137

Drainpipes (R.I.P.)

CHAIN OF CRATER

Mauna Ulu
1061m

Mauna Ulu View

Kupapau Point

Wahaula Heiau

Hokuma Point

KA'U DESERT

Lookout

Puu Loa
Petroglyphs

Laeapuki Point

Holei Sea Arches

Naula Sea Arches

Petroglyphs

Kaena Point

Kibuka Nene
Campground

696m

Lookout

Halape
Shelter

Seabird Sanctuary

KAEOI ISLAND

Halape

Keauhou
Shelter &
Landing

Kahue Point

Apua Point

Keauhou Point

Kakiwai Point

Kalue Point

Kaaha
Shelter

Naliikakani Point

PACIFIC OCEAN

Surfing in Hawaii

Sacred and Sublime

In this editors' *aloha*, we would like to emphasize that what has been included in these pages is not the entire Hawaiian surfing story, but what we hope is a respectful introduction to one of humanity's most sublime relationships with nature. To tell the entire waveriding story about surfing's birthplace would require much more space than is available in this volume, given in particular surfing's role in Hawaii's oral tradition, recorded history and contemporary everyday society. Surfing in Hawaii is not just a sport or a form of recreation. It is one of a very few cultural phenomena that has somehow survived the many shocks—both physical and psychological—that have been visited upon Hawaiians during more than 200 years of colonization and com-

mercial exploitation. Indeed, surfing ranks with the Hawaiian language and the classical *hula* dance as icons of what was in ancient times a unique, highly sophisticated Pacific/Polynesian culture.

Even in its most ancient forms, surfing as it has evolved in Hawaii is one of our most wondrous discoveries. Just imagine that moment long ago in ancient Hawaii when the first surfer conceived the idea of a surfboard, and then—in a remarkable fulfillment of a new concept—paddled out into the sea and tapped the energy of an incoming wave. Imagine what it was like to surf that first time, and to continue doing so until the joy of it grew and grew with the passing of time. Latter-day surfers such as us

should also ask why was it only the Hawaiians who were able to do this for hundreds of years of early human history.

Surfing is a unique physical and cultural phenomenon. With this in mind, we have purposely left much unsaid in this book. Some things that belong to the realm of the secret and the sacred we have left for you to discover and enjoy.

We hope that you find this study of Hawaii accurate, sensitive, captivating, informative and interesting to read. No matter what time of year you choose to visit the great surfing islands of Hawaii, we're sure that you'll have a great time and be charged with surf-stoke for evermore.

—*Leonard and Lorca Lueras*

A tasty little unidentified surf spot lost somewhere in the Hawaiian Islands. Go on, see if you can find it. *Photo: Brett Uprichard*

Try these other titles in Periplus Editions' line of Surfing Guides

ISBN 962-593-313-1

Leonard and Lorca Lueras' *Surfing Indonesia* is probably the most comprehensive guide ever written on the Indonesian island chain . . . Whether you are traveling to the Mantawais in a luxury yacht or slumming it in Kuta, this book is a must.

Surfer magazine, January 1998

I've had *Surfing Indonesia* on my desk the last two years and in that time I've picked it up again and again, sometimes to glance at it for a moment, sometimes to pore over it for an hour. I always take it with me when I leave Bali to go surfing again, and always get it out when friends on holiday in Bali visit me. The great amount of research that has obviously gone into *Surfing Indonesia* and its wide range of contributors means it offers a wealth of information and a variety of writing styles and perspectives on surf breaks and surfing.

Surf Time magazine, September 2000

ISBN 962-593-322-0

Five Stars
The classy layout and glossy action photos [*Surfing Indonesia* and *Surfing Australia*] would make these titles ideal for a coffee table, but these guidebooks are small enough to fit in a backpack or the glove box of a Sandman panel van. They even have waterproof covers.
Both have comprehensive maps to each country's surfing spots, with guides to local conditions, the best surf season, special gear you'll need, and what's going to hurt you—"watch out for great white sharks." The books are also dotted with feature articles that are more interesting and down-to-earth than the stuff that fills the pages of most surfing magazines.
If you're planning a surfing trek through either country, they're worth every cent.

Ralph magazine, July 2000

Available in 2001

ISBN 962-593-593-8

Available in 2001

ISBN 962-593-541-X

Periplus Diving Guides

Diving Indonesia (Third Edition)
ISBN 962-593-314-X

"*Diving Indonesia* has to be the most fascinating book published in the last year."

BBC World

"*Diving Indonesia* comes described as "A guide to the world's greatest diving," and lives up to its promise. This guide features 120 color photographs, up-to-date travel information, maps of all major dive sites, essays on reef life and ecology, charts of site conditions, plus information on local geography, history, and lore."

Ocean Realm

Diving Southeast Asia (Second Edition)
ISBN 962-593-312-3

"Perhaps no other region in the world presents such clear waters and abundant undersea life as Southeast Asia. The azure seas, a bounty of reefs, submerged wrecks and fabulous coral gardens should get even the most hardened land lover into a wetsuit and mask.

This guide to the best dive sites in Malaysia, Indonesia, the Philippines and Thailand maps out the watery worlds that await the enthusiastic diver. The detailed information—whether it's a walk-in dive, a night dive, diving in remote locations or from live-aboard boats—provides everything you need to take the plunge: the visibility, the current, the type of fish, the quality of the coral, the choicest spots."

Going Places

Diving Australia (Second Edition)
ISBN 962-593-311-5

"An unbelievable collection of dive sites and information brought from renowned dive authors, Neville Coleman and Nigel Marsh. This handy book covers every state with detailed information on the sites. Every site has a map and an icon-based guide to tell you what you can expect to see, the reef life, the visibility, reef and pelagic fish, drop-offs and pinnacles. It has over 200 lovely colour photographs and most importantly, is easy to follow.

Basically, there is an awesome amount of information in this book. As a general guide to diving in Australia—this is the business."

Scuba Diver

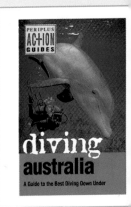

ISBN 962-593-323-9

ISBN 962-593-064-7

CONTENTS
PRACTICALITIES

Opposite: A splendid Hawaiian surfing mood at sunset. Be sure to look out for the "green flash." And, as always, *aloha. Photo: Steve Wilkings*

Travel Advisories for Surfers

Hawaii is unique as a surfing destination. Besides being the ancient birthplace of modern stand-up boardsurfing, it also happens to be home to what are arguably the finest rideable waves in the world. Other places in the world have their perfect 10 point moments and days, but when Hawaiian waters are good for surfing, well, they are very, very good. And when Hawaiian swell, wind and water conditions are perfect, well, don't even ask. Just dive in and enjoy the surfing experience of a lifetime. As Hawaiians are fond of saying about their home, "Hawaii no ka oi"— "Hawaii is da best."

When visiting "Da Islands," however, don't arrive with a mind full of sugarcoated ideas about the place. Be casual of mind, but also be prepared to take many practical things into consideration. Although Hawaii is beautiful, tropical, laidback and many miles from the West Coast of the US mainland (at least a five-hour plane ride), remember that it is first and foremost an American State (the 49th state of the US union, gaining admittance in 1959). While exotic, Hawaii is socially, economically and politically still very much a part of America, despite the stereotypical visions of it as an island dotted with palm trees swaying in the trade wind, with dark-skinned Hawaiian girls in grass *hula* skirts, green sugarcane, prickly pineapples, and, of course, Waikiki Beach and naughty beachboys. In Hawaii's capital, Honolulu, and even on Hawaii's outer islands, you'll find urban areas that are just as modern, built up and freewayed as any other big city in the world.

You will also find, despite recent downturns in the economy here, one of the most expensive places in the world. The "Paradise of the Pacific" of old is now a Paradise Paved that can only be had for a price. Gone are the days when you could arrive here with a modest amount of money, boardshorts, T-shirts and a surfboard and spend a hedonistic summer beachbumming your way around the islands. These days, as the Boy Scouts marching song advises, you should "Be Prepared" before you visit these faraway islands. Money (plenty of it) and guns (as in big-wave guns) are both required.

What to Expect

The following information is intended not only for surfers; it also applies to anyone who happens to be island-hopping or attempting to beachbum their way across the Aloha State. There are many exotic things that you will encounter on your first visit here, and, with luck, you will continue to have many other first-time experiences on future journeys.

Waves The first thing on a surfer's mind will definitely be the world-renowned ocean swells that make Hawaii the top surfing destination in the world. Hawaii is situated thousands of miles from any significant land masses, so strong Pacific Ocean swells glide onto and pound her many coastlines, coral and limestone reefs with continuous vigor. Nearly all of Hawaii's shores get whacked by unreal surf regardless of what time of the year you happen to come here. Even the occasional tsunami (or tidal wave) rocks into town. Such freak waves can cause great devastation and have been known to reach heights of up to 28 feet off the coast of Hawaii's southernmost island, also called the Big Island.

Wintertime, from the months of October to March, is prime time because Hawaii gets bombed by monstrous swells that bring life to the legendary North and West shores of all the islands. These strong ocean pulses can arrive from a variety of angles from straight west to north, and even winding around to northeast. Some swell directions can absolutely ignite certain surfing breaks, leaving others just down the road sputtering on the same swell. These bands of oceanic energy, generated by angry cyclonic storms that brew in the vastness of the Northern Pacific Ocean east of Japan and the Aleutian Islands, march straight for the Hawaiian Island chain in (usually) neatly-intervaled wave sets. Since the Hawaiian Islands are basically volcano peaks that emerged from the deep central Pacific Ocean, there is no continental shelf to slow the approach of these charging swells. This makes for fast-breaking, radical wave action with plenty of punch. During the winter months, you can definitely count on witnessing some of the tallest waves ridden—and oftentimes just watched and unridden—in the world.

Summertime is a huge downshift from the raging winter madness. From April to September, the surf spotlight is focused on the islands' south facing beaches. Summer swells generated by Southern Hemisphere storms off New Zealand and north of Antarctica make a long trek due north from the frozen extreme south, passing through other exotic locales such as Tahiti and Fiji before arriving at Hawaiian coasts. Swells are to be expected from the southwest, south, and southeast, bringing with them the promise of stoking summertime fun. These southerly wave pulses are usually nowhere near in size to waves on the North Shore during the winter. That's not to say that south shore waves suck; they are definitely as capable of producing world-class waves, only smaller. Besides, it's not the size that counts. Western coasts also benefit from these these regular and pleasurable Oahu summer swells.

On rare occasions, **off-season swells** will make a cameo appearance out of nowhere, creating waves on shores that are usually dead flat at that time of year. For instance, south swells in the middle of winter can send a wave of relief to those tired of battling it out with North Shore crowds, and vice versa. Da boys up north could be tucking into Pipe bombs in the middle of summer, while the townies try to outsnake each other in 2-foot crumblers.

The **transition season** is the best time to witness what must be one of the greatest wonders of the surfing world. When Hawaii receives swell from all sides and the winds are dead (or variable), reefs start to come alive and yield waves on all sides, causing local islanders to go stir crazy deciding which break they desire. Should they stay and surf their local fave, or check out that one secret spot on the other side of the island they've always heard so much about? It's quite an amazing phenomenon—perfect waves surrounding you on all sides. It's enough to drive a sane surfer loony.

Winds The winds blowing over the Hawaiian Islands dictate where you'll find the best surf of the day.

Trade winds are prevalent year-round and blow at least 70 percent of the time. They have a north-northeast flow to them and fan most spots along the north, west and south shores with offshore blowing gusts. When storms from the North move in, cold, northerly winds that accompany rain are the norm. This makes things sideshore on the North Shore, but still straight offshore in the south and west.

When storms push up from the south, so-called **kona winds** from, yes, the south, prevail and create offshore conditions on the eastern and northwestern sides of the islands (which are covered with onshore chop for most of the year).

Variable winds are another strange phenomenon that occurs when winds are almost at a standstill. During this period, the whole of the islands experiences offshore winds until late morning when the land heats up and draws the air back from the sea, creating onshore breezes on all coasts. Finally, before dark in the late evenings, the entire process is reversed and the coastal waters glass off. Forecasts of wind conditions are a great advantage and should be taken note of.

Tides Time and tide wait for no man, and that's true even in laidback Hawaii. Many surfing breaks are better on certain tides than others, and it is very useful to know where to go and when. On the other hand, some spots in Hawaii will go off on high tides, low tides and just about everything else in between.

As is true of any coast in the world, tides experience their most extreme drop and rise during the full moon. The least movements occur during half moons, or neap tides. According to a spokesperson from the University of Hawaii's Department of Geography, "Hawaii has a mixed tide with a low range. Spring tides nowhere exceed 3 feet (a little less than 1 meter)."

Buoy Reports Buoy reports are an integral part of surfing intelligence in Hawaii. Buoys strategically located off the coasts of Hawaii are the mechanisms by which scientists determine and predict wave heights. Recordings are made of wave heights and intervals by coastal weather surveyors who then announce them to the public via phone recordings. Most surfers begin their mornings with an early call to hear the latest data from the buoy reports. On-the-spot personal prognostication takes practise, but it's a valuable skill to have.

The four elements of waves, winds, tides and buoy reports are crucial in choosing which surf spots will dish up the best waves of the day. It takes years of surfing in Hawaii to accurately make the right call for the day, but by knowing what Mother Nature is up to, you can greatly increase your possibilities. Note: **Surf report hotlines/recordings** from the National Weather Service give you readings and data for wave, wind, tide and buoy reports several times a day. Refer to the specific Practicalities sections for information on how to find out any of the above while you are surfing in Hawaii.

What to Bring Along

Surfing equipment for Hawaii covers a broad spectrum and includes surfboards, boogeyboards, McDonald's trays and even straight bodysurfing. What it all boils down to is your level of surfing, how much equipment you want to carry and how hard you want to push it once you're here. Hawaii is well-stocked for all a surfer's needs, but be sure to bring along the following items to ensure a pleasant and hassle-free visit.

Surfboards For summertime surf, your favorite hotdogging shortboard will suffice, or perhaps something with a little more length for those odd bigger days. Depending on your weight, height and surfing style, you'd use a 6'1" (shortboard), and then a 6'5". These will cover the day-to-day fun stuff associated with Town surf. Of course, there are always those rare huge days when the South Shore gets bombed with swell and reaches winter-like proportions, but those are usually blue-moon occurrences.

As the winter season starts to kick in, you may want to increase your selection.

Some hardcore hitters arrive at the airport with a dozen boards, while others show up with a few trusty sticks. For smaller, "flat" days, a shortboard will do just fine at the many performance-perfect sandbars and reefs. On bigger days, things become more more complicated. Many seasoned pros and those in the know have boards specially suited for the breaks they surf. For instance, your average touring pro will probably have a set of boards specifically shaped for threading gaping Pipeline barrels, being more pulled in or having extra rockers and other additional features. Sunset boards will be shaped differently, with extra thickness for heavier deepwater waves and for punching through chop. Waimea boards are pretty much made for getting you on, down and out alive, and are usually thick, long beasts. 7'6", 8'4", 8'6", 9'6", 10'6"(!)—it doesn't matter how big a board you have, there will always be someplace for you to ride it.

And if you don't happen to have the right board for the given conditions at a spot, Hawaii has one of the most extensive collection of surfshops, boardmakers and board factories around. New or second-hand, there's bound to be a board out there perfectly suited to you. It just requires a bit of shopping around. If you have a bit of extra cash to splurge, you may even consider ordering a custom-made pipe shooter or big-wave rhino chaser. Hawaii is not just home to some of the best surfers in the world, it also has some of the most gifted shapers to ever wield a planer.

Because Hawaii has humongous surf, the big, big boards you depend on here won't do you a whole lot of good back home, unless you come from a place where your home break hits 20 feet and goes off. So, as the season winds to a close, the obvious move most surfers make is to stash their beloved guns away until the following winter. That's when having good ties with local surfers is important, as there aren't too many people who'd be stoked to help you babysit your eight-board Hawaii quiver until the following year.

Board Bags It's a good idea to bring a good-sized board bag on your trip. There are dozens of different types, but whatever you choose should fit all your boards snugly and protect them from hard suitcases and other baggage. Be sure that your boards are packed so that if they are dropped from a height of, say, 4 feet, they will stay in place and undamaged. Board bags are also handy for stashing extra belongings or clothes that can double as padding. Best option is 7'6" to 8' triple (or more) bags.

Wetsuits Despite its tropical climate, Hawaii can sure bring on the chill factor, especially when the winds start to howl. A springsuit will adequately shield you from the cold and make your surfing sessions a lot more enjoyable and bearable.

Wax Hawaiian waters are tropical, so wax up your stick accordingly. Some companies manufacture a good "tropical" water wax, and even special Hawaiian formulas.

Legropes and Leashes The legendary winter waves of Hawaii have lots of push, so be sure to pack a longer, thicker leggie for the bigger days. Comp-lite leashes are usually sufficient for smaller surfing days.

Helmets Proven time after time to be effective, helmets are definitely nothing to be scoffed at. Worn by some of the top surfers in the world such as Tommy Carroll and Liam Mcnamara, who have almost created a fashion of it, helmets are worth their weight in gold when it comes to shielding your dome from a brush with the nasty reefs below.

Sunscreen Surfing and sunbathing are two of Hawaii's most popular pastimes, but to prevent dangerous sunburn, be sure to liberally rub on a lotion containing a sunscreen (e.g. aloe vera or PABA) before exposing yourself to the intense ultraviolet rays found in these latitudes. Also, tan slowly: take no more than 30 minutes of direct sun exposure the first day out, 40 minutes the second day, and 50 minutes the third to slowly build up a tolerance for tropical sunlight. For the treatment of sunburn, various commercial remedies are available, but locals often rub on the gooey juice of a freshly cut aloe vera cactus plant.

Protection from the sun is essential to make sure you don't go home looking and feeling like a California raisin. Save your skin and protect it from peeling. Your face, lips, ears, the back of your legs, and any other delicate extremity you choose to expose are all at risk. Make sure to use at least 15 SPF.

Diving Equipment Hawaii's coastal waters offer more recreation than just surfing. For flat days or even for a change of pace, don a mask and snorkel and check out a fish's perspective of life. If you're feeling adventurous, take along a handsling (a spear shot from the hand) or a speargun and shoot for dinner while you're at it.

Respect Hawaiians have a rep for being some of the friendliest, cruisiest people around. However, always treat them with respect as you are a guest on their island. Punchouts and tensions in the lineup are a daily thing at some places, so keep your cool and just go with the flow.

Additional Items

The following items will help to ensure that you don't get stuck during your journey. A **Swiss Army or multi-purpose knife** is handy in a multitude of situations. **Duct tape** is another must-have in any surfer's inventory. This stuff can seal and solve a lot of unexpected problems. A **camera/video recorder** is great for the memories and for showing your friends what happened on your trip.

Your **driver's license and credit cards** are handy documents here (as they are in most of America), especially if you are planning to drive or book into a hotel. In many places, you are *persona non grata* without these bits of plastic. Finally, bring your **cojones** along—no point showing up here without them. Don't be afraid to push your surfing to the limit and to expand your wave horizons.

Hawaii Water Hazards

Hawaii is generally a safe place to surf— that is, if you don't mind the odd shark attack, being sucked into the Pacific by a raging current or having a punchout with one of the boys. As long as you are aware of the hazards of surfing in Hawaii and of what to look out for, your sessions will be that much more enjoyable.

Sharks What a topic to start with. Yes, sharks are definitely present in the coastal waters of the Hawaiian Islands, and, though rare, shark attacks do occur. Tiger sharks (*Galeocerdo cuvier*) are the main worry here as they are ferocious when feeding, although there is no serious evidence that these predators specifically hunt for surfers or swimmers. Boogeyboarders and kneeboarders, on the other hand, are often inadvertently at the top of their food chain, but then, tiger sharks seem to go for anything that crosses their paths during a lunch run, even garbage. Tiger sharks can grow up to 18 feet long, so if you happen to see one, try to exit the water as hastily as humanly possible.

Other sharks common to the *aloha* waters include the grey hammerhead, Galapagos, and white- and black-tipped reef sharks. These critters are all over the ocean, but are more strongly attracted to river mouths and harbors where fishermen clean their catch, and other places where runoff occurs and dead organisms are expelled into the sea.

Murky waters are always a good sign to stay clear. The prime feeding times for sharks have traditionally been at dusk, night and dawn. This isn't always a good thought to have when you're enjoying a dawn patrol or evening glass-off session, but it is not an absolute fact, so don't fret (too much). Some Hawaiians consider the shark (or *mano*) a spiritual ally, or a sacred *aumakua* creature, so you are well-advised to pray Hawaiian-style if you encounter one.

Though shark attacks are decidedly rare in Hawaii (as in most parts of the world), several recent freak attacks have occurred at Chun's Reef on Oahu's North Shore. One incident involved a surfer named Gary Chun (no relation to the spot), who was attacked but fortunately escaped without being bitten. Another involved a boogeyboarder who disappeared when going for an early sesh at a neighboring spot called Leftovers; all that was later recovered was his sponge with a huge shark bite taken out of it. And due north of Oahu, on the south shore of Kauai, another boogeyboarder was recently attacked and lost a leg.

Coral Reefs Some of the reefs you will be surfing over here are ridiculously shallow, so take extreme caution or avoid them completely. Within recent memory, at least one surfer has died of a reef-inflicted head injury while surfing Backdoor Pipeline, and dozens of others have been planted or bounced off the bottom at various reefs, causing quite a bit of discomfort, gouges, slashes, stitches, etc.

Given the danger, make sure you know how much water you're surfing over and consider the wisdom of wearing a protective helmet. If you are unfamiliar with a spot and its hazards, be sure to check with the local lifeguards before paddling out. These guys are there to make sure you don't get in over your head (or under your head), so heed their words. Keep in mind that even minor coral cuts can become infected and do not heal easily.

Currents Hawaii's remarkable waves produce some of the heaviest river-like rip currents around. Close-breaking waves like Pipeline have tremendous rips. Rip currents are caused by the energy of breaking waves. As the waves peak and break, the energy is pushed toward the beach. At the end of the set, this energy rushes back out to sea via a channel. Should you get caught in a rip, don't panic and do not swim against its pull. Instead, swim perpendicular to it, or let it drag you out to sea where it will die out, then swim back in.

Jellyfish Another one of an oceangoer's worst enemies, jellyfish are not mushy creatures to be taken lightly. These real-life blobs normally drift onto coasts plagued by strong onshore winds, blowing in like little translucent submarines from the deep blue sea and making life very uncomfortable for anyone who encounters even a piece of them.

Hawaii's warm and hospitable waters are home to a number of jellyfish, but the most pesky of the poisonous ones is the Portuguese man-of-war, or *Physalia*, which hovers on or below the surface of the water and often seems to sneak up on you when you least expect it. This creature's prey-seeking tentacles can sting like hell if you are unlucky enough to ever touch one. Even brushing against part of a jellyfish can cause red and painful skin welts and, in some people, bring about a severe allergic reaction.

If you are whacked by one, clean yourself thoroughly with fresh water and then rinse your wounds with a solution of either ammonia and water or baking soda and water. If you should experience extreme allergic symptoms, head to a doctor for further consultation and treatment.

Sea Urchins Not the most pleasant thing to step on, these purple-black balls of poisonous and sharply barbed spikes are no strangers to Hawaii. Known here as *vana* or *wana*, these guys are regularly found in offshore shallows and here and there atop coral and limestone reefs. Booties help; otherwise, tread softly before paddling out.

If you should accidentally step on one, try to pluck the spikes out as soon as possible. This is usually best done with a sterilized needle. Some surfers simply crush the spikes and then ceremoniously apply some kind of acidic liquid (urine and vinegar are favorites) onto the offending barbs. This helps to melt them down, so don't be reluctant to piss on yourself as a quick and usually handy first-aid remedy.

Eels You'll find sea eels galore in and around the reefs of the Hawaiian Islands. They have extremely sharp and jagged teeth and very strong jaws, but rarely attack other creatures, including human beings.

Eels tend to hang out in crevices and holes and usually only strike out at something in self-defense when they are disturbed or feel threatened.

Surf and Buoy Reports

Surf Reports Recorded surf reports are updated several times a day and will come in extremely handy. They summarize wave trends on all sides of the island, along with tide and wind conditions, buoy reports and sunrise/sunset times. Best of all, surf reports are free and just a phone call away. Some surf reports are sponsored by companies for the winter season only, and as such are strictly temporary. Some are even broadcast by local radio stations. Talk about being informed! Try dialing the following reports for more information:

The National Weather Service   973-4383
The Surf News Network   596-SURF (7873)
Tropical Rush Surf Shop   638-RUSH (7874)

Buoy Reports Recordings from the National Weather Service (these guys are on it!) give you the latest on all buoy movements. Very handy for those in the know and completely mindboggling for clueless souls. Call for information at Tel: 973-6114.

Traveling to and around Hawaii

By Air Hawaii is serviced by the **major**

American airlines as well as a number of **foreign air carriers**. Most of these planes arrive at Honolulu International Airport and touch down on Oahu's Reef Runway (which was completed in 1977 on a shallow reef-lagoon between Honolulu Harbor and Pearl Harbor). A few American airlines also fly from mainland US cities to the Big Island (landing at either Hilo or Kona) or to Maui (landing at Kahului).

If you have plans to surf on an island besides Oahu, be sure to inquire about special incentive plans (in conjunction with either Aloha Airlines or Hawaiian Airlines, Hawaii's two main carriers). These offer sharp discounts on inter-island fares if you have already purchased a round-trip ticket from the US mainland to Hawaii. Savings through these plans can be considerable, but keep in mind that the cost of flying to an outer island also includes a surcharge of from $20 to $25 extra per surfboard being brought. No matter how well you pack your boards or how little extra baggage you have, it makes no difference to the airlines, unless you happen to be served by an attendant with the *aloha* spirit.

Airlines Servicing Honolulu International Airport Airlines with 800 numbers can be dialed toll-free from anywhere in the State of Hawaii, and, in some cases, from anywhere on the US mainland. The following are the major airlines offering regular air services to Hawaii. Note that those numbers that are not 800 numbers are for telephone contact points on Oahu:

Air Canada	800-776-3000
Air Marshall Islands	949-5522
Air Micronesia	800–231-0856
Air New Zealand	800-262-1234
All Nippon Airlines	695-8008
Aloha Airlines	484-1111
Aloha Island Air	484-2222
America West Airlines	800-235-9292
American Airlines	833-7600
Asiana Airlines	943-0200
Canadian Airlines	800-426-7000
China Airlines	955-0088
Continental Airlines	800-523-3273
Delta Airlines	800-221-1212
Garuda Indonesia	947-9500
Hawaiian Airlines	838-1555
Japan Air Lines	521-1441
Korean Air	800-438-5000
Mahalo Air	833-5555

Northwest Airlines	955-2255
Philippine Airlines	800-435-9725
Qantas Airways	800-227-4500
Singapore Airlines	800-742-3333
Trans Air	836-8080
TWA	800-221-2000
United Airlines	800-241-6522

Inter-Island Air Services There are a number of small **commuter airlines** in Hawaii that prop-fly passengers at lower altitudes and along more scenic inter-island routes. These fly over pineapple fields, volcano craters, fern forests and secluded valleys. Hawaii's three most popular regional airlines are listed below. Note the various outer island and US mainland numbers.

Aloha Airlines
On Oahu, Tel: 484-1111; on the Big Island, Tel: 935-5771, on Maui, Tel: 244-9071; and on the Garden Isle of Kauai, Tel: 245-3691. From the US mainland, Tel: 800-367-5250 (toll-free).

Aloha Island Air
On Oahu, Tel: 484-2222; can be reached toll free from the outer islands at Tel: 800-652-6541. From the US mainland, Tel: 800-323-3345 (toll-free).

Hawaiian Airlines
On Oahu, Tel: 838-1555; on Maui, Tel: 871-6132; on the Big Island, Tel: 326-5615; on Kauai, Tel: 245-1813; on Molokai, Tel: 553-3644; and on Lanai, Tel: 565-7281. From the US mainland, Tel: 800-367-5320 (toll-free).

Airlines and Surfers All Hawaii inter-island flights charge **$20 to $25** per board for every scheduled flight. Any traveling surfer worth his board wax will want to arrive with a quiver of at least two to three surfing sticks, an equipment list that means a one-way charge for surfboards that may end up costing you more than what you paid for your inter-island plane ticket. Even worse are some international airlines who will charge even more per board, and who are completely anal and non-cooperative about this policy. Golfbags okay, but surfers suck. You can hope for a lenient check-in attendant, but be ready to reach deep into your pocket for moolah.

By Sea Sailing into Honolulu Harbor deep in the downtown district of Oahu is still a gracious and romantic way to arrive at the island. Sadly, these days, only a few old-style passenger liners make this a port-of-call, and they are usually very expensive.

Immigration
Visitors from most foreign countries need to show a valid passport with a **US visa** in order to enter this most un-American of American states.

Animals and Plants Hawaii is rabies-free, so all incoming animals that are allowed here must be placed in a quarantine station for 120 days at the owner's expense. In a state that is snake-free, snakes are taboo so keep your pet python at home. As for plants, Hawaiian authorities are completely paranoid regardless of whether you want to bring plants in or take them out. Note that at the airports, baggage is inspected on both inbound and outgoing flights.

It is forbidden to import or export certain fresh fruits and plants, except for coconuts and pineapples. Avocados, bananas, and papayas must first be fumigated at Hawaii's plant quarantine (Tel: (808) 586-0844), and mangoes and lychees must be pitted and peeled before they can be taken to the US mainland. Fumigated fruits bound for foreign countries may be purchased at the airport. Most flower *leis* may also be worn to the mainland. Those restricted outside Hawaii include roses, gardenias, jade flowers, *maunaloa* and all plants in soil.

Climate
Seasonal Weather As a writer once said, Hawaii is, "a land of eternal June." Most of Hawaii experiences balmy **73 to 88 degree Fahrenheit** weather from April through October, with cooler and wetter 65 to 83 degree weather during other months. Rarely does the mercury drop below 60 degrees, and the sea and northeasterly trade winds serve as a huge air conditioning system.

Now and then, rare southerly or westerly winds cause a sticky-humid weather situation popularly called a *kona* condition. This mugginess, however, is usually temporary, and before long, prevailing Pacific trade winds do their cooling thing as usual. It is always raining somewhere, but some areas on every island—particularly the windward side of mountains—receive more rainfall than others. Indeed, the wettest spot on Earth is located atop Mount Waialeale on Kauai, a place that has been pummeled by as much as 486 inches of rain in a year. At higher altitudes (such as at Kula and Haleakala on Maui, and Kokee on Kauai), temperatures range from 48 to 72 degrees Fahrenheit. At the mountainous regions of the Big Island, the average temperature drops down to 31 to 58 degrees during the winter, so bring warmer clothing if you intend to tour these areas. In fact, slopes near the peak of Mauna Kea on the Big Island even receive snowfall at times in the heart of winter. Yes, this picturesque peak is actually snowboardable/skiable, though when snow-horny people ski here, it's more of a novelty than a proper session at, say, a true ski destination. Still, snow in Hawaii?—go up and see for yourself.

Sometimes when there is a volcanic eruption on the Big Island, a smoky pall hangs over the islands for a few days. Islanders call this volcanic haze "vog." Surfers don't much like this condition because it can make breathing difficult while one is paddling at sea.

Severe Weather Hurricanes rarely strike Hawaii. When they do, however, they can cause massive damage and rearrange landmarks and reefs. Hurricanes Iwa and Iniki were the latest in recent memory. The latter ravaged Kauai, destroying homes and property and changing the reef configurations at certain surfing spots.

Earthquakes occur more often and sometimes precede a tsunami (a seismic or tidal wave). Local telephone directories conveniently publish Civil Defense tsunami inundation maps, as well as related emergency information regarding such hazards.

Time Zones
National time differences are staggered as follows:

Hawaii Standard Time	12 noon
Pacific Standard Time	2 p.m.
Mountain Standard Time	3 p.m.
Central Standard Time	4 p.m.
Eastern Standard Time	5 p.m.
Atlantic Standard Time	6 p.m.

When the US mainland sets its clocks forward for Daylight Savings Time (usually from May through October), add an hour

to the above time zones except Hawaii's. International calculations are based on Greenwich Mean Time plus 10 hours.

Money and Banking
Hawaii is one of the most expensive states in the good ol' US of A. Because most food and other necessities are shipped here from far away, they cost more than they generally do on the US mainland, and the price of certain items can even vary between Town and the North Shore. As such, it's always good to have an extra stash around.

Hawaii does not have private money changers such as you will find on the streets of most international cities, but you can convert currency (usually at an embarrassing loss) at the International Airport and at some bank branches at the airport and in downtown Honolulu. Certain hotels also offer this service, but their exchange rates are also very bad. Best to arrive here with American greenback dollars.

Most non-American currencies only elicit rather provincial stares from local bankers and merchants. Islanders, however, love **major credit cards** about as much as they do cash. **Bank cards** also have quite a good away-from-home afterlife.

Tax, Service and Tipping
As with the rest of the US, a **4 percent tax** is levied on all purchased goods. That's 4 cents to every dollar.

Tipping is expected in Hawaii. No ifs, ands or buts about it; if you want to avoid stinkeye and bad karma, leave an offering of at least **15 percent** of your bill for all service personnel. Cab drivers are included as well, especially when heavy bags are involved. Generally, airport porter's baggage handling fees run about a dollar per bag while cab drivers get tipped 15 percent plus about 25 cents per bag.

Communications
International and Local Calls From the middle of the Pacific, you can dial direct to almost any place in the world. A multilingual staff of operators will assist you with your calls. Long-distance telephone rates are listed in the green pages of the Honolulu Telephone Directory, or just dial "0" and an operator will assist you. Note that the international telephone code for Hawaii is **808**, a number that also has to be

used for inter-island phone calls. In other words, you do not have to dial 808 in order to call someone on the same island as you. However, if you wish to call someone on another island, you have to dial 808 first. International long distance calling is available everywhere there is a phone (unless blocked by the owner).

Prepaid **phonecards** are generally the easiest and most common method of calling long distance, and they can be used from normal house phones and pay phones. You can find phonecards at most supermarkets and other various shops. Telephone booths are located in most towns, and local calls cost 25 cents. The use of cellular phones is widespread in Hawaii.

The following is a list of telephone services you can turn to for assistance:

Operator Assistance	0
Time of Day	543-3211
Free Interpreting	595-7267
Oahu Directory Assistance	411
Inter-Island Directory Assistance	1+555-1212
Mainland Directory Assistance	1+Area Code+555-1212

The Internet Local access numbers are available for America OnLine, GTE.net, and other major providers. Temporary hookups are also available via Aloha.net and Hawaiian.net. Most hotel rooms have modem-connectible phone jacks for web access, and internet/cyber cafes are gaining in popularity.

Electricity
Before plugging in your expensive video camera or cellphone for a recharge, remember that Hawaii's power-current is the standard US voltage of **110-120 volts, 60 cycles**. Carry a versatile adapter plug and voltage converter if you hail from a faraway land.

Security
Sad but true, but theft is a problem here, so great precaution should be taken at all times (unless you don't mind getting ripped off). After parking your car, it's a good idea to take all important or expensive items with you. If this is not possible, make sure all goods are stashed well out of sight. Anything and everything is fair game, including car stereos, bags, cash, boards,

etc. Rental cars are at an even greater risk, as they are a telltale sign that someone is from out of town and a potentially easier target. Around the house, be sure to lock all doors and windows when stepping out, and, once again, keep all goods out of sight (and preferably indoors). Stolen boards are as common as the monster swells here, and no house is theft-free (not even Mr Lopez's Pipe House). It may sound boring and repetitive, but, as the saying goes, forewarned is forearmed.

Medical/Emergencies
If you have any emergency problems that require the assistance of police, ambulance or firefighting personnel, go straight to the nearest telephone and dial 911 or 0 and ask for the emergency service you need. Coast Guard Search and Rescue Services can by reached at Tel: (800) 552-6458.

For more information about specific emergency services for the different islands, please refer to the specific Travel Advisories for that island.

Accommodations
For decades, Hawaii has been hosting millions of visitors a year and it has literally hundreds of different kinds of accommodations, ranging from expensive and chic resorts to reasonably-priced hotels to hostels and campsites. Indeed, according to one recent survey, Hawaii now has more than 75,000 hotel and condo rooms available for renting and leasing (and in many cases, even for sale).

Prices vary considerably, depending on the season, special corporate discounts and package rates, which are usually arranged by licensed travel agents. Unfortunately, the prime winter surfing months of December to March also coincide with the peak visitor season in Hawaii (yes, lots of people want to get away from the winter woes back home), so be advised to have some kind of accommodation worked out in advance before you arrive. Otherwise, you might just find yourself frustrated and homeless in Paradise.

Brave souls can sometimes save a lot of money by simply showing up at a hotel and asking for a non-rack rate on the spot, but don't always count on such impulsive generosity from hotel owners.

Perhaps the best single source of information regarding hotel bookings is the

Hawaii Visitors and Convention Bureau, which can either be reached at Tel: (808) 923-1811 or through its very active websites at www.gohawaii.com or www.visit.hawaii.org. The HV&C sites list a mindboggling array of accommodations available to the general public, but to publish their entire listing here would require a separate book.

Also worth contacting for additional information is the **Hawaii Tourism Authority** at Tel: (808) 586-2550. Again, there is something for everybody available under classifications that range from hostels, backpacking and outdoor campsites to bed & breakfast hotels, condominiums, hotels and resorts, reservation and broker services, time-share houses and apartments, vacation rentals, and even private homes and cottages.

Most surfers who visit Hawaii are young and on a budget, so many of the listings in this book are those that (if available) won't unnecessarily break your bank account and take money away from your surfing holiday funds. If you are a high-roller, flush adult surfer or an in-the-bucks yuppie-exec surfer, you might want to opt for more posh hotel or resort style accommodations.

Camping/Campgrounds Hawaii offers campgrounds operated by the US National Park Service, the State of Hawaii, the four island counties and some private organizations. Many are extremely beautiful, but you have to plan for and make reservations for the use of such places way in advance. State parks require a 7-day advance application for permits, plus a shelter fee. Rates and rules vary, so refer to the proper agencies for information.

Federal Parks in Hawaii Visit the NPS website for more information on national parks in Hawaii.

National Park Service
300 Ala Moana Boulevard
Suite 6305, P.O. Box 50165
Honolulu, Oahu, HI 96850
Tel: (808) 541-2693

Haleakala National Park
P.O. Box 369
Makawao, Maui, HI 96768
Tel: (808) 572-4400

Hawaii Volcanoes National Park
P.O. Box 52
Hawaii National Park, The Big Island, HI 96718
Tel: (808) 985-6000

Kaloko-Honokohau National Historical Park
73-4786 Kanalani Street, #14
Kailua-Kona, The Big Island, HI 96740
Tel: (808) 329-6881

Puuhonua o Honaunau National Historical Park
P.O. Box 129
Honaunau, The Big Island, HI 96726
Tel:(808) 328-2326

Puukohola Heiau National Historic Site
P.O. Box 44340
Kawaihae, The Big Island, HI 96743
Tel: (808) 882-7218

State Parks in Hawaii Address correspondence to the Department of Land and Natural Resources, Division of State Parks.

Island of Oahu
P.O. Box 621, 1151 Punchbowl Street
Honolulu, Oahu, HI 96809
Tel: (808) 587-0300

Island of Maui
54 South High Street
Wailuku, Maui, HI 96793
Tel: (808) 984-8109

Island of Kauai
P.O. Box 1671, 3060 Eiwa Street
Room 306
Lihue, Kauai, HI 96766
Tel: (808) 274-3444

The Big Island
P.O. Box 936, 75 Aupuni Street
Hilo, The Big Island, HI 96721
Tel: (808) 974-6200

County Parks in Hawaii Address correspondence to the Department of Parks and Recreation.

City and County of Honolulu
650 South King Street
Honolulu, Oahu, HI 96813
Tel: (808) 527-6343

1580 C Kaahumanu Avenue
Wailuku, Maui, HI 96793
Tel: (808) 243-7383

Molokai (County of Maui)
P.O. Box 1055
Kaunakakai, Molokai, HI 96748
Tel: (808) 553-3204

County of Kauai
4444 Rice Street
Moikeha Building, Suite 150
Lihue, Kauai, HI 96766
Tel: (808) 241-6660

County of Hawaii
25 Aupuni Street
Hilo,The Big Island, HI 96720
Tel: (808) 961-8311

Direction-Telling

Hawaiian islanders share a common language for determining directions that has nothing in common with anything else on Earth. Orienting oneself in Hawaii has to do with a purely local sense of geography and with using prominent local geographical features. The two most common directional terms are *mauka* and *makai*. *Mauka* means "upland" or "towards the mountains" and *makai* means "towards the sea."

In the Honolulu area, directions are also given in relation to Ewa (a plantation town just west of Pearl Harbor) and Diamond Head (the landmark crater to the east side of Waikiki). These four directional terms—*mauka, makai*, Ewa and Diamond Head—make eminent sense to island people. Attempt to use the conventional terms north, south, east and west and a local person will probably shake his or her head and say something like, "Eh, how you figgah, brah?"

Clothing

Dress is extremely cool, casual and laid-back throughout the islands. The brighter and louder your *aloha* shirts, the better, especially on Aloha Friday when such outrage is encouraged even in Honolulu's stuffy financial district.

Slippers (or, to the rest of the world, "rubber thongs") are typical footwear for Hawaii: just go to any party/gathering and check out the array of "slippahs" by the doormat. These precious items are a must for anyone trying to fit in here, and generally retail for around 2 bucks and up at most department stores. Popular brands include Locals and Surfah.

Local Transport

Public Buses Oahu is the only Hawaiian island with a regular islandwide bus system. For more information, refer to the Oahu Practicalities section.

Tour Buses, Limousines and Taxis Your next best transportation bets are tour buses and car-pool limousine taxis that, for a modest fare, transport passengers directly to any hotel in Waikiki and to other tourist resorts throughout Hawaii. The biggest such islandwide company in Hawaii is Gray Line.

There are also metered taxis that will take you anywhere you want, provided you pay the metered price and tip the driver for baggage handling and general services. Taxis, however, are rare and very expensive on all of Hawaii's islands.

Car Rentals Rental cars are the norm for most independent travelers. For those on a budget, a van can double as transportation and living quarters. Rentals generally go for around $30 or less per day for a car, but it is cheaper to rent by the week. Most rental agencies have offices at or near the main airport on every major Hawaiian island.

The yellow pages of the Honolulu Telephone Directory are a good place to check too. Reservations can be essential, especially during the peak season. Peak season can also see dramatic increases in prices, as well as a dearth of cars.

As in most of the US, you must have a valid **driver's license** plus (invariably) a valid **major credit card** in order to rent a car. For foreigners, an international driver's license is required. On Oahu, the minimum age requirement for renting a car is 21. On the neighboring islands, the minimum age is 25. Book in advance and ask companies for their best possible deals. Some have deals for those traveling to and driving on different islands. Drivers under the age of 25 may run into certain restrictions and/or extra charges.

Alamo	(800) 327-633
	www.goalamo.com
Avis	(800) 321-3712
	www.avis.com
Budget Rent a Car	(800) 935-6878
	www.budgetrentacar.com
Dollar	(800) 367-7006
	www.dollarcar.com
Hertz	(800) 654-3011
	www.hertz.com
National	(800) 227-7368

Campers and 4-Wheel-Drives Campers are available on all the islands except Lanai. 4-wheel-drive vehicles are rarely available. Reservations are advisable. Try Budget Rent a Truck (Oahu) at 735 North Nimitz Highway, Honolulu 96817, Tel: 524-4000.

Campers and Coaches For campers and coaches, consider the following options:

Beach Boy Campers (Oahu, Kauai, Maui, Hawaii), Suite B2-A, 1720 Ala Moana Blvd, Honolulu 96815, Tel: 955-1849.
Holo Holo Campers (for the Big Island), Box 11, Hilo, Hawaii 96720, Tel: 935-7406; (for Oahu) 28 Lagoon Drive, Honolulu 96819, Tel: 936-2202; (for Maui) 20 Wharf Street, Lahaina, Maui 96761, Tel: 553-5337 (Molokai), Tel: 245-4592 (Kauai).

Other Transportation Options For other transport options, call for information at these companies:

MTL City Bus, Schedule and Information Tel: 531-1611.
Open-Air Pedicab Co., Waikiki, Tel: 923-3106.

Liquor Law

The legal drinking age in Hawaii is 21 years, up from 18 before. Unlike many States on the US mainland, it is permissible to bring your own beer, wine or spirits into restaurants that do not have a proper liquor license (with the proprietor's approval). However, it is illegal to drink alcoholic beverages in public parks and beaches, or to have an open bottle or can of alcohol in your vehicle.

Places of Worship

Hawaii is host to a spectrum of religious beliefs, the main ones being Christianity, Buddhism, Shintoism and Judaism. Numerous other religious faiths and esoteric spiritual movements are also represented. For more information, contact the Hawaii Council of Churches (Tel: 521-2666) or check local telephone directories.

The Saturday editions of *The Honolulu Advertiser* and *The Honolulu Star-Bulletin* also print special sections on religion covering special religious activities and scheduled services.

Talk Story Like a Local

To actually master the Hawaiian language or even the pidgin English spoken in this State takes a lifetime of being here and absorbing its nuances. Forget about trying to get it down as you'll just make a fool of yourself (or as the locals say, you will "make ass"). Even if you manage a few elementary phrases, as soon as a conversation starts to develop, you'll immediately be found out as an imposter. Instead, just try to master a few Hawaiian words, some of the surf slang, a little of the pidgin, and, well, do the best you can, brah. What follows is but a random sample of local talk.

Ahi — Yellowfin tuna
Alii — Hawaiian royalty
Aina — The land
Aloha — Usually said as a greeting or farewell; also signifies a feeling of love, compassion; literally "to face" (*alo*) "the breath of life" (*ha*)
Bruddah/brah/cuz — Used as noun for describing a friend

Calabash — A bowl
Coast *haole* — California *haole*
Cruising — Hanging/chilling out
Da kine — A noun commonly used to describe anything: "You know, like da kine?"
Diamond Head — Direction; towards the Diamond Head headland/landmark
Donkey — A less than able surfer
Ewa — Direction; towards Ewa town
FOTB — Fresh Off The Boat; said of newcomers
Going mental — Description of really good surf
Got ___?(wax, change, *poi*, etc.) — Do you have?
Hana hou — Do it again; one more time
Haole — A foreigner, usually but not necessarily white
Hapa — Half
Hapa haole — Half *haole*
Heenalu — Surfing, literally "wave sliding"
Howzit--(brah/cuz)? — How are you, (man)?
Hauna — Smelly
Hui — A club
Hula — Traditional Hawaiian dance
Imu — Underground oven
Jersey — Rash guard/lycra shirt
Kahuna — A priest or shaman
Kamaaina — A longtime local
Kane or *Kanaka* — a man/male
Kau kau — Food
Keiki — A child
Koko Head — Direction; towards the Koko Head headland/landmark
Kokua — Help, or to help
Lanai — A porch or terrace
Lei — A flower garland
Like — Want: "I like sample da *poi*."
Long shot — Description of a wave that peels off a good distance
Luau — Traditional Hawaiian feast
Mahalo — Thank you
Mahu — A transvestite
Makai — Direction; towards the sea
Make — Dead, to die
Malihini — A newcomer
Mana — Power
Mauka — Direction; towards the mountains
Mele Kalikimaka — Merry Christmas
Menehune — Babies, mythical little dwarves

Nalu — Wave or waves
Oahana — Family
Okole — Rear end, butt
Ono — Delicious
Pakalolo — Marijuana
Paniolo — Hawaiian cowboy
Pali — A cliff
Papa Heenalu — Surfboard, literally "a board (for) sliding on waves"
Pau — Finished: "I like go surf when work's pau."
Pau hana — Finished with work
Pikake — Jasmine flower
Piko — Belly button
Poi — Pounded taro paste
Puka — A hole
Pupu — Finger foods
Shaka — A hand signal and greeting
Shoots — For sure
Slippers — Rubber thongs, zoris
Stay — Means location: "Brah, where you stay?" "I stay at the beach."
Tutu — Grandparent
Wahine — A girl/woman/female

Useful Phone Numbers

Note: All numbers listed below are for Oahu island. Seek operator assistance for outer island numbers.

Airport Visitor Information, Tel: 836-6413

AAA (The Automobile Association of America), 590 Queen Street, Honolulu, Tel: 528-2600

Hawaii State Civil Defense, Tel: 733-4300

The Hawaii State Library, Tel: 586-3500

Hawaii State Parks, The Division of State Parks, Box 621, Honolulu, HI 96809, Tel: 587-0300

The Sierra Club, Box 2577, Honolulu, HI 96803, Tel: 538-6616

The University of Hawaii, Tel: 956-8111

US Customs, Tel: 522-8060

US Immigration, Tel: 532-3721

US Passport Agency, Tel: 522-8283

Oahu

General Information

Oahu, Hawaii's third largest island, is known as "The Gathering Place" because it and the city of Honolulu are the social, financial and political center of the State of Hawaii. It has a land area of 593.6 square miles, and more than 80 percent of Hawaii's residents live here. Honolulu International Airport is Oahu's link to Hawaii's neighboring islands, and to the rest of the world. Tourism is the island's primary industry, though the island has many sugar and pineapple plantations as well as a large military presence.

Getting There

For specific information about airlines and cruise ships that call at Oahu's Honolulu International Airport (which is synonymous with the Hawaiian Islands or Hawaii), please refer to the preceding general Travel Advisories section.

On-Island Transport

For specific information about rental cars, limousines and other forms of individual or mass transport, please refer to the preceding general Travel Advisories section.

Taxis A commentary about taxi service in Hawaii is included in the preceding general Travel Advisories section. The following numbers are useful if you need to book a cab in Oahu:
Aloha State Cab, Tel: 847-3566; Charley's Taxi, Tel: 531-1333; Sida Taxi, Tel: 841-0171; Sunset Taxi, Tel: 537-9760; and Waikiki Charley's Taxi, Tel: 955-221.

Buses Honolulu's/Oahu's TheBus system may seem slow and sleepy compared to such systems in other parts of the world, but it is reliable and a reasonable way to roll around Town and Oahu. For schedules and route information, call TheBus Customer Service at Tel: 848-4500 or 848-5555. The main office is at 8ll Middle Street, downtown Honolulu.

Unfortunately, TheBus is not designed for—or of much practical use to—itinerant surfers because surfboards are not permitted on board. Bicycles can be transported on the bike rack on the front of the bus, but surfboards are *kapu*. Passengers are usually allowed only a very small piece of hand luggage while on these yellow, brown and orange commuter beasts. TheBus fares are a buck ($1) for whatever the distance you intend to travel on the bus route. If you intend to jump on more than one bus to reach your destination, ask the driver for a transfer. No eating, drinking or smoking is allowed any of TheBus vehicles.

Accommodations

On the North Shore Surfers coming to Oahu will generally be staying in one of two places, in Town or in the Country. There are tons of places to stay on the North Shore, ranging from styling it to budgeting it. The only problem is that most places get booked-up for the season. Beachfront—or as close to beachfront as possible—is the call, but this is not always available or affordable. However, there's always something up for grabs, and the bulletin board at Foodland is a good place to start hunting. Other supermarket bulletin boards are a smart call too. Word of mouth works as well, so ask around. Rooms generally go for around the $400 per month mark. You can also crash at one of the few budget hostels around the country.

Across from Three Tables by Waimea, try **Backpackers Vacation Inn and Plantation Village** at 59-788 Kamehameha Highway, formerly owned by the late Mark Foo. Prices start around $15 per person for a dorm-style room shared with one or two others. Tel: 638-7838, Fax: 638-7515, Email: backpackers@aloha.net.

Breck's on the Beach Hostel, located right at Backyards, 59-043 Huelo Street, offers affordable beds to crash in. Talk to Sandy there who can set up all kinds of places to stay from Haleiwa to Sunset, depending on group size and budget. Two- to three-person studios start at $45 and up. Contact details are: Tel: 638-7873, Email: brecks2000@yahoo.com.

If you really want to go big, check into the **Turtle Bay Hilton**. Situated on the edge of Kahuku just after Velzyland, it is the most styling and expensive place to stay on the North Shore. Rooms go for just under $200 to $330, and $400 and up for the suites. Included in the package are golf courses, tennis courts, swimming pools, horse stables and waves out front. Tel: 800-445-8667; on Oahu, Tel: 293-8811, Fax: 808-293-9147.

Camping is permitted at Kaiaka Beach Park near Haleiwa and at Mokuleia Beach Park. Be sure to have your permits if you intend to camp. Please refer to the preceding general Travel Advisories section for further information about Hawaii's national, county and state parks.

Down in Town Honolulu has all sorts of accommodations, ranging from cheap to unimaginably costly. No matter where you're staying in Waikiki, you're already right by the beach and in the middle of it all. Big-name hotels cover this area, as do lesser-known ones. Where you stay depends entirely on your budget.

The Banana Bungalows, located in Waikiki, has dorm rooms for $17, with ocean/surf check views. Private rooms are also available. 2463 Kuhio Ave. Call toll free 888-2-HOSTEL, or Tel: 924-5074, Fax 924-4119, Email: hires@bananabungalow.com.

The **YMCA** is also here, and, as they say, is always a fun place to stay. $29 will get you a single room, $40 for a double. Other rooms are also available, just ask. 401 Atkinson Drive, Tel: 941-3344.

A short walk from Waikiki Beach is the **Hawaiian Seaside Hostel**. Around $15 will score you a bed for the night with better rooms available as well. 419 Seaside Avenue, Tel: 924-3306, Email: seaside@powertalk.com.

The Outrigger owns a stack of hotels in the Waikiki area, with reasonable deals for all of them. Prices go for around $75 a person and up. Tel: 800-688-7444, and be sure to ask about any special rates or deals they might have.

Of course, you could style it at one of the grand hotels in the area including the Hilton, the Hyatt, The Sheraton, etc., if you've got extra bucks to spend. They're all there, right in the heart of Waikiki. Just stroll around and pick one to your heart's content. A list of accommodations could go on forever here, so our recommendation to you is to check out the gohawaii.com website for all your sleeping needs.

Dining

On the North Shore Pickings are pretty slim for fine dining in the Country. Around Sunset Beach, you can get various plate lunches at the **Sunset Diner** by Kammies. **Ted's Bakery** just opposite Backyards is actually one of the best bakeries on Oahu, but make sure you get there early as the pastries go quickly. Plate lunches and other foods are also available.

Probably the best eats on the North Shore are at **Aloha Joe's** by the boat harbor in Haleiwa. The pricey dishes are worth every cent though, and it's a cool place to have dinner and to check out the celebrities in town. For those post-dawn patrol sessions, or just for a killer breakfast, check out **Cafe Haleiwa** across from McDonalds, which also gets packed with hungry surfers. Out by the Kahuku Sugar Mill is the legendary white shrimp truck that is **Giovanni's Aloha Shrimp**, makers of some of the best shrimp plates around. Across from the fire station and and Pupukea Beach Park is the institution known to the world as **Foodland**. Here you can stock up on household needs and foods, as well as buy cooked meals. **Starbucks** opened up recently next to Foodland, bringing a smile to all the caffeine-Jonesers of the North Shore. The **North Shore Marketplace** has all kinds of places to eat (and shop). For the quick and easy, **KFC** never ceases to please. **Cholo's** has the best (and only) Mexican dishes on the North Shore. **The Coffee Gallery** has da kine coffee, breakfast, pastries and vegitarian dishes. Further towards the boat harbor is **Matsumoto's**, world-renowned for their shave ice and multitude of flavors.

Down in Town Town has the widest imaginable range of foods to choose from. There's tons of good stuff, depending on what type of cuisine floats your boat. Restaurant Row, off the corner of Punchbowl and Halekauwila, is a good place to start eating. The Ala Moana Center, Hawaii's biggest shopping mall, also has an awesome array of dining spots in its food court. Good for the post-Bowls food rush. Others picks include **Shipley's Alehouse and Grill** on the second floor of the Manoa Marketplace (2756 Woodlawn Drive) which is a killer place for dinner or a drink at the bar. Different nights of the week have different themes, such as live music or disco night. Actually, the dance floor here goes off with UH students, so check it out and give them a call at Tel: 988-5555. As far as burgers go, it's tough to top the **Kua'aina Sandwich Shop** at 1116 Auahi. Veteran Honolulu eat-outers also recommend the **Olive Tree Cafe** at 4614 Kilauea Avenue, Kahala, for casual Middle Eastern food; **Maui Tacos** at 95-221 Kipapa Drive in Mililani for fine budget Mexican *comida* and **The Pipeline Cafe** at 805 Pohukaina Street for a great 4 p.m. to 4 a.m. combination of food, happy hour and live dance bands.

If Hawaiian-style *kalua*, *pipikaula*, *poi* and *lomi-lomi* salmon are your day's craving, why not try the *ono kau kau* at **Helena's Hawaiian Foods** at 1364 North King Street or the **Aloha Poi Bowl** at 2671 South King Street. You can enjoy a sit-down *luau* for two (or even one). Not exotic enough? Then you are a candidate for Thai food at either **Mekong** (1295 South Beretania) or **Mekong II** (1726 South King Street), upscale Hawaiian regional fare at **Alan Wong's** (1857 South King St.) or what is usually great Japanese sushi and sashimi at **Yanagi** (at 762 Kapiolani Boulevard). Honolulu town is one of the world's true meeting places of East and West, so go food-searching here and you'll find that the world is here for you to enjoy.

Entertainment
Town is *the* place on Oahu for partying and general entertainment. Whatever you're into, Town has got it. Be it live punk shows, art openings, all-night raves, concerts, movies or strip bars, it's all here. Check fliers for the latest word, or tune into local radio stations. The local newspapers—above and underground types—are also good sources of info.

Other North Shore Amenities and Attractions Around Sunset Beach, at Kammies, is a coin-operated laundromat for all your washing needs. Foodland is the best bet for grocery shopping, but is still more pricey than Town. Costco is the best place for bargains, but you have to be a member. If you know of anyone with a membership card and you need to buy in bulk, go for it. There is an interesting *heiau*, just up the road from Foodland. Drive up Pupukea Road and take the turn off to the *Puu O Mahuka Heiau*. The heiau itself is interesting, but the panoramic view of Waimea, its surrounding valley and Kaena Point makes the spot breathtaking.

Money and Banking
Hawaii in general and Oahu/Honolulu specifically are as sophisticated as any other modern city in the world, meaning its cities and towns are replete with banks of international standing. Regarding money and banking here, please refer to the preceding general Travel Advisories section for more details.

Medical/Emergencies
Police, ambulance and firefighting personnel can be reached at 911, or dial "0" and ask for the emergency assistance you need. Coast Guard Search and Rescue Services can by reached at Tel: 552-6458.

Hospital services are very good in Hawaii, so keep in mind the following in case you have an accident in Hawaii, surfing-related or otherwise:

The Queen's Medical Center, 1301 Punchbowl Street, Honolulu, Tel: 538-9011. The **Kaiser-Permanente** clinics, main office at 1010 Pensacola Street, Honolulu, Tel: 593-2950.
The Straub Clinic and Hospital, 888 King Street, Honolulu, Tel: 522-4000.
The **American Red Cross**, Tel: 734-2101.

Communications
For general communications services, please refer to the general Travel Advisories section for more information.

Post Offices Normal American postal rates apply. While on the North Shore, do your postal duties at the main post office in old Haleiwa town just up from the North Shore Marketplace. Every decent-sized town on Oahu also usually has a proper US Post Office. Ask a local if you need directions. The following is a list of the more handy ones: The **Main Branch** is in the Federal Building, downtown Honolulu, Tel: 546-5625. Downtown general delivery is open 7.30 a.m. to 4 p.m. on Mondays to Fridays, 7.30 a.m. to noon on Saturdays. Other services are open 8 a.m. to 4.30 p.m.

on Mondays to Fridays, 8 a.m. to noon on Saturdays. The **Ala Moana Center Branch** is at the Ala Moana Shopping Center off Ala Moana Boulevard, Tel: 946-2020. It is open 8.30 a.m. to 5 p.m. on Mondays to Fridays, 8.30 a.m. to 12.30 p.m. on Saturdays. The **Waikiki Branch** is located on Saratoga Road, Tel: 941-1062. It is open 8.30 a.m. to 5 p.m. on Mondays to Fridays, 8 a.m. to noon on Saturdays. Another good place where you can arrange for personal or special postal or monetary services while you are on Oahu is the **American Express Clients' Mail**, 2222 Kalakaua Avenue, Tel: 922-5547. It is open 8.30 a.m. to 4.30 p.m.

Surf Shops and Boardmakers

Because surfing has such a tremendous tradition and presence in Hawaii, it's only natural that there should be myriad surf shops to support the community of local and visiting waveriders. These shops and board factories are located throughout the State on all the major islands, and they cater to whatever it is a surfer could ever possibly need and more.

In this listing of Oahu surf shops, the letters DR following an entry denotes that ding repair services are available. There are also a slew of underground "Ding Doctors" around the islands with board-repair skills that range from masterly to moronic. Among the best ways to locate these guys is by good ol' word of mouth or by checking in at reputable surf shops or scanning general bulletin boards in surf areas. The following listing is a current one, but be sure to keep your eyes open for new and underground places. Such shops, often operated by top shapers, are opening their doors all the time.

On Oahu/In Town

Blue Hawaii
1446 Kona Street, Tel: 943-2583

Blue Planet
813 Kapahulu Avenue, Tel: 922-5444 (DR)

Boardriders Club Hawaii
International Marketplace, 2301 Kuhio Ave. 922-5900, Tel: 926-5800

Classic Surfboards
451 Kapahulu Avenue, Tel: 735-3594

Downing Hawaii/Get Wet
3021 Waialae Avenue, Tel: 737-9696 (DR)

Hawaiian Southshore Outlet
320 Ward Ave, Suite 112, 597-9055

HIC
Ala Moana Mall, Tel: 973-6780
King's Village, Waikiki, Tel: 971-6715
Pearlridge Center, Tel: 483-6700

Inter Island Surf Shop
PO Box 235365, Honolulu, 96823, Tel: 945-2982

Local Motion
1714 Kapiolani Blvd, Tel: 955-7873
2164 Kalakaua Ave, Tel: 926-7873

Roxy Quiksilver
1116 Auahi Bay 3, Tel: 596-7699

T and C (Town and Country)
Kahala Mall, Tel: 733-569
Ala Moana Mall, Tel: 973-5199
Waikiki Trade Center, Tel: 971-5599
The Ward Warehouse, Tel: 592-5299
Uptown Pearlridge, Tel: 483-5499

Turbo
1673 Kalakaua Avenue, Tel: 946-1303

Waipahu Racquet Surf and Sports
1831 South King Street, Rm 201, Tel: 941-4911

On the North Shore

Barnfields Raging Isle
66-250 Kamehameha Highway, Tel: 637-7707 (DR)

BK Ocean Sports
66-215, Kamehameha Highway, Tel: 637-4966

Hawaiian Surf
66-250 Kamehameha Highway, Tel: 637-8316

Hawaii Surf and Sail
66-214 Kamehameha Highway, Tel: 637-5373

Hawaiian Trades
66-249 Kamehameha Highway, Tel: 637-7873

HIC
Haleiwa, Tel: 637-0991

Jammin Hawaiina Kine Surfboards
66-617 Kaupe Road, Tel: 637-7663

JC Hawaii Surfboards
66-437 Kamehameha Highway, Suite 101,
Tel: 637-3238

North Shore Ohana Surf
59-176 Kamehameha Highway, Tel: 638-5934

Patagonia
66-250 Kamehmeha Highway, Tel: 637-1245

Quiksilver Boardriders Club
66-250 Kamehameha Highway, Suite G-100, Tel: 637-5026

Rainbow Bridge Gift Shop
62-620 Kamehameha Highway, Tel: 637-7770 (DR)

Strong Current Surf Design
66-250 Kamehameha Highway, Suite C-103, Tel: 637-3406

Surf-N-Sea
62-595 Kamehameha Highway, Tel: 637-9887 (DR)

Tropical Rush
62-620A, Kamehameha Highway, Tel: 637-8886

X-cel Wetsuits Hawaii
66-590 Kamehameha Highway, Tel: 637-7663

On the West Side/Waianae-Makaha

BK Ocean Sports
86-120 Farrington Highway, #C305, Tel: 696-0330

Local Motion Waikele Center
Tel: 668-7873

Makaha Planet Surf
85-876 Farrington Highway, Tel: 696-5897

Maui

General Information

Maui, Hawaii's second largest island, is known as "The Valley Isle" because eons of erosion and volcanic activity have covered it with many lush and expansive valleys. Maui's population is concentrated in two neighboring towns, Kahului and Wailuku. Wailuku also serves as the Maui county seat, and Maui's main airport is located just outside Kahului town. Maui has a land area 728.6 square miles in size, including two huge shield volcanoes (Puu Kukui, elevation 5,788 feet, and Haleakala, elevation 10,023 feet). Tourism is the island's primary industry, followed by agriculture and horticulture, primarily of sugar, flowers and pineapple.

Getting There

Unless you sail here on a luxury yacht or put in on a rare visiting cruise ship, you will probably arrive like just about everybody else—by airplane from a mainland city, Honolulu or one of Hawaii's other neighboring islands—and land at Maui's main airport just outside Kahului.

On-Island Transport

If you are flush with bucks, you can rent either a helicopter or biplane at Kaulu Airport for doing initial surf checks, but that is a very self-indulgent and expensive go. More logical would be a friend's car, a rental car or (also expensive) a taxi.

Rental Cars Rentals can be obtained at the airport by calling to book one in advance, or simply booking one upon arrival. Try one of the following: Alamo, Tel: 871-6235; Avis, Tel: 871-7575; Budget, Tel: 871-8811; Dollar, Tel: 877-6526; Hertz, Tel: 877-5167; National, Tel: 871-8851. Please refer to the preceding general Travel Advisories section for more information.

Taxis Fares here are controlled by the local government. The initial drop on the meter costs $1.75, a first mile costs $3.50, then each additional mile is $1.75. At these rates, it would cost you about $45 to get to Lahaina Town near the Kaanapali Coast.

Buses There is no proper island bus system on Maui. The only things resembling a bus are the special tourist shuttle buses provided by hotels, either free or for a fee.

Accommodations

Banana Bungalows in Wailuku offers cheap dorm beds for around $15 and more for private rooms, though it is not quite near the beach. Tel: 244-5090 or 800-746-7871. **The Hookipa Bayview Cottage** is right at Hookipa, and has rooms for $70 and up. Tel/Fax: 575-7888.

If you plan on hitting up Maalaea, then why not stay right there at **Ocean Breeze** with rooms for $65 and up with breakfast? Tel: 888-463-6687 (toll-free) or 879-0657. Otherwise, money-savers, try camping at either a national, state or country park. refer to the general Travel Advisories section for more information.

Dining

Maui caters to a wide variety of tastes. Of course, there are the multitude of fast food joints in all the major towns, but we have chosen to list some of the better grinds around, be it breakfast, lunch or dinner. For openers, try some of the following:

In Paia Charley's on the Hana Highway has killer breakfasts. The pancakes, eggs benedict and pizza are all good. **Mama's Fish House** in Kuau is the place for *ono* fresh (you guessed it) fish dishes. **Mana Foods**, one of the few health food stores on Maui, is found on Baldwin Avenue and has a nice salad bar and a variety of healthier, feel-good foods. To satisfy your munchie attack, stock up at the **Kuau Store** or hit the assortment of pastries and other delights at either **Picnics** or the **Peach's & Crumble Cafe & Bakery** on Baldwin Avenue.

In Lahaina-Kaanapali Lahaina's Front Street is at the forefront of action on the Maui scene, featuring most of the top bars, shops, art galleries, restaurants and other forms of entertainment found here. During the Halloween festivities, Front Street is closed off and a Mardi Gras-like parade takes over, featuring all kinds of freaks in costume who rule the street for a night. **Hard Rock Cafe** and **Planet Hollywood** have locations worldwide, even on Maui, right on Front Street. **Kimo's** packs in the crowds, probably because of their excellent steaks, seafood, and chipper hosts. **Bubba Gumps** is the spot for tasty shrimp dishes. **Maui Brews**, like the name says, has very drinkable homemade brews, but is also a happening restaurant and nightspot. For Mexican food, try out **Compadres Bar and Grill** at the Lahaina Cannery Mall. The **Hula Grill** at Whalers Village in the nearby Kaanapali resort has authentic Hawaiian and seafood dishes, but gets packed so call 667-6636 for reservations.

Up-Country and Other Places

On the way into Makawao via Baldwin Avenue, get your fill at the **Makawao Steak House**. In Makawao proper, **Casanova** has authentic Italian grub and is also a nightclub. Wednesday nights are so-called ladies' nights, and weekends go off as they should.

Any decent local place with "plate lunches" is usually worth an eating try, but while at the winding Hana Highway's end, in "Heavenly Hana" itself, try a local da kine at **Tutu's** at the Hana Bay beach park.

Entertainment

For everything you ever wanted to know about Maui, call 244-1337 and speak to a representative of the **Maui Visitors Bureau**, or, better yet, go check out their wares at 1727 Wili Pa Loop in Wailuku. Other good sources of local intelligence are Maui's many enthusiastic publications, including newspapers such as *The Lahaina News*, *The Maui Bulletin*, *The Haleakala Times* and *The South Maui Times*. The gratis tourist magazines *This Week on Maui* and *Spotlight's Maui Gold* are also worth picking up and checking out.

Money and Banking

Banks on Maui are spread out and generally open from 8 a.m. to 3 p.m. on normal weekdays, sometimes later. Saturdays are open half days, meaning the doors are shut at noon. Sundays, of course, are closed.

The following are a few of the larger and more accessible banks that you can find on the Valley Isle.

In Lahaina Bank of Hawaii, at Lahaina Shopping Center; and First Hawaiian Bank, at the corner of Papalaua and Wainee streets, and on Honoapiilani Highway.

In Kahului Bank of Hawaii, 27 Puunene Avenue

In Wailuku Bank of Hawaii, 2105 Main Street

In Honokowai Bank of America ATM at the Food Pantry

In Kihei Bank of Hawaii, Azeka Place II.

In Paia Bank of Hawaii, on Baldwin Avenue, heading towards Makawao town.

In Hana There is a part-time Bank of Hawaii near the Chevron Gas Station.

Medical/Emergencies

Police, ambulance and firefighting personnel can be reached at 911, or dial "0" and ask for the emergency assistance you need. Coast Guard Search and Rescue Services can by reached at Tel: 552-6458. You can also call a helpful Maui County crisis and help line at 244-7407.

Maui's largest hospital is the **Maui Memorial Hospital** at 221 Mahalani Street, Wailuku, Tel: 244-9056. There is also a small hospital at Hana, the **Hana Medical Center**, Tel: 248-8294. You can go to either of these facilities 24 hours a day.

Communications

Further widespread use of pesky but handy cellular phones. Particularly handy for relaying surf spot info from remote areas. Telephone booths are located in most towns, and international long distance calling is available everywhere there is a phone. **Alii Mocha** is a cybercafe located at 505 Front Street Shopping Center. Internet cost is 20 cents per minute, or $12 an hour. Printing is $1 per page, $1.75 for color, Tel: 661-7800. In Kahului, **Kinko's** will take care of all your communication and printing needs at 395 Dairy Road, Tel: 871-2000.

Post Offices In Wailuku, the post office can be found at 250 Imi Kala Street. In

Kahului, it's on Puunene Avenue. In Lahaina, try Highway 30, on the way from Lahaina to Kaanapali. There is also a small substation at the Lahaina Shopping Center. In Kihei, the post office is at Azeka Place on South Kihei Road, and in Paia, it is along Baldwin Avenue. In Honokowai, the post office is opposite Honokowai Beach Park in the Food Pantry. In Hana, it's near the Chevron Gas Station.

Weather

The **National Weather Service** gives daily recorded weather conditions for Maui, Molokai and Lanai. Call 877-5111. For daily recorded surf and wind reports, marine forecasts and other useful meteorological information, call 877-3477. For more detailed surfing-related info, try to chat up a nice guy at a local surf shop.

Surf Shops and Boardmakers

Next to Oahu, Maui is Hawaii's second most-visited island. It is also the site of very spectacular surfing venues (Jaws and Honolua Bay), windsurfing (Hookipa and Sprecklesville) and even bodysurfing (Baldwin Beach Park, Fleming Beach Park and Kihei). As such, Maui has more than its fair share of surf shops and boardmakers. The following is a partial listing of some of the the better-known surfing establishments. New and underground surf shops open regularly. To learn more about these places, seek out local surfers in the know. Visiting windsurfers, meanwhile, should ask for special Maui windsurfing publications, as well as about the locally active Maui Boardsailing Association.

In Lahaina

Boss Frog
150 Lahainaluna Road, one block off Front Street, Tel: 661-3333

Honolua Surf Co.
845 Front Street, Tel: 661-8848; at the Whalers Village, 2435 Kaanapali Parkway, E1, Tel: 661-5455; or at the Lahaina Cannery Mall, 1221 Honoapiilani Highway, Tel: 661-5777; and at the Honolua Wahine-Whalers Village, 2435 Kaanapali Parkway, D8, Tel: 661-3253

Local Motion
Lo' Mo' is right smack on Front Street

Quiksilver Boardriders Club
Front Street

Reef Divers
578 Front Street, Tel: 667-7647

In Kahului

Hawaiian Island Surf and Sport
415A Dairy Road, Tel: 871-4981

Hi-Tech Surf Sports
One of Maui's biggest, if not the biggest surf shop. 425 Koloa-Kahului, Tel: 877-2111

Lightning Bolt
On the Hana Highway across from the Maui Mall

Local Motion
Second floor, Kaahumanu Mall, right next door to Shapers, Tel: 871-7873

Maui Mistral
261 Dairy Road, Tel: 871-7753

Maui Windsurf
520 Keolani Place, Tel: 877-4816

Sailboards Maui
397 Dairy Road, Tel: 871-7954

Second Wind Sail and Surf
111 Hana Highway, Tel: 877-7467

Shapers
Second floor, Kaahumanu Mall. A true hardcore surf shop, Tel: 877-7873

In Kihei

Boss Frog
2395 South Kihei Road, next to Mack & Jack's Lobster Shack, Tel: 875-4477

Honolua Surf Co.
2411 South Kihei Road, Tel: 874-0999

Reef Watchers
61 South Kihei Road, Tel: 874-3467

Kauai

General Information

Kauai, Hawaii's fourth largest island, is known as "The Garden Island" because of its lush tropical vegetation. Kauai has a land area of 549.4 square miles, and its main airport and administrative seat are situated in the town of Lihue. Lihue and Kapaa are the two largest towns, and the island's main industry is tourism, followed by sugar production.

Getting There

From Honolulu and the other Hawaiian Islands, Aloha Airlines and Hawaiian Airlines fly to Kauai from dawn to dusk with jet flights departing approximately every hour. Note that surfboard transport is charged on inter-island flights.

From the mainland, United Airlines flies direct to Kauai from San Francisco and Los Angeles. The fare is higher than the standard mainland-Honolulu-Kauai airfare, but is worth it for those who are tight on time. During certain seasons, some large tour companies such as Pleasant Hawaiian Holidays offer reasonably priced seats on West Coast charter flights. Check with your agent for more details.

On-Island Transport

Rental Cars Most of the major rental car companies have an office at Lihue Airport. Cheapo rental car companies faded away during the economic downturn following Hurricane Iniki in 1992. Making reservations well in advance is highly recommended. During peak tourist seasons such as the Christmas holidays and school breaks, economy rental cars can be scarce.

Cheap bombers and moderately priced used cars are also available at lots near the airport, and you can also try the classified ads in *The Garden Island* newspaper and on kauaiworld.com, as well as private sellers along busy roads.

Taxis Expect to pay Honolulu-level taxi rates.

Buses The Kauai Bus runs daily from Mondays to Saturdays from Kehaka to Hanalei; however, backpacks and suitcases are not allowed on board. Some hotels offer an airport pickup service.

Accommodations

Long gone are the days when crews of touring surfers could rent cheap Kauai plantation houses and live for months on poverty-level budgets. Now, except for those who make use of the limited number of camping sites, visiting surfers book rooms alongside the tourists. Over 6,000 hotel rooms are available on Kauai, plus dozens of vacation rentals and bed & breakfast operations. Major resort destinations include Princeville, which overlooks Hanalei Bay; the Coconut Coast from Kapaa to Wailua; the Nawiliwili Bay area; and Poipu Beach Resort on the South Shore. First-timers are advised to join package tours with room, airfare and car included.

Princeville accommodations range from $100-a-day condos to luxury suites at the tony **Princeville Hotel**. Gas, food, dining and supplies are generally more expensive on the North Shore than in Lihue and the surrounding towns.

The Kapaa-Wailua tourism corridor along Kuhio Highway is the island's moderately priced resort area. Hanalei is about 30 to 45 minutes to the north and Poipu is about 30 minutes to the south. The **Marriott Resort** at Kalapaki is the major hotel at Nawiliwili. Cheaper rooms can be had at nearby low-rise hotels and guest houses. Rooms in Poipu runs from expensive digs at the **Hyatt Regency Resort** to moderately priced B&Bs. The **Waimea Plantation Cottages** just north of Waimea town offers visitors 1930s-style plantation cottages at super-deluxe prices. Try **www.kauaivisitorsbureau.org** for links to major hotel chains, vacation rentals and B&Bs.

Campgrounds are more organized and patrolled now than in past decades. Parks where camping is allowed are located on the North Shore, East Side, and West Side, and in the cool, damp forests up in Kokee.

Some parks are run by the County of Kauai, others by the State of Hawaii. Permits are available in Lihue during weekday working hours. It's best to contact the offices in advance regarding availability and location. Call Kauai County Parks & Recreation Division, Tel: (808) 241-6660, or the State of Hawaii's Division of State Parks (Kauai), Tel: (808) 274-3444.

Dining

Restaurants in Kauai have grown in number and become somewhat more sophisticated. The **Pacific Cafe** next to Safeway in Waipouli is rated as one of the best restaurants in Hawaii serving Pacific Rim cuisine. Fast food can be had in the major towns, but not on the North Shore or in Waimea. Mexican, Italian, Chinese, Thai, Korean, Hawaiian, and American restaurants are popular. Low budget dining is available at joints like **Hamura Saimin** in Lihue. Grocery store prices are higher than in Honolulu; sticker shock prices include $5 for a gallon of milk.

Money and Banking

Again, as on other neighboring isles, the major banks have branches throughout Kauai. Refer to the local yellow pages for a complete listing of bank services in Kauai.

Medical/Emergencies

The main emergency room for the island's hospital services is located at **Wilcox Memorial Hospital** at 3420 Kuhio Highway in Lihue, Tel: 245-1100. Limited emergency medical treatment is also available at the **Veterans Memorial Hospital** at 4643 Waimea Canyon Road. Ambulance service is privately run and satellite bases are located throughout Kauai. Solar powered emergency telephones are located about every mile or so along major highways. Helicopter rescues are not uncommon, especially in remote and diffficult-to-reach wilderness areas.

Communications

The use of cellular phones became popular following the destruction caused by Hurricane Iniki. Cybercafes are also growing in number, and you can check your e-mail at **Bubba Burgers** in Kapaa and at the **Atomic Clock Cafe** in Hanapepe.

Post Offices Each major town on Kauai has a proper US Post Office. Parcel companies such as FedEx, UPS and DHL also service Kauai. However, some services are slower so deliveries might take a day or two longer than they would on the US mainland.

Surf Shops and Boardmakers

Brewer Surfboards
Dick Brewer, designer, Tel: 826-9033

Deja Vu
Kukui Grove Shopping Center, Tel: 245-2174

Doctor Ding Surf Shop
Hanapepe, Tel: 335-3805

Hamilton Surfboards
Bill Hamilton, shaper, Tel: 826-6960

Hanalei Surf Company
Hanalei Town, Tel: 826-9000

Hawaiian Blades
Max Medeiros, shaper, Tel: 245-9441

Kai Kane
Hanalei, Tel: 826-5594; Kukui Grove Shopping Center, Tel: 245-7337

Liko Kauai Cruises
Waimea, Tel: 338-0333

Miura Store
Kapaa (cousin to the famous Miura Store boardshort makers of Haleiwa), Tel: 822-4401

Nukumoi Surf Co.
Poipu Beach, Tel: 742-8019

Progressive Expressions
Koloa Town, Tel: 742-6041

Tamba Surf Co.
Kapaa, Tel: 823-6942

Wellman Surfboards
Mike Wellman, shaper, Tel: 338-0888

Westside Sporting Goods
Waimea, Tel: 338-1411

The Big Island

General Information

The island of Hawaii, more commonly referred to as "The Big Island", is, uh, the largest of the Hawaiian Islands. It is made up of an area 4,034.2 square miles in size and includes five large shield volcanoes, including Mauna Kea (elevation 13,796 feet), Mauna Loa (13,677 feet), Hualalai (8,271 feet) Kohala (5,480 feet) and Kilauea (4,093 feet). Mauna Loa and Kilauea, which are both part of the Hawaii Volcanoes National Park, are very active volcanoes, often producing stunning eruptions that are one of nature's greatest spectacles.

Tourism is an important industry in Hawaii, as it is on all of Hawaii's isles, but The Big Island also has great expanses of agricultural land, primarily for sugar production and cattle ranching, but also for the growing of coffee, papaya, macadamia nuts, coffee and horticultural products. The island's two main airports are situated at Kona and at Hilo. Hilo is the island's county seat and its largest town.

Getting There

Unless you sail to The Big Island on a yacht or a rare visiting cruise ship, you will probably arrive here by airplane. You will most likely land at one of the isle's two major local/international airports, Kona International Airport at Keahole on the island's dry west coast or Hilo International Airport on the wetter and lusher east coast.

Some visitors also arrive on the Big Island on smaller aircraft, landing in the middle of *paniolo*/cowboy country at the Waimea-Kohala Airport.

On-Island Transport

Again, if you are swimming in bucks, you can rent either a helicopter or biplane at one of the Big Isle's two major airports for doing preliminary surf checks. Other options are a rental car or a taxi.

Rentals Rental cars can be obtained at either of Hawaii's two airports in advance or upon arrival. Try the following car rental companies:

At Kona International Airport at Keahole
Alamo, Tel: 329-8896; Avis, Tel: 327-3000; Budget, Tel: 329-8511; Dollar, Tel: 329-2744; Hertz, Tel: 329-3566; National, Tel: 329-1674.

At Hilo International Airport
Alamo, Tel: 961-3343; Avis, Tel: 935-1290; Budget, Tel: 935-6878; Dollar, Tel: 961-6059; Hertz, Tel: 935-2896); National, Tel: 935-0891.

If it's a 4-wheel-driving experience you're looing for—thanks to the combination of surfing, cowboy and volcano countries—try calling the Harper Car & Truck Rentals company in either Hilo, Tel: 969-1478, or in the Kailua-Kona area, Tel: 329-6688.

Taxis Fares here are controlled by the local government. The initial drop on the meter costs $2, and the meter charges $1.70 per mile thereafter. Distances here are long so the price of a taxi fare can spiral.

Buses There is a charming **Hele On** bus firm that carries passengers between Hilo and Kona via Waimea along the northerly Hawaii Belt Road. These buses also run along other constantly-changing routes in and around the Hilo and Volcano areas, so it would be advisable to telephone them at 935-8241 to find out what's going on when you want to take a ride.

Accommodations

You can book yourself into nearly any type of hotel room imaginable, and the following are places that we would suggest you stay while on surfari on the Big Island. If you are the outdoors type or on a budget, try tent-camping at either the Kalopa, MacKenzie or Manuka state parks or, better yet, book an A-frame shelter at **Hapuna Beach** or proper little cabins in the mountains at Mauna Kea, Kalopa and Kilauea.

Permits are required, so call the national, state or county parks office to make proper reservations.

In Kona, **Patey's Place** (Tel: 326-7018) has one of the best budget deals around, with dorm beds and simple rooms from $15 to $35 respectively. Patey's Place has a counterpart on the Hilo side of the island called **Arnott's Lodge** (rates from $17 to $40) at 98 Apapane Road, Tel: 969-7097. The **Kona Tiki Hotel** on Alii Drive has quaint beachside accommodations from around $60 and up, Tel: 329-1425. Kona also has a slew of condos, all comfortable and decent, at varied but most are usually priced at relatively expensive resort-style rates.

Dining
Whatever your fancy, the Big Isle has something to suit your taste. Fast food joints dot the major towns, and no matter where you are on the Big Island, you will never be far from one. In a bid to move beyond the usual fare, the following is a sample of grinding venues that are guaranteed to please even the most diffident of surfers.

Kona Try the **Sibu Cafe** for Indonesian-style food or **Lu Lu's** for a sports bar/restaurant with a cheerful ambience. Both are on Alii Drive. At Kopiko Plaza, off Palani Road, seek out the **Big Island Bagel Co.**, which is known for its specialty bagels, coffee and sandwiches. If the caffeine and starches there don't satisfy your innermost cravings, you can repair to **The French Bakery** at Kaahumanu Plaza or to **Island Java Java** at Alii Sunset Plaza, where you can coffee out to da max (be sure—of course, brah—to try the local Kona coffee). **Oodles of Noodles**, meanwhile, has noodles of all types (from Italian to Chinese to Greek, and everything that can noodle in-between) available for slurping at the Crossroads Shopping Center on Henry Street. If you feel like splurging a bit, go for a bite at the **Chart House** at Waterfront Row, or **Jameson's by the Sea** on Alii Drive.

Heading into South Kona, be sure to make a stop at the **Aloha Cafe** for their great sandwiches, omelets and carrot cake.

Hilo If you're downtown, you've got to go at least once to the funky **Cafe 100** at 969 Kilauea Avenue, where until very recently you could still enjoy quite a substantial local-style meal (including coffee!) for under $3. Try the house *loco moco*, a local-boy (and even local-girl) specialty of the house. Japanese food freaks swear by **Miyo's** in the Waiakea Villas complex, while ice-cream lovers can never get enough of the exotic and creamy stuff scooped up at the **Hilo Homemade Ice Cream** emporium alongside the Hilo Tropical Gardens.

After ice cream, you can go tastefully native by eating onolicious Hawaiian food at the **Kuhio Grille** (at the Prince Kuhio Plaza), or you can meditate your way through a smoothie and eat, uh, "real food" at the aptly-named **Abundant Life Natural Foods** store at 292 Kamehameha Avenue. Whatever you decide to eat around here, be sure to try the *loco moco* at least once before leaving.

Money and Banking
Banking on Hawaii is very much like everywhere else in Hawaii. Main branches are found in every major town, with Bank of Hawaii and First Hawaiian Bank being the local favorites. ATMs are found throughout the Big Island as well. The easiest way to find them is to ask around. Refer to the local yellow pages for a complete listing of bank services in Hawaii.

Medical/Emergencies
One of the Big Island's main hospitals is in Hilo, at the **Hilo Medical Center**, 1190 Waianuenue Avenue, Tel: 969-4111. The number for the emergency room there is 969-4100. The other main hospital on the island is at **Kona**, Tel: 322-9311. The Big Isle also has special crisis and help phone numbers, so dial 969-9111 in Hilo or 329-9111 in Kona if you have a serious personal or emergency problem.

Communications
Further widespread use of cellular phones around here too. They are especially handy for relaying surf spot info from remote areas, as well as for emergencies.

Post Offices Most medium to major towns on the Big Island have a proper US Post Office. Parcel companies such as FedEx, UPS and DHL also service The Big Island. As with the other Hawaiian islands, some services might be slower, so deliveries might take a day or two longer than they would on the US mainland.